THE STRANGE REBIRTH
OF
LIBERAL BRITAIN

THE
STRANGE REBIRTH
OF
LIBERAL BRITAIN

IAN BRADLEY

WITH A FOREWORD BY

THE RT. HON. DAVID STEEL MP

CHATTO & WINDUS

THE HOGARTH PRESS

LONDON

Published in 1985 by
Chatto & Windus · The Hogarth Press
40 William IV Street
London WC2N 4DF

British Library Cataloguing in Publication Data
Bradley, Ian, 1950-
The strange rebirth of Liberal Britain.
1. Liberalism——Great Britain——History
I. Title
320.5'1'0941   JC599.G7

ISBN 0 7011 2670 1 (hardback)
ISBN 0 7011 3005 9 (paperback)

Typeset at The Spartan Press Limited
Lymington, Hampshire
Printed in Great Britain by
Redwood Burn Ltd
Trowbridge, Wiltshire

This book is dedicated to that hardy and indomitable breed who, when pressed as to their political affiliations, describe themselves, often rather apologetically, as 'old-fashioned Liberals'. I hope it will make them feel that they have nothing at all to be apologetic about, and that they are anything but old-fashioned.

It is especially for Lucy who has waited so faithfully.

CONTENTS

FOREWORD
BY
THE RT. HON. DAVID STEEL, MP

———————

This is a book which has been waiting to be written. In its earlier chapters it admirably re-states the fundamental principles of Liberalism. The second section reminds us of the departures from Liberalism taken by British public policy, coincidental with the decline of the Liberal Party as a force in British politics. The third part traces the rebirth of Liberalism with both a small and a capital 'L', and the fourth suggests some worthwhile Liberal directions for the future.

It all makes valuable reading, especially I found in pointing out how far we have departed from some of the basic principles which guided the Liberal founders of the welfare state. We have forgotten two of the Beveridge principles: selectivity rather than universality in welfare benefits, and co-operation between the public and the private sector in health care. 'A basic precondition for the successful operation of such a (national) scheme would, Beveridge recognised, be the maintenance of full employment, without which the demand for benefits would exceed the amount of contributions', writes Ian Bradley.

Ian Bradley seems to feel that full employment as it has been conventionally understood is no longer possible to achieve. I broadly disagree. We should at least secure fuller employment. The present pouring of North Sea oil resources into massive welfare benefits, instead of public investment to stimulate employment, is the very antithesis of Liberalism; which is why I disagree with those, including the author, who suggest that via Hayek and Friedman, Margaret Thatcher has embraced parts of Liberalism: the parts are very small indeed. For the true Liberal, the present authoritarian class-war climate in Britain is the very reverse of the co-operative society valuing every individual personality and contribution. For the true Liberal also, Mrs Thatcher's conduct of European affairs must be anathema.

The author freely draws on the rich seam of Liberal literature which deserves to be disinterred. Its influence should not be under-estimated. I recall being taken aback on my visit to Moscow in January 1984 to see in Lenin's study – the inner sanctum of the Kremlin preserved almost as a shrine – one of Ramsay Muir's volumes gracing the shelves.

I wonder, though, if Dr Bradley's optimism about the future of small 'l' liberalism can be fully justified. In his interesting chapter on the assault on the liberal spirit, he writes accurately of the 'brutalising pressures of collectivism and commercialism and the enervating and de-humanising influence of the mass media', yet falsely in the name of liberalism so many people welcome the current media explosion via cable and satellite broadcasting. This is one area where the superficial arguments about 'greater individual choice' are overwhelmed by the virtual certainty that it will simply be a greater choice of trivia, and that lowest-common-denominator pressures will lead to a further lowering of standards, or in Richard Hoggart's words 'render its consumers less capable of responding openly and responsibly to life'.

Today's liberal has to rely on government as a controlling and stimulating mechanism much more than Ian Bradley would wish. The American liberal J. K. Galbraith said some years ago that it was pointless liberals trying to apply basic doctrines unchanged to cope with a real world which included monopoly trade unions, state sectors of industry and international regulation of trade, none of which existed in the days of the earlier Liberal philosophers.

I agree with all that he says about the failure of nationalisation as a doctrine, but if we are to break down state ownership into people ownership we have to get our hands on the levers of power to do it.

The smaller units of industry in the new technologies give us a fresh opportunity to put Liberal ideas of common ownership and partnership into practice, and to extend these in the context of a counter-inflationary strategy on incomes generally.

Rather than force industry into new legislative strait-jackets I believe modern Liberals should seek to use our sophisticated tax system to create an 'enabling society' by encouraging people to adopt the policies we want. Co-operatives, for example, are sometimes derided as failures: both the *Scottish Daily News* and Triumph Motorcycles went out of production. Yet there is some evidence that what was lacking in these two cases was demand for the product, and that compared with previous performance in these workplaces productivity itself was revolutionised. So if the co-operative theory is applied instead to products for which there *is* a demand, there is every ground for optimism.

Ian Bradley is a little harsh on 'statutory incomes policies'. Yet he is right also to move us on from these centralised notions to a theory of partnership employment where the individual in industry should earn a greater part of his remuneration from a share in the fruits of his endeavours rather than free collective bargaining. Hence my adoption in recent years of the phrase 'incomes strategy', which I hope he finds more acceptable. That includes of course his view of the need for a guaranteed national income or social dividend.

I must admit that I cannot concur with all of the author's conclusions. He rejects some recent developments in the Liberal Party as over obsession with tactics. In my view he is wrong. The change of recent years has been to rescue Liberalism from the fireside of Oxford studies to be once again a relevant movement appealing to a mass electorate. Hence our rise from 2½ per cent of the popular vote in two general elections in the 1950s to 25 per cent in 1983, in alliance with the SDP, whom the author too lightly derides in the best manner of what Jo Grimond called the 'wee free' streak of Liberalism.

The author quotes the gloomy backward-looking worries of

Simon and Rowntree during the Second World War as to whether Liberal philosophy was applicable at all in today's world. This volume reinforces my confidence that fifty years on it is not only applicable but sorely needed.

INTRODUCTION

May I begin by asking you to play one of those games so beloved of the BBC's *Transatlantic Quiz*, or *Round Britain Quiz* as it was in radio's more modest days. Can you find a common factor that links the Greenham Common peace women and the gentlemen at the Institute of Economic Affairs, the rising circulation of the *Guardian* newspaper and the falling membership of trade unions, increased concern about excessive drinking in Britain and the success of the Campaign for Real Ale, microchip technology and the growth of organic farming, and which takes in David Steel, David Owen and, to some extent at least, Margaret Thatcher and Tony Benn as well?

You give up – or, perhaps, having pondered the title of this book, you have already guessed. What I will be arguing in the pages that follow is that they are all manifestations of a profound but curiously little-noticed movement which is transforming our national life and which can, perhaps, best be described as the strange rebirth of Liberal Britain.

But hasn't Liberal Britain been long dead and decently buried? It is, after all, fifty years since George Dangerfield wrote his eloquent obituary.* In much of the ensuing half

---

* *The Strange Death of Liberal England*, first published in 1935 and still in print. I wanted to follow Dangerfield and call my book 'The Strange Rebirth of Liberal England', even though it deals with Great Britain as a whole. However

1

century the values which he saw dying in the years before the First World War have shown few signs of coming to life again. Those who have remained true to the principles of Liberalism have often felt themselves to be survivors from a lost world living in an increasingly alien and hostile environment. This was the gloomy view taken by Jo Grimond, for so many the personification and the hope of post-war British Liberalism, in a lecture which he delivered a few years ago:

> British liberalism in the next decade or so must now ask itself how liberals should behave in a basically illiberal society. Three quarters of the world is in practice indifferent or hostile to liberalism and Britain is moving in the same direction . . . Tolerance, respect, care for other things than power, all that goes to make civilization, are under attack . . . We live in a country which is internally slipping into corporatism which ultimately has always led to some form of authoritarian rule. Externally, and by some elements in the country itself, we are threatened by aggressive communism.[1]

While I share some of Jo Grimond's fears, I take an altogether more cheerful view both of the present state of liberalism in Britain and of its future prospects. Whatever pressures we face, we are still one of the most liberal societies in the world. Visitors to this country from abroad may well detect a peculiar malaise in our economic performance and our industrial relations, but they are almost universally impressed by our tolerance, our fair-mindedness and our attachment to the ideal of freedom. Almost uniquely among the industrialized nations of the world, our police still go about their normal duties unarmed. Speaker's Corner in Hyde Park remains open to all comers and amazes tourists from countries where such freedom of speech is unknown. The broadcasts which go out round the clock from that massive island temple in the Strand which houses the External Services of the BBC are respected throughout the world for their impartiality, free comment and calm authority. These are among

---

I have bowed to the wishes of my publisher and included Britain in the title. Liberalism has, indeed, survived much better in the more bracing climes of Scotland and Wales than in the softer air of England, and southern England in particular. In some ways, indeed, it can never really be said to have died in the Celtic lands.

the enduring legacies of our liberal tradition, a tradition which is explored in the first part of this book.

It is true that we have come perilously close to extinguishing liberalism in Britain in the twentieth century, just how close I attempt to show in the second part of the book. But we have stopped ourselves just in time and, as I try to show in the third part, the liberal flame is burning more brightly now in our land than it has for many years. One manifestation of this has, of course, been the dramatic recent revival in the electoral fortunes of the Liberal Party, although I shall be arguing that it is by no means the only, nor even perhaps the most significant sign. The rebirth of liberalism which we are now witnessing is a much deeper and more complex phenomenon than the percentage swings of opinion polls and by-election results which so obsess television commentators (and, one might add, many Liberals).

This book is only partly about the Liberal Party. The decidedly catholic list of movements and individuals at the beginning of this introduction will, indeed, already have alerted readers to the fact that its subject is liberalism as much with a small as with a capital 'L'. The two concepts are by no means the same: there are many liberals who would never consider themselves Liberals, indeed not a few who would never dream of voting Liberal. At the same time, the Liberal Party, although it has historically been and still remains the best political vehicle for the transmission of liberal values into practice, contains a number of people who are not, I fear, true liberals.

Most of those great Victorians who established the distinctive tradition of British liberalism were actively associated with the Liberal Party: Cobden, Bright, Mill, Gladstone, Acton, Green and Morley. So were many of those who kept liberalism alive through the darker days of the twentieth century: J. A. Hobson, L. T. Hobhouse, G. M. Trevelyan, Gilbert Murray, Ramsay Muir, Elliott Dodds and Jo Grimond. But it has to be said that the present liberal revival owes at least as much to members of other political parties, Conservative, Labour and Ecology, and to those with no party affiliations, as it does to active Liberals.

It would be presumptuous to present this book as a call to the Liberal Party, and to the Social Democrats with whom it is now in alliance, to return to liberal principles. Those principles undoubtedly guide both parties, but there can be no denying that in certain areas they have been buried under some distinctly illiberal and unradical thinking. The manifesto which the Liberal-SDP Alliance presented to the British people at the last general election was the most conservative offered by any of the major parties. It offered little more than a rehash of that cosy, corporatist, social democracy which nearly sank this country in the 1960s and 1970s. To use the memorable phrase coined by that great European Liberal, and admirer of the British liberal tradition, Professor Ralf Dahrendorf, it promised a better yesterday. Yet, as Dahrendorf has said:

> The issue today is not how to be social democratic . . . The issue is what comes after social democracy. If this is not to be a Blue, Red or Green aberration, it will have to be an imaginative, unorthodox and distinctive Liberalism which achieves the common ground of social democratic achievements with the new horizons of the future of liberty.[2]

The last part of this book attempts to offer some thoughts about the forms that this new liberalism might take. It can be read in part as a kind of personal manifesto for the Alliance – as what one Liberal would like to see his party standing for in the closing years of the twentieth century. But it is not, I hope, just conceived and written in party terms. This book celebrates and commends something that is not and never has been the sole preserve of one political party. Nor, one might add, is it that mixture of trendy permissiveness and shallow irresponsibility which passed for liberalism in the 1960s and 1970s and with which the word is still often associated today. It is rather a deeply spiritual quality, a state of mind, a way of life, a faith. That is the real nature of liberalism. I can do no better than quote Ramsay Muir's eloquent definition:

> Ultimately it has a religious character. For many of us, at all events, it rests on the conviction that the Spirit Who has guided man in his toilsome struggle out of the mire of animalism is perpetually working upon every mind, goading it by means of those insatiable aspirations after rightness which are the torment and the glory of man; after the rightness of form which is beauty, after the rightness of fact which is truth, and after the rightness of relations which is justice. These

4

aspirations are the source of all advance. But they assume an infinite variety of form, according to the varying texture of the minds in which they work. What man or group of men dare presume to decree that some among them are to be exalted, others condemned or forbidden? This is the ultimate faith of Liberalism, a belief in the supreme value of individuality, because individuality is the medium through which God works; an eager welcome for variety of type, character and effort, because variety is fruitful and desirable in itself; a distrust of all attempts at the authoritative regimentation of human activities, beyond what is necessary for common needs.[3]

Many people have contributed directly or indirectly to the writing of this book. The principal debt of gratitude which I must record is to all those whose own liberalism has influenced and inspired me over the past twenty years or so. Chief among them are my parents who between them represent the two different sides of the British liberal tradition: my father, christened William Ewart like his father before him, open-minded, rational, supremely tolerant, ever-interested in his fellow human beings and their eccentricities and foibles; my mother, born and brought up in the West Highlands of Scotland, holding to the more romantic and passionate idealism of Celtic radicalism. Others whose liberal values have inspired me, and to whom I would like to record my gratitude, include my aunt, Mrs Margaret Duckett, Miss Dorothy Peirce, Edward and Bertha Bradby, David Mayhew, Michael Meadowcroft, David Alton, Richard Wainwright and the late Sir Christopher Cox.

I owe a special debt of gratitude to David Steel for his foreword to this book, and to Tim Congdon, William Wallace and Arthur Seldon who have long encouraged me to set down my thoughts on liberalism past, present and future and who have contributed several ideas to this present volume. My publisher, Hugo Brunner, who himself comes from a distinguished Liberal family, has made many valuable suggestions and given me much encouragement. I have also gained much from conversations with fellow members of the editorial board of the *New Universities Quarterly*, particularly Boris Ford, Richard Hoggart, David Holbrook and Krishan Kumar, and with fellow members of the Youth Call working party, particularly Nicolas Stacey and Alec Dickson.

I first developed my thesis about the strange rebirth of Liberal Britain in a lecture given under the auspices of the Acton Society in 1980. I was able to develop my thoughts further in talks to the Unservile State Group and the Athena Society at Tonbridge School in 1983. I am grateful to those bodies for giving me the chance to air my ideas and for some penetrating criticism and questions.

The bulk of this book has been written in what some might consider the distinctly illiberal atmosphere of an English public school. I have to say that I have found the environment liberal in the best sense of the word. To all my colleagues at Cranleigh School, who include not a few old-fashioned Liberals, I say a particular thank you for making the period in which I have been engaged in writing this book so enjoyable.

PART ONE

THE BRITISH LIBERAL TRADITION

1

THE PURSUIT OF LIBERTY –
A HISTORICAL AND
PHILOSOPHICAL EXCURSION

At the heart of liberalism is a passionate commitment to the pursuit of liberty. To start with that statement is to say everything and at the same time to say nothing. What is meant by liberty? And surely it is too widely valued a principle to be regarded as the defining characteristic of a particular political and philosophical tradition – is it not a common ideal of all who are not totalitarians?

An attempt to answer the first of those questions will occupy most of this first chapter. We shall discover that liberty as it has been defined and pursued by British liberals is a complex and rather specific quality which is not at all what it might first seem. The second question is rather easier to answer. Of course attachment to the principle of liberty is near-universal in those countries, like our own, which are not subject to totalitarian rule. But only for liberals is it the supreme and guiding principle before which all other considerations must bow. The conservative minded will tend to subordinate liberty to the claims of authority or tradition, while for socialists it must ultimately take second place to equality. Liberals alone will, in the words of the preamble to the British Liberal Party's constitution, make their chief care the rights and opportunities of the individual and in every sphere set freedom first.

The development and the defence of the ideal of human

liberty have been the most powerful and enduring contributions which liberalism has made to British life. They have also, perhaps, been Britain's most significant contribution to the world at large. As Elliott Dodds, a great liberal journalist and former president of the Liberal Party, put it: 'The argument of liberty from Locke to Mill, and on through Green and Hobhouse to Ramsay Muir, has been the characteristic gift of Britain to the world'.[1]

It is, of course, not just abstract intellectual concepts that we have exported but also liberal institutions as diverse as the rule of law, parliamentary democracy, free trade and public service broadcasting. And at a more personal level we have often beckoned to our shores those living in darker lands where the lamp of liberty no longer burned. From the Huguenot weavers who set up their looms in Kent in the sixteenth century to the East African Asians who brought their business skills to our cities in the 1960s and 1970s, those fleeing from persecution and oppression abroad have traditionally found a refuge in Britain. We have provided a safe haven for many exiles who have gone on to spread the gospel of liberty in their own lands, including such great national liberators as Giuseppe Mazzini, founder of the movement to create a unified and independent Italy, Lajos Kossuth, instigator of the Hungarian revolt against Austrian rule, and Charles de Gaulle, leader of the Free French movement during the dark days of Nazi occupation of our nearest Continental neighbours.

Although the idea of liberty has always been at the core of liberalism, the application of that idea has not remained fixed and immovable over the years. As liberals have perceived new and different threats to liberty, so they have changed their perspective and emphasis. Since at least the seventeenth century, as we shall see, British liberals have perceived liberty first and foremost as an intellectual and spiritual quality, but at different times other aspects have also been stressed. Initially they concentrated on securing the liberty of the person and basic legal rights, moving on later to freedom of speech, freedom of conscience and freedom of association and public meeting. Side by side with these campaigns went the championship of economic liberty, the right to private property and to free trade. Once these were achieved, liberals began to see the need to promote the cause of liberty in the area of social and material conditions and to work for freedom from poverty, disease, idleness and poor physical surroundings.

Many historians have argued that this new 'social' liberalism which showed itself in the latter part of the nineteenth century represented a fundamental shift in the idea of liberty away from a negative concept of freedom as the absence of all external restraints, including government intervention, and towards a much more positive emphasis on freedom to develop one's capacities which envisaged a major role for state action to create the conditions where such development was possible for everyone. There is no doubt that there was a shift of emphasis in liberal thinking, as we shall see, but arguably it was not quite as great as it is often portrayed. To some extent, both the negative and the positive ideas of freedom have always been present in the British liberal tradition. The struggle for liberty has been fought on many different battlegrounds and against many different enemies, but it has always had one overriding aim – to enable people to lead free and full lives and to develop to the maximum the talents with which God has endowed them.

It is difficult to know quite how far back in history to go in seeking the origins of the British liberal tradition. They could be said to lie in Anglo-Saxon society with its established property rights, its system of justice and its attachment to the idea of local democracy epitomised in the institution of the village moot. The Middle Ages saw the establishment of some of the most important elements of English liberalism: the assertion in *Magna Carta* of the rights of the people against arbitrary rule, the championship of representative government by Simon de Montfort, and, perhaps above all, the institution of the Common Law, with its insistence on the impartial adminis-tration of justice on an equal basis to all citizens and its concern with human liberty expressed in the writ of *habeas corpus* and in the principle that a man is innocent until proved guilty. By Tudor times at least liberty of the person, that most basic of all freedoms, was fairly well secure in Britain and the status of a free man, independent in body, mind and spirit and calling no man his master, was one to which many aspired.

It was the Puritan fathers of the seventeenth century who first gave expression to the particular view of liberty which has, perhaps, been the distinguishing characteristic of British liberalism. It sprang directly from their religious faith. Regarding the words of the Bible rather than the teachings of the Church as the ultimate source of truth, they believed it to be of the first importance that the individual should be free to interpret the Gospel for himself and in his own way. To make him subject to the authority of priests, and particularly the priests of a single Church established by the law of the land, was, they felt, wholly contrary to the spirit of Christianity. For this belief John Bunyan and many others were sent to prison.

The Puritans' notion of liberty was very soon applied in both the political and economic spheres. Taken up by John Pym, John Hampden and Oliver Cromwell, it became a rallying cry for those who opposed the absolutist powers and 'Divine Right' of the monarchy and sought to increase the role of Parliament in the government of the country. Parallel demands for economic freedom were also made by merchants and manufacturers who sought liberation from protectionist restrictions on trade and industry. But it is important to remember that liberty was first and foremost perceived and championed in Britain as an inner quality of the spirit and the intellect. So for liberals it has always remained – too much so, indeed, for the critics of liberalism who see it as putting insufficient stress on material factors and external circumstances.

The first and most eloquent exponent of this view of liberty was John Milton. His writings provide the first clear exposition of the case for allowing free thought and free speech and as such, perhaps, give him a better claim than any other single individual to be regarded as the father of British liberalism. Appropriately, a copy of the pamphlet in which he put forward his argument, *Areopagitica*, was placed on the high altar of Westminster Abbey at the special service to mark the centenary of the British Liberal Party in May 1977. The work also serves as the symbol of office of the party president. Every new incumbent receives a bound copy from his predecessor at the annual assembly.

Milton wrote *Areopagitica* in response to an ordinance passed by Parliament in 1643, shortly after the beginning of the English Civil War, which established a system for the regulation of printing and publishing and the licensing of books. He was deeply disappointed that those who had opposed such illiberal institutions as the Court of Star Chamber were now showing themselves to be as antipathetic to the free interchange of ideas as the absolute monarch whom they had overthrown. So he set out to argue the case against censorship, taking the title of his pamphlet from the name of the hill on which the democratically elected 'Upper Council' of ancient Athens met to decide on political and religious matters.

Milton took as his starting point the teaching of Christianity. When God created Adam, He gave him freedom to choose either good or evil. Free choice was the supreme gift which God had given to man. It enabled him to discover the truth for himself, using his own mind rather than the ideas imposed on him by someone else, and obeying the dictates of his own conscience rather than some externally imposed authority. Any attempt to censor the free thoughts and words of individuals was doubly pernicious: it prevented them from reaching the truth and it denied the most important faculty which God had given to man.

Areopagitica laid down clearly for the first time three key principles which lie at the heart of the liberal faith. The first is that liberty is essentially about moral choice. Its possession is vital because it alone enables individuals to realise their true human potential as independent moral beings with both the sense and the power to be able to decide for themselves how they wish to live. Liberalism is strongly opposed to a determinist view of life; it holds that men and women are morally free and are able to influence events for good or ill through their freely held ideas and convictions. This central feature of liberalism has been particularly stressed in the twentieth century by Isaiah Berlin, a philosopher who belongs in many ways to the British liberal tradition.

The second principle follows from the first. It is the confident conviction that out of free debate and the discussion of different viewpoints each person will find his own truth. In the words of

Jo Grimond, Liberalism 'must start from the position that only the actions and states of mind of individuals voluntarily arrived at can have value'.[2] Liberals eschew universal truths and final solutions, holding rather that each individual must work out his own position, even though this will involve agonising moral choices and the possibility of moral uncertainty. They therefore believe with Milton that it is totally wrong to fear or suppress the opinions of others, however odious or repugnant one may feel them to be. They revel in argument and dialectic and seek the widest possible dissemination of ideas and opinions. The creation of a free and cheap press was, as we shall see, one of the most outstanding and characteristic achievements of nineteenth-century British liberalism.

This attitude rests, of course, on an optimistic view of human nature. It presupposes that most people are at least potentially, if not actually, influenced more by reason and argument than by prejudice and convention. Liberals see men and women as rational and intelligent beings with the capacity for understanding and discovery, not as creatures of habit who are content to take all their ideas from others and never work things out for themselves.

From this optimistic view of human nature stems the third and most important principle which Milton established in *Areopagitica*. This is that liberty does not mean licence. It is not the freeing of people to do what they like regardless of the consequences, but the enabling of them to make the best of themselves and contribute to the well-being of the community of which they are part. Once again, the principle derives from Christianity. Christ came into the world to free men from the slavery of sin not so that they could follow their selfish wills and gratify their baser appetites, but so that they could lead good and full lives motivated by a spontaneous desire to follow Him in whose service they would find perfect freedom.

Liberty, then, is a condition of self-rule in which thought and behaviour are governed by reason, conscience and other human faculties rather than by blind obedience to externally imposed authorities or slavish adherence to habit, prejudice or custom. Lord Acton, the great nineteenth-century Catholic historian and Liberal statesman who worked throughout his life on a vast history of liberty, put it succinctly: 'Liberty is not the power of doing what we like, but the right of doing what we ought . . . (it) is ultimately founded on the idea of conscience'.[3] It is not, of course, necessary to believe in Christianity or any other religion in order to take this view of liberty. It is the common starting point of all the great British liberal theorists, including such convinced free-thinkers as John Stuart Mill and John Morley.

To equate liberty with mere licence would, after all, be to say that everyone should pursue their own selfish interests regardless of the interests of others. As we shall see in later chapters, such a narrow individualistic view has never been part of the British liberal tradition. Milton and his fellow-Puritan fathers did not preach an atomistic individualism which took no account of man as a social being. It is true that in the intellectual and spiritual sphere they stressed that man must work out his own salvation for himself and not depend on the will of others. But they also had a strong communal sense, rooted in their conception of the gathered church and the community of believers. Moral worth was to be found as much in the community as in the individual, and Christ's example showed that man's life on earth was not just to be lived for himself alone. This sense has always been strong among liberals. In the words of Elliott Dodds: 'Liberty does not lie merely in freedom from restraint. Still less does it involve freedom to assert anti-social "rights" against the interests of the community. True freedom means that opportunity shall be given to every man, woman and child in the commonwealth to live out the best that is in them and to develop their faculties for the service of their fellows'.[4]

The notion of abstract natural rights, popular with many liberals on the Continent and with certain modern protest movements, is indeed largely alien to the British liberal tradition. As we shall see in Chapter Three, Victorian Liberals who campaigned for the extension of the franchise did not see the vote as a natural right but rather as a trust and a recognition of responsibility and maturity to be given to those who had shown themselves worthy to receive it. Responsibilities are just as important as rights in the liberal's scale of values. Indeed, the liberal ideal of a free man is one who is independent-minded, self-directing, responsible and outward-looking towards his fellows.

In practice, of course, the rule of law is needed to prevent liberty from being turned into licence. Not everyone is equipped or inclined to lead a responsible life and there will always be abuses of liberty and anti-social behaviour. Liberty depends on law and can only exist under its protection and regulation. What liberals insist on is that law is made with the consent of the people and that it is administered impartially and applies equally to all. That sturdy maxim first enunciated in the seventeenth century and applied so effectively in our own times by Lord Denning, 'Be you never so high, the law is above you', remains one of the most important safeguards of liberty in these islands.*

If John Milton was one of the earliest writers to define the moral and spiritual basis of liberty, John Locke was one of the first to extend the idea into the economic and political spheres. There are many, indeed, who regard Locke rather than Milton as the father of the British liberal tradition. This is true if liberalism is seen primarily as a political and economic doctrine. But as I have already made clear in my view at least liberalism in this country has always been conceived of first and foremost in moral and spiritual terms. It is for that reason that I regard Milton and the Puritan fathers as the founders of the British liberal tradition. But it is also right to acknowledge Locke as the author of some of the most important principles of British liberalism, including the case for private property, the notion of government by consent, and the idea of representative democracy with the principle of majority rule tempered by respect for the rights of minorities.

Locke developed these principles in his *Two Treatises of Government* which were published in the aftermath of the Glorious Revolution of 1688 which ended the Stuart experiment in absolutism and established constitutional monarchy in Britain. In these works he described the essence of political

* The earliest published source for this maxim which I have come across is Thomas Fuller's *Gnomologia* (1732). Lord Denning, whom I have consulted, is of the opinion that the maxim dates from the trial of Charles I.

liberalism in terms which are clearly reminiscent of Milton's defence of religious and intellectual liberty:

The liberty of Man in society is to be under no other legislative power but that established by consent in the commonwealth, nor under the dominion of any will, or restraint of any law, but what that legislation shall enact, according to the trust put in it. Freedom for man under government is not for everyone to do as he lists but to have a standing rule to live by, common to everyone of that society, and made by the legislative power erected in it; to have a liberty to follow his own will in all things where the Rule prescribes not, and not to be subject to the inconstant, uncertain, unknown arbitrary will of another man.[5]

Locke defined the three basic rights of man as life, liberty and property. His remarks on the last of these subjects are particularly important as they laid the basis for later liberal economic theory. Locke based his case for private property on the argument that the individual is the proprietor of his own person and capacities, and therefore of the labour of his body and the works of his hands. Whatever he mixes his labour with, be it land or other natural products, he makes his own property. This argument is fraught with inherent difficulties and contradictions, of both a practical and a theoretical nature, and it has been interpreted in several different ways. It may be too much to conclude, as the distinguished Canadian political scientist, Professor C. B. Macpherson, has done, that Locke's is a theory of 'possessive individualism' which specifically sets out to justify the unequal possession of property and to argue that society is a series of market relations. Certainly that is not how all liberals have interpreted it. But there is no doubt that Locke's work was of considerable importance in the formation of the British liberal tradition, not least in establishing the right to own property and in putting the pursuit of liberty before that of equality.

By 1700 Britain displayed many of the basic features of a liberal society which were to take other European countries another 150 years or so to achieve. There was, broadly speaking, religious toleration, an independent judiciary and a largely free press. During the eighteenth century the broad principles of freedom of conscience and free speech were defended by the Whigs. Towards the end of the century, under the leadership of Charles James Fox, they committed themselves to certain specific campaigns in the field of civil liberty, such as the political emancipation of Roman Catholics and Protestant Nonconformists, the abolition of slavery in the British Empire and the limited extension of the franchise. Fox himself strenuously opposed efforts by William Pitt during the war with Revolutionary France to suspend *habeas corpus*, gag the press and suppress public meetings and political clubs. The Whigs carried several of their campaigns to a successful conclusion in the first half of the nineteenth century. 1828 brought the repeal of the Test and Corporation Acts which prohibited Nonconformists from serving in local government or in public offices, 1829 the political emancipation of Roman Catholics and 1832, of course, the Great Reform Act and the first step towards a fully democratic system of government. A further important liberal achievement came in 1833 with the abolition of slavery throughout the British Empire.

These achievements in the fields of religious and civil liberty were paralleled by a similar victory for the principle of economic liberty. In the early seventeenth century trade and industry in Britain were fettered by protectionism, monopolies and Government regulation. The Puritan merchants and manufacturers began the battle for free trade. Industrial monopolies were abolished by the Long Parliament of 1640 to 1660 and were not re-introduced at the Restoration. Commercial monopolies, which had been sold by the Crown as a source of revenue, also gradually disappeared in the later seventeenth century as trading companies lost their exclusive rights and privileges.

Many restrictions on economic activity remained, however. The dominant economic system of the seventeenth and eighteenth centuries was that of mercantilism, the regulation of all economic activity by the Government which spun a web of protection and restriction around trade and industry. Bitterly criticised by Adam Smith in his famous work *The Wealth of Nations* (1776), the mercantilist system was only gradually dismantled in the first half of the nineteenth century. During the 1820s liberal Tories like George Canning, Frederick

Robinson and George Huskisson began to reduce the thousands of duties on imports and exports and swept away such protectionist measures as the Navigation Acts, which forbade carriage of goods to or from England or the colonies in foreign ships, and the laws prohibiting the export of machinery and the emigration of artisans from Britain. Reciprocal treaties were signed with other countries reducing or totally abolishing tariff barriers and trade with the colonies was thrown open. The work of establishing a free system of trade was largely completed by Sir Robert Peel and his able lieutenant William Ewart Gladstone in the 1840s and 1850s.

The battle for free trade, which was fought in the teeth of strong opposition from the powerful landed interest which dominated Parliament and the Tory Party, culminated in the famous struggle over the Corn Laws. Opposition to these restrictive measures, originally imposed in the aftermath of the Napoleonic Wars to protect British farmers by keeping out cheap foreign wheat, grew among merchants and manufacturers and was led by the two great radical politicians of the mid-nineteenth century, Richard Cobden and John Bright. Their argument was essentially threefold: that the Corn Laws kept the price of bread artificially high to the detriment of the consumer; that they caused the wheat-growing lands of Eastern Europe and America to impose reciprocal tariffs against imports from Britain and thus closed off major export markets; and that the whole system of protection was inimical to international harmony and world peace.

With the repeal of the Corn Laws by Sir Robert Peel in 1846, in a move which split the Conservative Party down the middle and led to those Tories who supported repeal joining the emerging Liberal Party, Britain's economy became the freest in the world. It remained so, in an increasingly protectionist world, for the next eighty-five years, thanks in no small measure to the continuing sway of the arguments which Cobden and Bright had deployed so forcefully.

The economic liberalism espoused by these two men and their followers in what came to be known as the Manchester School, was not just confined to the sphere of international trade. It opposed protectionism, regulation and interference in many other areas of the economy. Putting his faith in 'that great principle of competition which God has set up in this wicked world as the silent arbiter of our fate', Cobden strenuously opposed attempts to control wages and prices by legislation. He attacked monopolies and privileges, whether public or private, and was a severe critic of what he saw as the growing menace of collectivism and the gradual move of the state into the roles of manufacturer and employer.

Cobden and his fellow mid-Victorian Liberals are sometimes portrayed as harsh and unfeeling advocates of the doctrine of *laissez-faire*. This is not fair. It is true that they rejected the Tory notion of state paternalism and preferred to rely rather on a combination of self-help, mutual support and philanthropy to elevate the condition of the poorer sections of society. But they were not doctrinaire anti-statists, content to leave everything to market forces regardless of the human consequences. Cobden, for example, supported state intervention to regulate the hours and conditions of work for children in factories, and to control the railway construction industry in the interests both of safety and of securing a standard gauge of track. He also argued for the establishment of a compulsory national system of education. Doctrinaire anti-statism, of the kind propounded in the middle of the nineteenth century by Herbert Spencer, was not the philosophy of the Manchester School.

One should, perhaps, go further and point out that such a philosophy has never, indeed, been part of the mainstream liberal tradition in Britain. Doctrinaire adherence to the principle of *laissez-faire*, or 'Donothingness' as Carlyle called it, is often attributed to British liberals, and Victorian Liberals in particular. In fact, it was an alien doctrine, invented by French economists in the mid-eighteenth century, which never found many convinced disciples in this country, certainly not in the main political parties. Not even the classical economists took it up as a cry. In *The Wealth of Nations*, a work in which the phrase *laissez-faire* is not once mentioned, Adam Smith indicated that he saw three major functions for the state: the defence of the realm, the protection of individuals from injustice and oppression, and the erection and maintenance of those public works and institutions which it could never be in the interests of any individual or small number of individuals to erect and maintain. A similar absence of doctrinaire anti-statism characterised the Whigs in the first half of the nineteenth century. Speaking in 1846 during a debate on a Bill to enforce a ten hour day in factories, for example, Lord Macaulay expressed the view that 'Where health is concerned, and where morality is concerned, the state is justified in interfering with the contracts of individuals'.[6]

The only major nineteenth-century Liberal to declare his faith in the principle of *laissez-faire* was, in fact, John Stuart Mill in his *Principles of Political Economy* (1848). However, he went on to make so many qualifications, particularly in later editions of the work, as to emerge in several respects as a strong interventionist. His overall position on the proper balance between the individual and the state was, like that of most of his contemporaries, one of flexible agnosticism. 'The interference of government is, with about equal frequency, improperly invoked and improperly condemned', he wrote. 'In the particular circumstances of a given age or nation, there is scarcely anything really important to the general interest, which it may not be desirable, or even necessary, that the government should take upon itself'.[7]

It is, incidentally, interesting to note that when two of the greatest Liberal thinkers of the twentieth century tackled the question of the proper balance between individual freedom and state action, it was in the same pragmatic and non-doctrinaire spirit. William Beveridge observed in 1922 that 'Liberalism in the economic sphere ought to stand for the empirical study of social questions', while John Maynard Keynes wrote four years later: 'We cannot settle on abstract grounds but must handle on its merits in detail, what Burke termed "one of the finest problems in legislation, namely to determine what the State ought to take upon itself to direct by the public wisdom, and what it ought to leave, with as little interference as possible, to individual exertion" '.[8]

Certainly a doctrinaire adherence to *laissez-faire* was not a feature of the first British administration which can properly be called Liberal, W. E. Gladstone's first ministry of 1868 to 1874. This was anything but a do-nothing government. It implemented a large number of reforms and had no hesitation in invoking state intervention where necessary while at the same time, as we shall see, retaining a strong preference for voluntary action wherever possible. The first Gladstone Government was strongly committed to promoting free trade, ending aristocratic privileges and extending religious and civil liberty. Among its achievements were the introduction of the secret ballot, the ending of the system of purchasing commissions in the army, the opening of the Civil Service to talent, the destruction of the Anglican monopoly on admission to Oxford and Cambridge Universities and the abolition of compulsory rates paid by all parishioners for the upkeep of the local Anglican Church.

With the passage of these and other measures establishing full civil rights for those who were not members of the Established Church the grievance which Milton and his contemporaries had felt more strongly than any other was finally and totally removed. People were no longer to be publicly discriminated against because of what they said or what they believed. Liberty, as Milton had defined it, was still very much under threat, however. In the oppressive moral climate of Victorian Britain people found themselves under tremendous social pressure to conform to conventional ideas and standards of behaviour. There were also all sorts of groups of moral busy-bodies around eager to interfere in other people's lives and impose their own values and style of conduct. It was to counter these two specific threats to liberty that John Stuart Mill wrote his famous essay *On Liberty* in 1859.

Mill is without doubt one of the greatest figures in British liberalism (and, it might be added, in British Liberalism too). Like those other Victorian giants, William Ewart Gladstone, Lord Acton and John Morley, he combined philosophy and practical politics and was both a thinker and a campaigner. He was, indeed, briefly in the House of Commons as a Liberal MP. Among the issues on which he campaigned were two which have continued to exercise a strong hold on liberal consciences: the emancipation of women and the civil liberty of coloured people. Mill's essay of 1869 on *The Subjection of Women* became something of a bible for the feminist movement throughout Europe. Since then British Liberals have demonstrated a growing commitment to improving the status of women, exemplified by the passage of the Married Women's Property Act by Gladstone's second government in 1882 and the redoubtable efforts of Baroness Seear to secure equal pay and pension rights a hundred years later. Liberal commitment to the civil liberties of racial minorities has been even more marked, not least in the courageous and consistent stand against racialism of the present Liberal Party leader, David Steel, who takes his stand on the words used by Mill in his famous debate with Thomas Carlyle in 1849 on the rights and wrongs of negro emancipation: 'We ought not to ordain that to be born a girl instead of a boy, any more than to be born black instead of white, shall decide the person's position through all life'.[9]

It is as a thinker rather than as a campaigner, however, that Mill takes a commanding place in the British liberal tradition. His great essay of 1859 still provides the clearest and fullest explanation in the English language of why it is that the liberal prizes liberty more than any other value. Mill rested his argument for liberty on the fact that it is the essential foundation for the rich and full development of the human personality. Like Milton, he believed passionately in the free interplay of ideas. Like Milton also, he saw liberty as the key which unlocked man's full potential as a thinking and choosing being and freed him from the slavery of believing and doing things because he was told to or because that was what was expected or customary.

To Mill, writing in the middle of Queen Victoria's reign, the main threat to liberty came from society rather than from the state. Only four pages of *On Liberty* are concerned with interference in people's lives and thought by the government, while over a hundred are devoted to interference from social and cultural pressures and particular sectional groups. Some modern liberals, it seems to me, have tilted the balance too far in the other direction and concentrated almost entirely on the threat to liberty posed by the state while losing sight of the often more insidious threats posed from within society itself.

As mentioned above, Mill had two particular targets in view

when he wrote his famous essay, and every liberal worthy of the name should still keep both of them squarely in his sights. He attacked his contemporaries' slavish adherence to the ideas of social acceptability and convention:

In our own times, from the highest class down to the lowest, everyone lives as under the eye of a hostile and dreaded censorship. Not only in what concerns others, but in what concerns only themselves, the individual or the family do not ask themselves what do I prefer? or what would suit my character or disposition?, or what would allow the best and highest in me to have fair play, and enable it to grow and thrive? They ask themselves, what is suitable to my position? What is usually done in persons of my station and pecuniary circumstances – or (worse still) what is usually done by persons of a station and circumstances superior to mine?[10]

We may think that we are less hidebound and snobbish than the Victorians, and in some ways we are. But there are still enormous pressures in our society, daily reinforced by advertisers and the mass media, to conform, to keep up with the Joneses, to follow fashion and not to do anything too original. *On Liberty* is a clarion call to us to lead independent lives, not to bother too much about what everyone else does, and to respect the 'awkward bugger' who refuses to do things in the conventional way. It is, indeed, a great hymn in praise of nonconformity and eccentricity.

Mill's other main target were those groups or individuals who sought to impose their own moral code on others and to curb activities which were properly no concern of any but those who took part in them. The example which he most frequently cited in *On Liberty* were the Sabbatarians who wished to see universally enforced their gloomy view of what should and should not be done on Sundays and who brought prosecutions against so-called offenders. Comparable examples in our own time might be those who harass and seek to bring criminal prosecutions against homosexuals or who would take away from parents the freedom to send their children to schools outside the state system. Mill insisted that everyone should be free to put forward his or her point of view, but he also insisted that 'the only freedom which deserves the name is that of pursuing our own good in our own way, so long as we do not deprive others of theirs'.[11]

Although most of *On Liberty* was concerned with threats to liberty posed by society, Mill was also very conscious of the damage that could be done by an over-mighty state. In the essay he listed three major objections to government interference: first, that generally speaking, those people personally interested in any business were the best people to manage it, and that therefore government should not, for example, interfere 'with the ordinary functions of industry'; secondly, that even where something could not necessarily be handled better by individuals than by the government, it was none the less preferable that it should be done by them 'as a means to their own mental education'; and thirdly and most importantly, that 'every function superadded to those already exercised by the government causes its influence over hopes and fears to be more widely diffused, and converts, more and more, the active and ambitious part of the public into hangers-on of the government.'[12]

Mill, then, had an instinctive dislike of over-interference by the state in people's lives. But, as we have seen, he was far from being a doctrinaire disciple of *laissez-faire*. Like Milton, he saw liberty as something fundamentally different from licence. There was one very important purpose for which he argued that power could and should be exercised over individuals, even against their wills, and that was to prevent harm to others. Whenever people invoked a so-called natural right to act in a way that was injurious to others, he saw the central principle of liberty as being violated. The example which he cited most frequently was the right of unrestricted procreation, which he regarded as injurious both to the offspring of irresponsible parents and to the interests of all who competed with them for scarce jobs. Fellow Victorian Liberals, following this principle, sought to curb other so-called 'freedoms' the abuse of which could inflict harm on others, such as drinking, drug-taking, gambling and free access to pornography. Unrestricted indulgence in these activities is, indeed, doubly to be condemned in liberal eyes – not only does it lead to anti-social behaviour but it also induces a state of dependence and of habitual enslavement which is just as destructive of the independence and integrity of the individual as political oppression and persecution.

Mill and other liberal theorists in the first half of the nineteenth century were primarily concerned with intellectual and civil liberty. In the second half a number of prominent thinkers extended the argument for liberty into other areas of life. These New Liberals, as they came to be called, never lost sight of the moral and spiritual basis of liberalism, but they saw that there were other evils apart from censorship, social pressure to conform, and the over-mighty authority of the Established Church and the state, from which men and women needed to be liberated. Poverty, illness, bad housing and inadequate education, they argued, were just as much of a hindrance to individual self-fulfilment and the exercise of choice, and to free people from those particular constraints would require the positive use of public authority.

The founding father of this New Liberalism was the Oxford philosopher, T. H. Green. In his view of liberty he stood firmly in the tradition of Milton and Mill. 'When we speak of freedom,' he wrote in 1880, 'we do not mean merely the freedom to do what we like irrespective of what it is we like. We mean the greatest power on the part of the citizens as a body to make the most and best of themselves.'[13] It followed that liberalism was about something more than the elimination of prohibitory laws and restrictions. 'The mere removal of compulsion,' he pointed out, 'the mere enabling a man to do as he likes, is itself no contribution to true freedom.'[14] A man imprisoned in slum conditions or enslaved by poverty was no more free than the habitual drunkard. He needed liberation, and that might well require the passing of laws, the redistribution of wealth and other activities of a positive and even a coercive nature by the state.

But if Green saw that public power might have a positive role to play in the pursuit of liberty, he was very far from being an enthusiast for the kind of all-embracing, paternalistic state favoured by many socialists and not a few Tories. As he put it: 'The real function of government being to maintain the conditions of life in which morality shall be possible, and

26

morality consisting in the disinterested performance of self-imposed duties, paternal government does its best to make it impossible by narrowing the room for the self-improvement of duties and for the play of disinterested motives'.[15]

A similar outlook informs the writings of the New Liberals of the early twentieth century, that distinguished group of thinkers of whom the most important were L. T. Hobhouse, J. L. Hammond, J. A. Hobson and Graham Wallas. They were deeply committed to efforts to liberate their contemporaries which involved considerable intervention by the state. In his influential book, *Liberalism*, first published in 1911, Hobhouse gave his view on the compatibility of coercive government and the principle of liberty:

> The function of state coercion is to override individual coercion, and, of course, coercion exercised by any association of individuals within the state. It is by this means that it maintains liberty of expression, security of person and property, genuine freedom of contract and the rights of public meeting and association . . .
>
> There is no intrinsic and inevitable conflict between liberty and compulsion, but at bottom a mutual need. The object of compulsion is to secure the most favourable external conditions of inward growth and happiness so far as these conditions depend on combined action and uniform observance. The sphere of liberty is the sphere of growth itself.[16]

The New Liberals are often bracketed with their contemporaries and friends, the early Fabians who founded the social democratic tradition in British politics. It is true that the two groups were on very friendly terms and worked closely together in their advocacy of many practical schemes of social reform. But there was a basic difference in their outlook which is well brought out in Peter Clarke's excellent book, *Liberals and Social Democrats* (Cambridge, 1978). The Fabian social democrats were first and foremost mechanical reformers who took a basically pessimistic view of human nature, had relatively little faith in the capacity of people to change either themselves or their societies, and therefore looked primarily to organisational and structural means to effect social progress.

The New Liberals, by contrast, were by temperament moral

reformers with an optimistic view of human nature who believed that progress came about primarily through the spontaneous, voluntary actions of individuals and communities. That is why they insisted, to quote Hobson, that 'the practical interpretation and realisation of moral and intellectual liberty for the people' is 'the most urgent and fruitful of all tasks'.[17] They held firm to the ideal of liberty which had inspired Milton and Mill and all the other great exponents of the British liberal tradition, to the conviction that, in the words of Hobhouse, 'the heart of Liberalism is the understanding that progress is not a matter of mechanical contrivance, but of the liberation of living spiritual energy.'[18] To a certain extent, this fundamental difference of approach still distinguishes Liberals from their Social Democrat allies today.

So where have we arrived after this all too brief historical and philosophical excursion? At a view of liberty as an essentially spiritual quality, founded on conscience and on the exercise of free moral choice, not at all the same as licence, and not necessarily set in perennial opposition to the state and to all coercive action. For liberals the individual human personality is the only ultimate source of virtue and moral worth, but that is not to deny that public authorities and communities have a very important role in providing the external conditions in which that moral worth can be developed. The individual is seen as creative, the state as regulative. The practical working out of this complementary relationship and its application in many areas of life by Victorian and Edwardian liberals to produce a coherent and distinctive British liberal tradition will be the subject of the next five chapters.

2

PRINCIPLE AND PASSION –
THE NONCONFORMIST CONSCIENCE
AND PROVINCIAL RADICALISM

On the Continent, and to some extent in the United States also, liberalism has been an essentially metropolitan and secular movement, self-consciously urbane, sophisticated and rationalistic. Liberalism in Britain has always had a very different character, rugged, restless and stubbornly anti-establishment, reflecting its origins in religious Puritanism and provincial radicalism. The nurseries of Liberalism in this country were not smart salons and pavement cafés but solid and severe Nonconformist chapels and temperance halls. Its finest exponents have been not so much clever philosophers or smooth talking intellectuals as straightforward, practical men and women with firm convictions and with fire in their bellies.

In their book, *The Liberal Tradition*, first published in 1956, Maurice Shock and Alan Bullock describe two fundamental principles which have characterised British liberalism. The first, as might be expected, is a belief in liberty. The second is a belief that principle ought to count for more than power or expediency. The historic role of Liberals, they argue, has been to modify policies and the exercise of power in the name of conscience. This is, of course, a reflection of the Christian roots of British liberalism and of the key role which the idea of conscience has occupied at least since the days of Milton. One particularly demanding conscience, that of Protestant Nonconformity, was, as we shall see, for long the guide and tutor of the British Liberal Party.

Allied to this strong sense of principle and conscience has been an element of passion. There is a tendency among historians to underplay this aspect of the liberal make-up and to portray Liberals simply as calm, reasonable men and women full of moderation and good sense. In this opening chapter on 'The Liberal Tradition' in a recently published book on British Liberalism, for example, Michael Brock lists as one of the characteristic Liberal attitudes 'the belief that moderation and reason are the prime requirements in the ordering of human affairs'.[1] This is certainly true – Liberals eschew extremism, fanaticism and bigotry and they seek to follow the paths of moderation and reason, accepting that those paths will often involve compromise and treading a middle way. But this is not to say that they are without passion or commitment. They are often people of strong emotions and fierce determination with a sense of mission in their lives. This was certainly true of William Ewart Gladstone, the first and greatest leader of organised Liberalism, who saw the Liberal Party as a great engine of change powered by the moral convictions of the people and who believed that 'good ends can rarely be attained in politics without passion'.[2] It is a noticeable characteristic of British Liberals, past and present, to believe that they are engaged not so much in a political movement as in a great moral crusade. As a rather disapproving Sidney Webb observed in 1901: 'A Liberal reform is never simply a social means to a social end, but rather a struggle of good against evil.'[3]

Both this stress on principle and the passion that goes with it derive from the origins of British Liberalism in religious dissent and provincial radicalism. We have already seen that it was the Puritan fathers who first formulated the characteristic British ideal of liberty. Two hundred years later it was the spiritual descendants of those Puritans, the Victorian Nonconformists, who created the British Liberal Party. It was out of their campaigns against the evils of drink, war and religious and economic protectionism that the impetus to form the party came, and from their distinctive brand of reforming zeal and moral earnestness that it took its spirit and character.

Few people epitomised this Nonconformist spirit better than John Bright, the Quaker cotton mill owner from Rochdale, Lancashire, who was prominent in nearly all of the great reforming campaigns of the mid nineteenth century and went on to sit in Gladstone's first two Governments. Bright came into political prominence when he led the campaign in his home town against the compulsory payment of rates to the Established Church. He went on to take a leading part in the campaign against the Corn Laws and to be a fierce critic of militarism and imperialism in Britain's foreign policy. His politics were grounded in his religion. As he put it, 'I could not be otherwise than a Liberal. I knew that I came from the stock of martyrs, that one of my ancestors had been in prison for several years because he preferred to worship in the humble meeting house of his own sect rather than in the church of the law-favoured sect'.[4]

Mr Gladstone observed in 1877 that 'Nonconformity supplies the backbone of English Liberalism.'[5] He might, without exaggeration, have gone rather further and said that it virtually dictated the policies of the Victorian Liberal Party. The strength of the Nonconformist Conscience made the Liberals the party of temperance, of disestablishment, of social reform and of peace. The licensing laws which bring down the shutters on British bars so firmly in the afternoons and late evenings are one of its most enduring legacies. So also is the tradition of protest against militarism and jingoism carried on today by the peace movement.

Even nowadays when both the Nonconformist churches and the Liberal Party are in rather reduced circumstances, the traditionally close relationship between them continues. Of the nine Liberal councillors serving in one Lancashire town in 1971, eight were Methodist lay preachers. One of the leading figures in contemporary Welsh Liberalism, Roy Roberts, is a Congregational minister (educated, appropriately, at the John Bright Grammar School in Llandudno), and at least three of the current batch of Liberal MPs are active chapel goers. Cyril Smith, a Unitarian, keeps up the Nonconformist tradition in John Bright's Rochdale, while both Alan Beith and Richard Wainwright are Methodist lay preachers. In an interesting

31

letter to the *Guardian* in June 1983, indeed, Richard Wainwright pointed to the close correlation between those areas of the country where Liberalism has survived and those with a strong Free Methodist tradition. Certainly the voters of his own Colne Valley constituency still provide some splendid examples of the liberalism of the chapel.[6]

The proud Pennine consciousness of the folk of the Colne Valley shows the survival of another strain which has long been important in British Liberalism. The creation of the Liberal Party was in many ways an expression of that great assertion of provincial self-confidence in mid-Victorian Britain which has also left us with such splendid monuments as the Free Trade Hall in Manchester and the great municipal buildings in the cities and towns of the Midlands and North. Liberalism has always been the creed of provincial England, of northern manufacturers and workers, west country small farmers and agricultural labourers. It has never been very popular in the metropolis, or among the rich landlords and businessmen of the softer south. Indeed, it is hard to think of a single famous Liberal past or present whose name is associated with the politics of London in the way that Jo Chamberlain's is with Birmingham, Lord Simon's with Manchester and Sir Trevor Jones' with Liverpool.

The Liberals have also, of course, historically been the party of Scotland and Wales. To appreciate this, one need only look at the background of the party's nine leaders in the present century. Four have been Scots (Sir Henry Campbell Bannerman, Sir Archibald Sinclair, Jo Grimond and David Steel), two Welsh (David Lloyd George and Clement Davies), and three English (H. H. Asquith – and he sat for a Scottish seat, Herbert Samuel and Jeremy Thorpe).

These provincial and Celtic roots account for much of the distinctive character of British liberalism. There is among most liberals a distaste for metropolitan smoothness and sophistication, for what John Bright summed up as 'society, smart people, hot rooms, elaborate meals and ceremonious observances'.[7] There is also a strong sense of local pride, a preference for devolving and decentralising power, and a natural sympathy for the small nations and peoples of the world and for all those struggling against over-mighty neighbours or oppressors.

David Lloyd George was, perhaps, the supreme exemplar of both the Celtic and Nonconformist strains in British liberalism. Brought up in rural North Wales by his strict Baptist uncle to hate English landlords and the Established Church, he first developed his oratorical powers in Band of Hope temperance meetings and first showed his radical streak when he refused to say the Anglican catechism at the church school which he attended. As a young politician, he devoted himself to the causes of Nonconformity and Celtic radicalism, leading the fight for the disestablishment of the Anglican Church in Wales, thundering against the evils of alcohol on temperance platforms up and down the country, and campaigning for land reform to remove the scourge of landlordism and create a nation of independent small proprietors. Himself born in poverty, his commitment to social welfare reforms, shown in his introduction of old age pensions and national insurance, was passionate and deep-rooted. So also was his devotion to peace and to the rights of small nations.

In his speeches Lloyd George showed himself to have a full measure of liberal passion. They were like sermons, filled with metaphors and images culled from the Bible, carefully fashioned to move audiences to tears and then to outrage, and usually ending with vehement tirades against the enemies of progress. None was more passionate than the great attack on the peers which he delivered to an audience of more than 4,000 at Limehouse on 30 July 1909, in the middle of the crisis over the People's Budget, and which set the rich trembling with anger and dismay. That more recent statement which has once again put Limehouse on the political map, the declaration by the founders of the Social Democratic Party on 25 January 1981, is, I fear, very dull and tame by comparison.

So much for the Liberal Party. Nonconformity and provincial radicalism have also had an impact far beyond the bounds of party politics. They have, for example, played an important role in the creation of two much applauded features of British life, the tradition of voluntary pressure groups and the institution of a serious, campaigning press.

Voluntary pressure groups, bringing together for the purposes of peaceful persuasion and campaigning individuals deeply committed to righting what they see as some major wrong, are a distinctive creation of the British liberal tradition which have long been held up by foreign observers as examples of that vitality and diversity which is at the heart of our national commitment to liberty. The first significant popular movement of this kind was the campaign for the abolition of the slave trade, and later for the extinction of slavery itself, which harnessed the moral indignation of Nonconformists and also Evangelical Anglicans. The second was the Anti-Corn Law campaign so effectively orchestrated by Cobden and Bright and infused with all the passion, and all the righteousness, of a great moral crusade. All subsequent pressure groups have, consciously or unconsciously, been modelled on these early movements. They have used the same techniques in their efforts to influence public opinion in general and legislators in particular.

Pressure groups do not always behave in a very liberal way, of course. They can abandon the tactics of persuasion and argument and take up those of force and bullying. They sometimes forget the right of their opponents to disagree with them and are tempted to impose their views on others. In these cases they are guilty of that group coercion which Hobhouse saw as fundamentally illiberal and for which he prescribed the remedy of state coercion. But the existence of these abuses does not detract from the great positive role which voluntary movements and pressure groups play in a liberal society, as expressions of the free and spontaneous anger and aspirations of the people, as agents in the interplay of ideas and debate, and as institutions which stand between the weakness of the individual and the power of the state.

The existence of a campaigning press is another expression both of the liberal assumption that people are susceptible to argument and persuasion and of an optimistic view of man's ability to change the world. The free interplay of ideas, and therefore the freedom of the press, is, as we have already seen, a key principle of British liberalism which was championed by the Puritan and Whig pioneers. In the mid-nineteenth century it was given an important boost when Gladstone removed all duties on newspapers, so bringing their price within range of every working man and woman. This abolition of the taxes on knowledge, as they had come to be called, unleashed a flood of newspapers, selling for a penny each, on the eager reading public. These papers, only a few of which survive today, were almost without exception Liberal in politics, Nonconformist in religious and moral stance and proudly provincial in outlook. They were edited by men of high ethical and intellectual standards who saw their job as a vocation and their business as a moral crusade.

This chapter has looked briefly at some of the great figures from the world of Nonconformity and provincial radicalism. I conclude it by mentioning two of these editors who, among many others, exemplify this important side of the British liberal tradition. The first is W. T. Stead, editor of the Darlington-based *Northern Echo* from 1871 to 1880 and later of the *Pall Mall Gazette*. The son of a Congregational minister, he declared as a young boy: 'I wish that God would give me a big whip that I could go round the world and whip the wicked out of it'.[8] The whip which he took up was journalism, and he used it with devastating effect against some of the most glaring injustices of his day.

The first major campaign which Stead mounted in the *Northern Echo* was over the brutal massacre by the Turks of some of their Bulgarian subjects in 1876. The publicity which he gave to this outrage provoked a national outcry over the Bulgarian atrocities, as they came to be called, and inspired Gladstone to come out of retirement and put himself at the head of the popular movement demanding British intervention to help the stricken Bulgars. Using the new techniques of bold headlines, pictures and frank, investigative exposures, but never sacrificing truth to sensationalism, Stead went on to mount campaigns on the evils of drink and bad housing and to crusade ceaselessly for peace, free trade and parliamentary reform. His most famous exposé, which landed him in prison, was of the 'white slave trade' in young girls who were lured to London as domestic servants and then shipped across to the Continent as prostitutes. Thanks to his fearless campaign, which was encouraged by Gladstone and Bramwell Booth of the Salvation Army, this grotesque trade was stopped.

The other great editor who epitomised both the Nonconformist Conscience and the radicalism of provincial England was the legendary C. P. Scott who for 57 years from 1872 to 1929 edited the *Manchester Guardian*. Like Stead's *Northern Echo*, Scott's paper was campaigning without being sensational or strident, high-minded without being dull or pompous, provincial without being parochial. It employed perhaps the most distinguished company of writers which has ever been brought together under one roof, a group which included the three leading exponents of the New Liberalism, Hobhouse, Hobson and Hammond, the poets Hilaire Belloc and John Masefield, and the historians R. C. K. Ensor and F. W. Hirst. Presiding over this talented company, and respected and revered by every one of them, was the gaunt, high-minded Unitarian who cycled to work, insisted that sex and murder should be accorded the lowest priority in assessing the value of a news story, held that comment was free but facts sacred, and thundered daily in his leaders against the evils of socialism, militarism and whatever else he felt to be bad for Manchester and bad for the world. There, indeed, was a striking blend of principle and passion.

3

TRUST IN THE PEOPLE –
THE DEMOCRATIC PRINCIPLE

Beneath the bust of William Ewart Gladstone which stands in the entrance porch of the National Liberal Club in London is carved an extract from one of his speeches: 'The Liberal principle is trust in the people qualified by prudence. The Tory principle is mistrust of the people only qualified by fear.' It is interesting to speculate what he might have gone on to say about the Labour principle had he lived long enough to see it in operation – perhaps management of the people qualified only by class feeling?

Like belief in liberty, trust in the people might seem to be a rather wide principle to attribute exclusively to just one political tradition. In a sense, of course, it is the common starting point of all democrats. But for Liberals it has a particular importance. This is because of their belief in the centrality of individual free choice and self-development and their conviction that people should be trusted as far as possible to pursue their own good in their own ways. Liberals are by nature distributists wanting to spread power, responsibility, wealth and ownership as widely as possible throughout society – not to establish absolute equality, for that is both impossible and undesirable, but to give everyone a stake in society and a say in the running of those institutions in which they have a direct interest, be it their local council, their place of work or

37

the government of the land.

The clearest expression of this commitment to the democratic principle, at least in the political sphere, is the notion of representative government. In origin, of course, this idea goes back to classical Greece. But its development and application in the modern world owes much to the work of liberal theorists and politicians in Britain. The call for government by consent and for parliamentary control over the actions of the executive echoes through British history from *Magna Carta* to the Petition of Right and on through the great reform acts of the nineteenth century. It was the cry of de Montfort and Langton in the Middle Ages, the Parliamentarians and Levellers of the seventeenth century, and the Whigs and Liberals of more recent times. Refined by John Locke and John Stuart Mill, popularised by John Bright and extended and passionately fought for by the suffragettes it has, perhaps, been the loudest and longest rallying cry of British liberalism.

The most concrete expression of that call was, of course, the extension of the franchise so that everyone had a direct say in electing the government. This took a long time to achieve. The principle of one person—one vote was not finally established in this country until 1948, more than a hundred years after the Great Reform Act of 1832 had first widened the franchise beyond its narrow aristocratic base. The slowness with which universal suffrage came was not just a reflection of the strength of opposition from the Conservatives and others opposed to parliamentary reform. Many Liberals themselves only gradually came to feel that the time was right for every man and woman to be given the vote. In the case of women's suffrage it has to be said that they largely shared the common prejudices of the age against the movement. This overall gradualism can partly be explained by the fact that Victorian Liberals saw the vote not so much as a natural right but rather as a trust to be earned. This view gave them a very exalted idea of the effect which conferring the vote on people would bring. John Bright and other enthusiasts for extending the franchise argued that the new responsibility which came with it would effect something little short of a moral transformation of the individuals concerned.

This view was also taken by J. S. Mill, whose essay on *Representative Government*, published in 1861, remains perhaps the best work on this subject in the English language. Mill regarded the act of voting in elections as the supreme exercise of the individual's capacity for making moral choices. His ideal was the active and continuous participation of every citizen in the business of government, as in the Greek city state, and for this reason he lauded institutions like the jury system and parish councils which offered similar opportunities in Britain. But he realised that in a large modern nation state such universal participation was impossible and in its place he recommended the principle of representative democracy.

For the modern Liberal Mill's essay has a particular interest. As well as being a superb exposition of the principle of representative government, it also points to the peculiarly unrepresentative nature of the British voting system:

> The pure idea of democracy is the government of the whole people by the whole people, equally represented. Democracy as commonly conceived and hitherto practised is the government of the whole people by a mere majority of the people . . .
>
> Real equality is not obtained unless any set of electors amounting to the average number of a parliamentary constituency, wherever in the country they reside, have the power of combining together to return a representative.[1]

Mill's proposal for a system of proportional representation based on a single transferable vote, which was later modified to include several multi-member constituencies rather than the single nationwide constituency he had originally envisaged, received remarkably little support from his fellow Victorian Liberals. He tried unsuccessfully to incorporate it in the provisions of the 1867 Reform Act, and subsequent attempts to introduce the scheme by Sir John Lubbock, great-grandfather of the present Lord Avebury, were opposed both by the Liberal establishment under Gladstone and by radicals like Bright and Chamberlain. In 1917 a Speaker's Conference on electoral reform recommended the introduction of proportional representation in borough constituencies but Liberal MPs were divided over the proposal and, with strong Conservative opposition, it failed to get through Parliament. As Vernon Bogdanor remarks in his excellent recent book on electoral reform, *The People and the Party System*, 'The Liberal failure to vote solidly for proportional representation must be accounted the Party's most disastrous decision this century'.[2] It was not until they found themselves consigned to the role of a third party in the 1920s that Liberals seriously took up the cause of electoral reform. Now, of course, it is a major priority.

It is both sad, and in some ways curious, that British Liberals did not show more interest in the idea of proportional representation until it was too late for them to implement it. The use of a single transferable vote accords much better than the first-past-the-post system with traditional liberal concern for widening the scope of individual choice and ensuring the representation of minorities. It also accords with an important strand of thinking in Liberalism which believes in diminishing the role and importance of party in politics. Proportional representation would have the effect of loosening the hold of the party whip and breaking down the primacy of party in British politics. As such, it must surely appeal to all those who believe, like Mill, that 'the constitution does not exist for the benefit of parties, but of citizens'.[3]

If their record over applying the principle of fully representative democracy to the government of the country is somewhat shaky, however, British Liberals have at least been prepared to apply it to their own affairs. In 1877, with the establishment of the National Liberal Federation, they became the first major British political party to introduce direct participation by all members in the formation and direction of policy. Just under a century later they became the first party to elect their leader democratically on the basis of one member, one vote.

Another long-standing Liberal commitment which is still very evident today is to open up the secrecy and élitism of government and bureaucracy. A significant breach of the closed, aristocratic wall around Whitehall was made by Gladstone's first ministry in 1871 when entrance to the Civil Service was thrown open to all comers on the basis of competitive examination. Gladstone himself was a considerable enthusiast for what would now be called open government. 'Publicity', he argued, 'is the great advantage, the great security of English public life'.[4] Following the lead given by Cobden and Bright, he waged a particular war against the secrecy which cloaked diplomacy and established a much greater degree of parliamentary control over the conduct of foreign affairs. This campaign was later taken up and extended by both Liberal and Labour radicals in the Union of Democratic Control who saw the horrors of the First World War as a direct result of leaving foreign policy to diplomats and politicians.

Liberalism has always stood clearly for the division and decentralisation of power. This principle underlay the campaign to give Home Rule to Ireland which engaged the Liberal Party for nearly forty years. Many Liberals have been equally keen to give self-government to the people of Scotland and Wales – indeed this policy appeared in a manifesto issued by Gladstone as early as 1886. The establishment of a democratically elected system of local government in Britain was another achievement of nineteenth-century liberalism. It began with the Whigs' Municipal Corporations Act of 1835 and was completed with a measure of Gladstone's last administration in 1894 which set up parish councils throughout the land. Now everyone, however humble, had a chance to take part in the process of government. In the words of J. Spence Watson, president of the National Liberal Federation, the principle of self-government had been brought to every cottage door.[5]

It is not only in the field of politics and government that Liberals have applied the principle of trusting people to run their own affairs. They have long been committed to the idea of industrial democracy and specifically to the introduction of employee participation in decision making, profit-sharing and co-operative enterprises. The first large scale profit-sharing schemes in Britain were promoted in the 1860s by two Liberal industrialists, Henry Briggs at Whitwood Colliery in West Yorkshire and Edward Greening at the Cobden Memorial Mills in Lancashire. Cobden himself enthusiastically supported the initiative of the pioneers in his own Rochdale constituency who launched the co-operative movement, and Gladstone announced that he 'looked to Co-operation as the new influence which should reconcile the mighty powers of capital and labour'.[6] Mill was also a strong advocate of co-partnership and predicted that it would eventually become the dominant form of ownership in British industry: 'The relation of masters and workpeople will gradually be superseded by partnership, in one of two forms: in some cases, association of the labourers with the capitalists; in others, and perhaps finally in all, association of labourers among themselves'.[7]

Implicit in these statements is an insistence that there is no necessary conflict between the interests of capital and labour, that employers and employees can co-operate together just as closely and successfully as groups of workers can. This was a fundamental tenet of Victorian Liberals and it explains their ambivalent attitude towards the emerging trade union movement. In so far as they were voluntary groups democratically representing working people, trade unions were welcomed as an extension of the liberal principle, but there was considerable concern over their use of coercion and pursuit of selfish sectional interests. Legislation passed by Gladstone's first Government in 1871 legalised unions for the first time and protected their funds while at the same time outlawing picketing and other forms of intimidation. The profoundly undemocratic structure of many unions appalled Liberals then as now, as did their opposition to co-operative ventures and their fostering of a spirit of conflict and division in industry. Cobden went so far as to describe them as 'founded upon principles of brutal tyranny and monopoly' and declared that he would rather live 'under a Bey of Algiers than a trades committee', while Mill expressed the hope that the extension of co-partnership in industry would lead to 'the true euthanasia of trade unionism'.[8]

Liberals have been equally unhappy about the exploitation of workers and the development of narrow sectional interests on the part of employers. Fundamental to the Liberal principle of trust in the people is the assertion of a common good which stands above and beyond narrow class and sectional interests. T. H. Green actually defined Liberalism as 'the cause of social good against class interests'.[9] This, of course, ties in with the unique historical position which the Liberals have occupied in British politics as a party of ideas rather than of class interests, drawing support evenly from right across the social spectrum, and appealing not on narrow sectional grounds, but on the basis of certain broad principles.

A concomitant of this view is, of course, the expectation that people in general will perceive the common good and will be prepared to put it before their own sectional interests. This particular aspect of the liberal's optimistic view of human nature characterised the approach of the Victorian Liberal Party to the emerging mass electorate. Unlike the Conservatives, who wooed the new working-class voters with a mixture of populism and bonhomie, giving them jingoistic slogans and subsidised beer, the Liberals appealed rather to their hearts and minds. The speeches which Gladstone delivered to the working people of Scotland in his famous Midlothian campaign just over a hundred years ago often lasted more than one and a half hours. They contained no appeals to the self- interest of his hearers, no easy bribes or promises, but rather complex disquisitions on the state of foreign affairs and impassioned outbursts on the plight of far off peoples and on the evils of imperialism. His audiences, who had come from as far afield as Shetland and the Western Isles and paid up to £10 to crowd into village halls to hear him, never went home disappointed.

The habit, so unfashionable in the twentieth century among politicians of all parties, of treating voters as concerned and intelligent human beings who can look beyond their own material self-interest, is an essential aspect of any real trust in the people. So also is another principle which is sometimes overlooked by present-day Liberals. The great Victorian democrats like Bright and Mill did not envisage an endless process of consultation and participation with no definite conclusions being reached. The opening up of government and the introduction of worker participation in industry should not, they believed, lead to any paralysis of action or will. Strong and decisive leadership would still be needed – Governments would still govern and managers would still manage, albeit that they would be more accountable and accessible.

This point remains valid today. If you are going to operate on the principle of trusting people, then you must trust them to do the job to which they have been elected or appointed and not constantly interfere with them and obstruct their actions. There is a tendency nowadays for certain groups, one thinks particularly of the police, to be subjected to incessant examination and to be frustrated and impeded in the performance of their work by mistrust and suspicion. There is a parallel tendency for enthusiasm for participation to reach such heights that the consultation process, on planning questions, for example, becomes endless and decisions are never taken. Of course, accountability and participation are vital – but so also is action.

There is another side to trusting the people which has been somewhat lost sight of by Liberals in recent times. Paternalism has ceased to be the prerogative of Tories to whom it historically belongs. Liberals are increasingly inclined to look to state agencies and to advocate protectionist remedies for social problems. They are also increasingly interested in the structure of the constitution and given to proposing complex reforms in the machinery of government. This approach is out of keeping with the tradition of British liberalism which, to repeat the distinction made in the last chapter, is one of moral rather than mechanical reform. It also betrays a lack of trust in the energies and capacities of the people.

4

A WELFARE SOCIETY –
THE VOLUNTARY PRINCIPLE AND
THE ENABLING STATE

Liberals put more stress on moral than on material values, but they are not blind to the physical condition of men. There is not much point, after all, in preaching the benefits of spiritual freedom and political liberty to someone who is shivering with cold and wondering where his next meal is coming from. Liberalism is founded on conscience and moral principle and as such it stands for the relief of suffering and the improvement of the human condition. The Latin word *liber* means generous as well as free, and altruism has always been a prominent feature of the liberal temper. The extent and vigour of voluntary activity in the field of social welfare in this country testifies to the strength of this aspect of the liberal tradition in Britain. As in so many other areas it is to the Victorian age that we must look for the development of a distinctively liberal approach to social welfare. It was of course the great age of private philanthropy, a period which saw charitable giving on a scale unequalled before or since and the foundation of many of the great voluntary organisations which are still active today. It was also an age of dedicated social reformers, campaigning for the spread of education, improvements in public health, land reform, temperance reform, better housing, better working conditions, and for a thousand and one other causes to improve the lot of humanity.

Underlying all this effort was the notion of voluntaryism. This is one of the most neglected and misunderstood components of the British liberal tradition. Although it is a rather ugly word it describes the attitude of Victorian Liberalism much more accurately than the commonly used phrase self-help, with its connotations of individualism and selfishness, or the equally hackneyed *laissez-faire*, the doctrine of do-nothingness. Unlike both self-help and *laissez-faire*, voluntaryism is a philosophy of social concern and social action which rests on the altruistic impulse in human nature. Wherever possible, the voluntaryist would have welfare promoted by the spontaneous and voluntary actions of individuals and communities rather than by compulsory government activity. But to back that voluntary action, and in cases where it is clearly inadequate to meet particular needs, he has no hesitation in enlisting public aid.

The best exposition of the principle of voluntaryism comes from the pen of John Stuart Mill. In his *Principles of Political Economy* (1848) he proclaimed his faith in 'the social feelings of mankind'. He went on: 'A people among whom there is no habit of spontaneous action for a collective interest. . . have their faculties only half developed; their education is defective in one of its most important branches'. It followed that 'the government should not only leave as much as possible to their own faculties the conduct of what concerns themselves alone, but should suffer them, or rather encourage them, to manage as many as possible of their joint concerns by voluntary operation.'[1] This encouragement, Mill suggested, should include public funding for voluntary activities and projects. The Government should only directly involve itself in the provision of social welfare in areas where it was clear that voluntary enterprise was inadequate to the task, and even then it should not try to supplant existing voluntary agencies but complement them. Thus state-provided schools should, where needed, be set up alongside private ones, publicly run hospitals complement voluntary clinics, and so on.

When it was first developed in the period of economic boom in the middle of the nineteenth century, voluntaryism was based on the confident expectation that private philanthropy, together with the extensive operations of friendly societies, trade unions and other agencies devoted to mutual aid and co-operation, would be adequate to combat the evils of ignorance, disease and poverty and to secure a decent standard of living for all. At the time this was by no means an unrealistic assumption. During the prosperous 1850s and 1860s voluntary schools set up mostly by the churches catered for the elementary education of many of the country's children, savings and insurance schemes run by friendly societies and trade unions tided many working men and their families through illness, unemployment and old age, and private philanthropy did much to relieve poverty and suffering. However, as the mid-Victorian boom gave way to the slump which started Britain's slow but steady decline as an industrial nation, it became clear that reliance on purely voluntary efforts would not be sufficient.

It was on the issue of elementary education that Liberals first conceded that the purely voluntary approach was inadequate and developed the notion of partnership between public and voluntary provision of services which has characterised the Liberal approach to social welfare over the last hundred years or so. During the 1840s and 1850s a vigorous campaign had been waged in favour of a totally voluntary system of schools. The leaders of the campaign, Edward Baines, a Leeds news-paper editor, and Edward Miall, a Congregational minister, argued that education was something which both could and should be provided entirely 'by individual talent and energy and the voluntary contributions of a free people among themselves'.[2] By the late 1860s, however, although they had lost none of their basic preference for voluntaryism, they had come to see that some publicly provided schools and state funding were necessary to meet the needs of the children of the urban poor who were not being reached by existing voluntary effort.

The measure which introduced universal elementary educa-tion in England, W. E. Forster's Education Act of 1870, is one of the historic Liberal achievements in the field of social welfare. It is also a splendid example of the application of the voluntary principle. Forster's Act ordained that there should be a school within the reach of every child in the land. It fulfilled that aim by authorising the establishment of publicly financed and organised Board schools in those areas which lacked voluntarily run schools. It further ordained that the voluntary schools should receive some public financial assistance. The aim, as Forster himself put it, 'is to complete the present voluntary system, to fill up gaps . . . not to destroy the existing system in introducing a new one'.[3] The Act faithfully fulfilled Mill's prescription of the proper use of state power and finance to complement and encourage voluntary community effort.

This idea of partnership between statutory and voluntary effort to promote social welfare underlay much of the work of Gladstone's governments. It can be seen, for example, in a minute issued in 1869 on the relief of the poor which proposed that the utterly destitute should be supported out of the compulsorily levied poor rates, while others should be helped by private charitable effort. It also lay behind measures to protect the funds of trade unions and friendly societies which were seen as important agencies of mutual aid and social insurance.

Gladstone himself never tired of repeating his own deeply held belief that it was through the spontaneous efforts of individuals and communities and not through the actions of the state that true social progress was achieved. But that did not stop him introducing legislation which considerably extended the scope of public intervention and public funding in the fields of health, education and welfare. His governments passed measures making attendance at school compulsory, regulating the hours of work of certain categories of workers and authorising the use of public money to establish libraries, public baths and recreation grounds and to purchase land for re-letting as allotments and smallholdings.

There were two important aspects of this legislation which kept it true to the Liberal tradition of liberty, trust in the people and voluntaryism. The first is that much of it was of a permissive rather than a mandatory kind. True to their democratic and decentralist principles, Victorian Liberals felt that the best public agency for securing the welfare of the people was local rather than central government. Local authorities were given wide enabling powers to tackle bad housing, poor sanitation and other social ills, and to raise the money for improvement schemes, but they were not actually compelled to do so. The initiative for action was left with local communities, local electors and local politicians.

In the hands of an energetic social reformer like Joseph Chamberlain the Liberal local government acts provided a spur for ambitious schemes of social improvement which involved taking essential public utilities like gas and water into municipal ownership and engaging in bold slum clearance and rebuilding programmes. Through his pioneering work in Birmingham in the 1870s Chamberlain established a distinctively Liberal style of democratic, decentralised urban social reform which has in our own time been taken up with considerable success in the city of Liverpool. In a statement which anticipates the approach of the community politicians of modern-day Liberalism he described it as:

a wise co-operation by which the community as a whole, working through its representatives for the benefit of all its members, and recognizing the solidarity of interest which makes the welfare of the poorest a matter of importance to the richest, has faced its obligations and done much to lessen the sum of human misery, and to make the lives of all its citizens somewhat better, somewhat nobler, and somewhat happier.[4]

The second important feature of this legislation is that in general it introduced state intervention only in areas where voluntary exhortation and effort had demonstrably proved to be inadequate, or where there was a weak party unable to protect itself against manifestly unfair treatment by a stronger party. We have already seen that Forster's Education Act was passed to fill in the gaps in the existing voluntary school system. Gladstone's last administration felt compelled for somewhat similar reasons to introduce a measure in 1894 (which was blocked by the House of Lords and did not reach the Statute Book until 1906) to make employers liable for injuries suffered by their workers and caused by faulty or inadequately protected machinery. Ideally, of course, this was a matter which Liberals would like to have left to the consciences of industrialists. But sadly not all employers had strong humanitarian instincts and legislation was necessary to compel them to do what natural justice demanded. Similar considerations prompted laws giving protection to Irish tenants against eviction and the imposition of unfair rents by their often absentee landlords.

Several prominent contemporaries, led by Herbert Spencer, A. V. Dicey, Sir Henry Maine and Sir William Lecky, regarded the increasingly interventionist social welfare legislation of Gladstone's later governments as marking a fundamental shift in British Liberalism away from *laissez-faire* individualism and towards socialist-style collectivism. This view, which has been echoed by a number of modern historians, is fallacious. As we have already seen, neither narrow individualism nor doctrinaire adherence to the principle of *laissez-faire* have ever been characteristics of the British liberal tradition. But if Liberals did not radically change direction in the last two decades of the nineteenth century, it is true that they placed a much greater emphasis on the whole subject of social welfare.

As urbanisation spread, and as the economic graphs turned downwards, the extent of poverty in Britain became painfully apparent to all who took any interest in their surroundings. This was in no small measure due to the work of a group of pioneer Liberal social scientists, led by Charles Booth and Seebohm Rowntree. Their carefully researched surveys revealed large pools of deprivation which had been left largely untouched by voluntary agencies and private philanthropy. Booth estimated that around thirty per cent of the population of London lived below a minimum level of subsistence. Nonconformists were roused by this domestic misery as they had been over injustices committed abroad and in publications like *The Bitter Cry of Outcast London*, written by a group of Congregational ministers, the Liberal conscience was stirred.

One of the leading exponents of this increased social emphasis was T. H. Green. In his writings he argued that the welfare of the people should stand alongside the promotion of liberty as the supreme Liberal goal. The two aims were intimately bound up, he suggested. Man was a social being who could only realise himself fully by participating in the community. True liberty meant 'the liberation of the powers of all men equally for contributions to a common good'. Green himself was actively involved in campaigns for temperance reform and for compulsory education which envisaged using the power of the state as an important agency of that liberation. In a key lecture which he delivered in 1880 he supported the interventionist measures of Gladstone's governments and put forward a clearly positive, but essentially voluntaryist view of the role of the state in the provision of social welfare:

> It is the business of the state, not indeed directly to promote moral goodness, for that, from the very nature of moral goodness, it cannot do, but to maintain the conditions without which a free exercise of the human faculties is impossible . . . We shall probably all agree that a society in which the public health was duly provided for, by the spontaneous action of individuals, was in a higher condition than one in which the compulsion of law was needed to secure these ends. But we must take men as we find them. Until such a condition of society is reached, it is the business of the state to take the best security it can for the young citizens' growing up in such health and with so much knowledge as is necessary for their real freedom.[5]

The idea which Green put forward can perhaps best be described as that of the enabling state. The power and resources of central and local government should be used to create the material conditions which enable that 'free exercise of human faculties' which Liberals seek for all people. The moral conditions, which the state can never provide, must come from the minds and hearts of the people.

The practical working out of this idea is clearly seen in the development in the late nineteenth century of a distinctive Liberal policy on the redistribution of wealth and property. Liberalism has never sought to take away the individual's right to earn and hold personal wealth and to own property. Quite the opposite in fact. What it has sought is to make everyone an owner by achieving a fairer and wider distribution of the earth's resources among its people. During the later Victorian period Liberals came to view the ownership of private property as a form of trusteeship which carried responsibilities and duties as well as rights. They also developed the notion of the unearned surplus, that often substantial part of an individual's wealth which did not owe its value directly to any effort he himself had made, but rather to the activities of society as a whole or to the accidents of geography. This notion of surplus value, or unearned increment, was taken as the justification for taxation which had as its aim the redistribution to the community as a whole of the wealth which was properly its to share and which had unfairly accrued to certain individuals.

Ideally Liberals hoped that the surplus wealth of the rich would voluntarily be transferred to the poor. This was always the great dream of Gladstone who proposed in 1890 the creation of a Universal Beneficent Society in which the rich would bind themselves to devote their surplus wealth to the good of the community as a whole and so avoid the necessity for compulsory redistributive taxation by the state.[6] It was not quite such a naive idea as it may seem today. It has been estimated that several Victorians contributed well over £1 million to charitable ventures. Liberal manufacturers were among the most generous givers. Joseph Rowntree, the York chocolate maker, set aside half of his wealth for charitable purposes, decreeing that a proportion should be used for the direct relief of distress and the rest for research into the long term causes of poverty, the promotion of temperance and the influencing of public opinion in favour of peace and the settlement of international disputes by arbitration. *The Times* noted in 1885 that charitable receipts in London alone came to more than the national budgets of Denmark, Portugal, Sweden or Switzerland and a survey in the 1890s found that middle-class families devoted more than ten per cent of their incomes to charity, a greater proportion than they spent on any other item except food.

Other Liberals, however, who believed like Green that they must take men as they found them, were less optimistic about the altruism of the well-off and more ready to use the state to share out their unearned wealth among the community. As early as the 1840s Mill had advocated taxation as a means of redistributing wealth and had specifically called for an inherit- ance tax. In 1894, the last year of Gladstone's last Government, W. V. Harcourt, the Chancellor of the Exchequer, imposed a graduated scale of death duties on both landed and personal estates. It marked the acceptance by the Liberals of a clear and positive role for taxation of private wealth by the state as an instrument of social reform.

The history of the campaign to promote wider ownership of the land, perhaps the most popular single social reform movement of Victorian Liberalism, shows a similar move from pure voluntaryism to the recognition of a role for the enabling state. Early land reformers like Cobden and Bright placed their faith largely in the removal of restrictions on the free sale and transfer of land. Later reformers called for the taxation of the land, and in particular of increases in value which could not be attributed solely to the efforts of the proprietor. This notion of site value rating, which was to be taken up by Lloyd George and is still enthusiastically canvassed by several Liberals today, is normally attributed to the American economist, Henry George, who wrote his famous book *Progress and Poverty* in 1881. The idea had, in fact, originally been developed by Mill more than thirty years earlier. Many late Victorian Liberals went even further and advocated the purchase of land by local authorities, compulsorily if necessary, for re-selling or letting as allotments and smallholdings. This last option, which fell only just short of nationalisation, was proposed by Chamberlain in his famous Unauthorized Programme of 1885 which promised 'three acres and a cow' to working men. Gladstone's 1894 Local Government Act did, in fact, empower local authorities to acquire land for this purpose, even without the owners' consent if necessary.

By the end of the nineteenth century, Liberals had worked out an approach to promoting social welfare which, while retaining their basic preference for voluntary action, envisaged a substantial role for central and local government. Specifically they had identified four areas where public intervention in an essentially free market economy and society was necessary to secure the welfare of the people. The first was to establish and enforce a legal framework for economic relations within the market, for example by defining the rights and responsibilities of employers and employees, or landlords and tenants. The second was to provide what economists call public goods like education and health, although there was an insistence that the state should not have a monopoly in the provision of these goods. The third was to control essential public services which were also natural monopolies like gas and water supplies, and the fourth was to promote social justice and a more equitable distribution of the earth's resources through redistributive taxation and the transfer of land.

The twin ideas of voluntaryism and the enabling state underlay the work of the last Liberal Government in Britain. This administration, presided over first by Henry Campbell-Bannerman and then by H. H. Asquith, inspired by the ideas of the New Liberal social scientists and philosophers like J. A. Hobson, L. T. Hobhouse, Charles Booth and the young William Beveridge, and galvanized by the restless energy of Lloyd George and Winston Churchill, almost certainly did more to promote the welfare of the British people than any other before or since. Among the features which it introduced were state old age pensions, national insurance against sickness and unemployment, labour exchanges, statutory minimum wage rates in certain industries, medical inspection of school-children, free school meals, publicly provided care for mal-treated and delinquent children and government-funded public works projects to provide employment and improve the physical environment. To help pay for this substantial package the famous 'People's Budget' of 1909 introduced graduated income tax, a new super-tax on high income earners, high sales taxes on alcohol and tobacco and a series of taxes on landowners. These last were part of an ambitious land reform programme involving a massive Domesday-style survey of the country and the creation of large numbers of smallholdings. Sadly, it was shelved when the war came and never really resurrected, although in 1918 Lloyd George succeeded in passing an Act which provided 20,000 smallholdings for returning soldiers to rent from county councils.

The 1906 to 1915 Liberal Government is often said to have laid the foundations of the Welfare State. Those involved would, I think, have preferred to use the phrase Welfare Society. They envisaged voluntary action, whether in the form of self-help, mutual aid or philanthropy, continuing to play a major role in securing the welfare of the people. Wherever possible they avoided setting up new public agencies and centralised bureaucracies, preferring to graft their new schemes on to existing voluntary agencies. Responsibility for administering the new system of national insurance, for example, was given to the trade unions, friendly societies and insurance societies. The new state old age pensions were made non- contributory so that their introduction would not damage the extensive existing voluntary savings and pensions schemes. The system of sickness and unemployment benefits was founded on the principle of insurance rather than state subsidy. The idea of personal responsibility was still seen as lying at the heart of social welfare.

The last thing which these Liberal reformers wanted to do was to create a great new Leviathan, an all-embracing, all-providing nanny state which would suffocate what Mill had called 'the social feelings of mankind' and turn them into dependent clients of a welfare bureaucracy. Their idea was rather to use public resources and power in an enabling sense to establish certain minimum safeguards and standards which would liberate men and women from the slavery of poverty, illness and ignorance and foster initiative and individuality. 'I do not want to see impaired the vigour of competition', Winston Churchill wrote in 1909, 'but we can do much to mitigate the consequences of failure. We want to draw a line below which we will not allow persons to live and labour, yet above which they may compete with all the strength of their manhood'.[7] Charles Booth based his argument for old age pensions on the grounds that they would guarantee to the elderly 'a security of position which will stimulate, rather than weaken, the play of individuality on which progress and prosperity depend'.[8] Hobhouse envisaged 'a kind of partnership between the individual and the community, the State affording a certain basis of material well-being on which it is left to the individual to build by his own efforts the fabric of his independence, comfort and even wealth'.[9] Hobson spoke simply of 'a fuller appreciation and realisation of individual liberty contained in the provision of equal opportunities for self-development'.[10]

The social reforms accomplished by the last Liberal Government to rule Britain were prodigious in their scale and effect. They banished want and misery from many homes. When Seebohm Rowntree went back to York in the 1930s to repeat the social investigation that he had carried out in 1901, he found that the proportion of working-class people living in abject poverty had been reduced by more than fifty per cent since his first survey, and he attributed this rise in the standard of living largely to the Liberal social reforms of 1906 to 1914. Yet those who brought them about had only a limited confidence in the efficacy of the new welfare system which they had created. They believed, with Gladstone, that it was not through the state that man was regenerated. They were, to repeat the distinction between the New Liberals and their Fabian and socialist contemporaries made in Chapter One, moral rather than mechanical reformers. Significantly, the 1906 general election, which brought the landslide victory which enabled the Liberals to push through their social reforms and to take on the House of Lords when it tried to block them, was not fought on the issue of social welfare at all. The issues on which Liberals, old and new alike, fought and won the campaign were the traditional ones of free trade, Nonconformist disabilities, and moral outrage over the use of Chinese slave labour in the South African gold mines. They did not approach the subject of the welfare of the people in the manner of more recent politicians, as a good election issue offering the prospect of a kind of Dutch auction with other parties, with promises of a higher pension here and a better benefit there. They had too much respect for the electorate to indulge in that kind of bribery, and an altogether deeper view of what made for real social progress – not the actions of the Government, but the community spirit and voluntary efforts of the people.

5

LIBERAL INTERNATIONALISM – THE DEFENCE OF FREEDOM AND THE PROMOTION OF PEACE

Liberals are naturally outward looking and internationalist minded. They aim to break down the barriers between countries created by suspicion and narrow nationalism and welcome the rich diversity that springs from the coming together of different races and cultures. Two principles in particular have traditionally animated British Liberals in the sphere of foreign affairs. Prompted by their love of liberty, they have been moved by the struggles for freedom and self-determination of small nations and oppressed political, racial and religious minorities. At the same time they have been lovers of peace, seeking the non-violent resolution of conflicts and the spread of international co-operation and rejecting the jingoism and xenophobia that make up one of the less pleasant sides of the British character.

These two principles are to some extent contradictory and over the past 150 years or so they have led to the development of two quite distinct, and sometimes conflicting, approaches to foreign affairs. The first, which springs directly from attachment to the pursuit of liberty, has seen Britain's role in the world as that of active champion of the cause of freedom and supporter of movements for independence and liberation. The second, which owes its origins to the pacifist promptings of the Nonconformist Conscience and the demands of the free trade lobby, has counselled a general policy of neutrality and non-intervention. Both these points of view still co-exist in the Liberal Party today as can be seen in recent differences of opinion over the rights and wrongs of the Falklands War and over the question of Cruise missiles and British membership of NATO.

The tradition of giving active support to the cause of freedom owes much to the work of the two outstanding foreign secretaries in the first half of the nineteenth century, the liberal Tory George Canning and the Whig Viscount Palmerston. Both championed and materially assisted national independence movements in Europe and Latin America. The idea that a continuation of this role should be a guiding principle of British foreign policy was strongly propounded by Mill who wrote in 1849 that it was the duty of every Liberal Government and people 'to assist struggling liberalism, by mediation, by money, or by arms, whenever it can prudently do so; as every despotic government, when its aid is needed or asked for, never scruples to aid despotic governments'. [1] National liberation movements like the Italian *Risorgimento* and struggles by oppressed peoples like the Bulgarians, Armenians and Montenegrins against their despotic Turkish rulers continued to excite Liberal sympathy and admiration throughout the nineteenth century and prompted not a few young Britons to go off and fight for freedom. It has to be said, however, that this sympathy was very rarely turned into large-scale assistance or military intervention.

One of the main reasons for this lack of direct assistance to those struggling for freedom around the world was undoubtedly the hold on the Liberal mind of the doctrine of non-intervention. This doctrine was first developed by Richard Cobden and John Bright in the 1840s and 1850s in opposition to some of the less liberal aspects of Palmerston's foreign policy, like his balance of power theory, his reliance on secret diplomacy and his tendency to counter the smallest slight to British pride with a dazzling show of military strength. They argued the case for minimal British involvement in the affairs of other nations on both economic and moral grounds, pointing to the high cost in both money and men of maintaining large armies and navies and engaging in imperial adventures. They castigated a style of foreign policy which they saw as bringing glory and prestige to the aristocracy who enjoyed secret diplomacy and war-mongering, but bloodshed and misery to the people who had to bear its consequences. In its place they proposed a new international order based on open treaties and democratic diplomacy ('as little intercourse betwixt the Governments, as much connection as possible between the Nations of the world' as Cobden put it), arbitration of disputes between countries, and the spread of commerce which, they confidently if somewhat over-optimistically expected, would turn swords into ploughshares and banish war from the face of the globe.[2]

This idealistic, anti-militarist approach has remained an important feature of British Liberalism. It sets itself against a rather unpleasant aspect of the national psyche, what Cobden described as 'the pugnacious, energetic, self-sufficient, foreigner-despising and pitying character of that noble insular creature, John Bull'.[3] Because of their opposition to imperialism and flag-waving military adventures, Liberals have often been portrayed as being anti-patriotic. This criticism was made of Cobden and Bright when they opposed the Crimean War, of Gladstone when he opposed Disraeli's jingoistic war-mongering against Russia, and of Lloyd George when he opposed the Boer War. The truth is that Liberals have a different kind of patriotism from that which expresses itself in the glorification of war and imperial conquests. It is well summed up in the words which Bright wrote as he sat contemplating the ruins of the Roman Empire:

From her history, and indeed from all history, I learn that loud boasting, great wealth, great power, extended dominion, successive conquests, mighty fleets and armies, are not immovable foundations of national greatness. I would rely rather on an educated and moral people, and on a system of government free at home, and scrupulously moral and just in its dealings with every other government and people.[4]

The potentially conflicting principles of Mill and Bright were to some extent at least synthesised later in the nineteenth century by W. E. Gladstone. Gladstone's ideas on foreign affairs have almost certainly had a more enduring impact than his pronouncements on any other area of policy. It is worth considering them in some detail as in many ways they remain to this day the guiding principles of British Liberalism. He conveniently summarised them in his 1879 Midlothian Campaign as 'to foster economy at home . . . to preserve to the nations of the world the blessings of peace . . . to strive to cultivate and maintain the Concert of Europe . . . to avoid needless and entangling engagements . . . to acknowledge the equal rights of all nations . . . and the foreign policy of England should always be inspired by the love of freedom'.[5]

Economy was certainly a major consideration in Gladstone's foreign policy. Throughout his administrations he kept defence spending down to what his opponents regarded as a dangerously low level. It was when his own Liberal Cabinet colleagues sought to raise spending on the Navy in 1894 that he finally resigned as Prime Minister and party leader. Economy was not, of course, the only consideration which led him to dislike military expenditure. While not actually a pacifist, he had strongly pacific leanings and regarded the maintenance of a large standing army and navy and the use of sabre-rattling diplomacy as immoral actions which increased the risk of war. To that extent, he was a dedicated disciple of Cobden and Bright.

He was also an enthusiastic follower of another principle which had first been developed by Cobden and Bright, that of settling disputes between countries by arbitration rather than by force. In 1849 Cobden had proposed a motion in Parliament inviting foreign powers to bind themselves to refer to external arbitration any future misunderstanding which could not be settled by amicable negotiation. Several other Liberals enthusiastically took up the idea, including W. T. Stead who called for 'the establishing of a High Court of Justice among the Nations, whose decrees would not merely be the recommendations of arbitrators, but would be enforced by the authority of the Court'.[6] In government, Gladstone insisted on settling by international arbitration the disputes between the British and United States governments arising out of incidents during the American Civil War. In 1872 five arbitrators in Geneva awarded the Americans more than £3 million compensation for the damage which had been done to their commerce by the activities of a British ship, the *Alabama*, which had been used for piracy by the rebel Confederate states. Although he regarded the award as somewhat excessive, Gladstone instantly ordered the money to be paid and incurred considerable unpopularity as a result. The sum involved, he said:

is dust in the balance compared with the moral value of the example set when these two great nations of England and America, which are among the most fiery and most jealous in the world with regard to anything that touches national honour, went in peace and concord before a judicial tribunal to dispose of these painful differences rather than resort to the arbitrament of the sword.[7]

As a result of the *Alabama* settlement the idea of using this method of settling disputes spread and 194 treaties binding countries to use arbitration were signed between 1872 and 1914.

On the subject of the British Empire, Gladstone shared both Mill's support for moves towards self-determination and Bright's dislike of colonial entanglements. Although as Premier he was not able completely to avoid such entanglements, feeling compelled to send troops to Egypt and the Sudan, his general policy was guided by the twin themes of granting self-government to existing colonies and resisting the acquisition of new dependencies. His first administration gave independence to the Cape of Good Hope and allowed Australia and New Zealand to decide their own levels of tariff. His second government withdrew British troops from Afghanistan, which had become a virtual British protectorate under Disraeli, restored the Transvaal to the Boers, and gave independence to Cyprus and Jamaica. It also saw a brief attempt, under the viceroyalty of Lord Ripon, to prepare the people of India for self-government.

In his strong support for movements of national self-determination Gladstone was closer to Mill than to Bright. It had, in fact, been his sympathy with the Italian struggle for unification and liberation from Austrian rule which in 1859 weaned the future Liberal leader from his early allegiance to the Conservatives. In his first period as Premier he was much concerned with preserving the independence of Belgium from possible aggression by either of the parties in the Franco-Prussian War and in opposing the proposed Prussian annexation of Alsace and Lorraine on the grounds that it 'involved the transfer of the allegiance and citizenship of no small part of the heart and life of human beings from one sovereignty to another without any reference to their own consent'.[8] He proposed a plebiscite supervised by the neutral powers of Europe to establish the wishes of the people affected. In later years he took up the cause of the Christian peoples of the Balkans struggling for liberation from their Turkish overlords. It was this struggle which inspired his leadership of the campaign against the Bulgarian Atrocities and which supplied the theme of the last great speech of his life, delivered in Liverpool at the age of eighty-seven and lasting an hour and twenty minutes, an impassioned demand for British intervention to avenge the Turks' massacre of Armenians.

Dear though the concept of national self-determination was to him, Gladstone was not blind to the dangerous and illiberal aspects of the nationalism which was beginning to grip Europe in the later nineteenth century. His friend, Lord Acton, had pointed out as early as 1862 that nationalism was by no means necessarily a liberal movement. Too often, indeed, it was accompanied by a harsh intolerance towards minority groups. 'If we take the establishment of liberty for the realisation of moral duties to be the end of civil society', Acton wrote in his unfinished *History of Freedom*, 'we must conclude that those states are substantially the most perfect which . . . include various distinct nationalities without oppressing them'.[9] Here was a powerful statement of the case for multiracial and multicultural societies of the kind that liberals in many lands have sought to champion in the twentieth century.

Gladstone's internationalism was rooted in an almost mystical sense of the harmony of moral interests between the nations of the world. It found concrete expression in his attempts to bring about a closer union between the countries of Europe. From his own deep immersion in its classical and Christian foundations, he conceived of Europe as having a particular

cultural and spiritual unity and a special role in the maintenance of peace and civilisation in the wider world. In the years
after the Crimean War he developed the notion of 'a European
conscience expressed by the collective guarantee and concerted action of the European powers' to check aggression and
oppression in any part of the world. [10] He went on to refine this
idea of the Concert of Europe, as he called it, as 'a tribunal of
paramount authority, the general judgement of civilised mankind'. [11] He was never entirely clear about the precise institutional form which the Concert would take, although he seems to
have envisaged a body somewhere between the United Nations
and the European Court of Human Rights which would act as
international peace-keeper, arbitrator and court of justice.

Despite repeated appeals to the collective moral sense of
Europe to forward the progress of peace and liberty in the
world, Gladstone got little support for his idea from fellow
European leaders. His only solid success in obtaining concerted action from the European powers came in 1880 when a
conference of ambassadors in Berlin produced an agreed policy
to safeguard the Greeks and Montenegrins against Turkish
threats to their boundaries. Among fellow Liberals at home,
however, his vision was taken up with alacrity. John Bright
expressed himself in favour of 'a more strict and generous and
peaceable political union among the nations of Europe', while
W. T. Stead bent his journalistic talents to 'the development
and strengthening of the principle of the European Concert
which seemed to me the germ of the United States of
Europe'. [12]

If support for European political union has been one
enduring Gladstonian legacy to British Liberalism, then
another has been a strong commitment to the establishment
and support of international agencies to promote peace and
practise arbitration. As early as 1875 Gladstone's faithful
lieutenant and future biographer, John Morley, had argued
that in the face of growing militarism world peace would only be
preserved, 'if it can be secured at all, by a league of pacific
powers, not afraid to wage war against the aggressor'. [13] In
the early years of the twentieth century he and other liberally minded individuals worked out the basic structure and

principles of such a league of nations which they fervently hoped would bring a new moral order into the conduct of international relations.

In the gathering gloom before 1914 Liberals clung resolutely to Gladstone's principles. The New Liberals spoke out against the evils of imperialism and tried to extirpate the heresy of Liberal Imperialism which had taken hold of some bold young spirits in the 1890s and split the party asunder over the issue of the Boer War. In his highly influential book, *Imperialism: A Study* (1902), J. A. Hobson suggested that delusions of imperial grandeur stood in the way of social reform at home, while L. T. Hobhouse, in his essay on *Liberalism* (1911), echoed the sentiments of John Bright: 'A nation may become great not merely by painting the map red, or extending her commerce beyond all precedent, but also as the champion of justice, the succourer of the oppressed, the established home for freedom'.[14] Meanwhile in Whitehall the members of Asquith's government, and none more so than the gentle, bird-watching Foreign Secretary, Sir Edward Grey, strove manfully in an atmosphere of increasing tension and jingoism to remain true to the creed of anti-militarism and non-intervention. When they finally abandoned that creed and declared war on Germany in September 1914 it was to defend the very principle which Gladstone had enunciated in the Midlothian campaign that 'the same sacredness defends the narrow limits of Belgium, as attaches to the extended frontiers of Russia, or Germany, or France'.[15]

— 6 —

THE LIBERAL SPIRIT

If you look up the word 'liberal' in the *Oxford English Dictionary*, you will find the following definitions:

1. Originally the distinctive epithet of those 'arts' or 'sciences' that were considered 'worthy of a free man', opposed to servile or mechanical. In later use, of conditions, pursuits, occupations: Pertaining to or suitable to persons of superior social station; 'becoming a gentleman' . . . Directed to general intellectual enlargement and refinement; not narrowly restricted to the requirements of technical or professional training.
2. Free in bestowing; bountiful, generous, open-hearted.
3. Free from restraint – free in speech or action.
4. Free from narrow prejudice; open-minded, candid. Especially, free from bigotry or unreasonable prejudice in favour of traditional opinions or established institutions; open to the reception of new ideas or proposals of reform.
5. Of political opinions: Favourable to constitutional changes and legal or administrative reforms tending in the direction of freedom or democracy.

It is significant that it is only the last of these definitions which introduces a political dimension. Liberalism is much more than a party creed. There are liberals in every walk of life and in every political party. What characterises them is not their particular political beliefs but their general tendency to exhibit those qualities of generosity, open-mindedness, receptivity to new ideas and also that robust and cheerful optimism which are the distinguishing features of the liberal spirit. The essence of that spirit is well summed up in another definition of liberalism by that great liberal thinker, Gilbert Murray. The Latin word *liberalis*, he pointed out, does not mean 'a believer in liberty', but rather 'like a free man'. He went on: 'Most men are not free; they are the slaves of their customs and prejudices, their passions, their interests, above all, of their fears. A Liberal is one who tries to throw off all those slaveries, and to think and act like a free man'.[1]

It is not inappropriate to describe Liberalism as a faith. Its foundations, as we have seen, are religious. A liberal society is not characterised by a particular social or economic structure but rather by a prevailing attitude towards the spiritual worth of the individuals within it. Liberals have never pinned all their hopes on the dismal science of economics nor measured human progress in terms of rises in the Gross National Product. Even the New Liberals of the early years of this century, more committed than most to economic and social reform, insisted, it may be remembered, that progress was ultimately a matter not of mechanical contrivance, but of the liberation of spiritual energy. In listing remedies to ease the plight of the poor, the New Liberal journalist C. F. G. Masterman left no doubts as to which he regarded as the most important:

Back to the land, from gigantic massed populations to healthier conditions of scattered industry; housing reform; temperance reform; a perfected system of national education; the elimination of the submerged; the redemption of women's labour – all these are immediate necessaries . . . but above all we need a real and living religion, some outpouring of spiritual effort.[2]

When Liberals have concerned themselves with questions of social and economic organisation it has been to insist that moral values take precedence over material ones. There is, for instance, a long tradition among British Liberals of questioning the wisdom of limitless economic growth. One of the most powerful statements of the case for a stationary-state economy is to be found in J. S. Mill's *Principles of Political Economy*. His argument is based not on the material consideration of the finitude of the world's resources, but on the moral effect on individuals of the unremitting pursuit of possessions and the destruction of the wildness and beauty of nature.[3]

There is nothing that Liberals value more than the individual human personality in all its richness and diversity. They revel in the infinite variety of its expression and in its durability and irrepressibility in the face of those forces which assault its integrity and which would reduce individuals to units in some grey and uniform social order. Liberalism in general, and British nineteenth-century Liberalism in particular, is often portrayed as a philosophy of individualism. This term, with its connotations of egoism and selfishness, is an inappropriate and misleading one to apply to an outlook which is essentially generous and sympathetic. I much prefer the word individuality with its sense of character and self-expression.

The celebration of individuality is the dominant theme of the novels of those three great masters of Victorian fiction, Charles Dickens, Anthony Trollope and William Makepeace Thackeray, and it is surely no coincidence that all three were active and committed Liberals.* Indeed, it could be argued that the English novel as a whole, with its enthusiastic evocation of character and its sensitive and loving exploration of the frailties, the complexities and the indomitability of the human personality, is the supreme literary expression of the liberal spirit.

From this fascination with the human personality comes a broad tolerance and an openness to all influences. Liberals revel in the variety of ways in which people live and express themselves. They recognise the diversity and complexity of the world and welcome the existence of many different faiths and beliefs and many different communities and organisations as an expression of human individuality. They understand and

* Thackeray and Trollope both stood as Liberal candidates, the former at Oxford in 1857 and the latter for Beverley in 1868. Dickens was asked to stand for Reading in 1841, but declined. Other Victorian novelists who actively espoused Liberalism included George Eliot, George Meredith, and Thomas Hughes, the author of *Tom Brown's Schooldays*, who was Liberal MP for Lambeth from 1865 to 1868.

excuse the quirks and foibles of human nature and do not attempt to shut themselves off from the new, the strange and even the disturbing.

This is not to say, however, that the liberal mind is just so much blotting paper, soaking up extraneous ideas and influences until it becomes a soft, soggy, shapeless mass with no clear identity of its own. Openness to the ideas of others does not necessarily imply a lack of personal convictions, just as being fair-minded does not have to mean having no mind of one's own. This important point is the theme of John Morley's powerful essay *On Compromise*, which was first published in 1874 and subsequently went through many reprintings. In this work he attacked what he described as his countrymen's 'flaccid latitudinarianism, which thinks itself a benign tolerance for the opinions of others, (but which) is in truth only a pretentious form of being without settled opinions of our own, and without any desire to settle them.'[4] Respect for the feelings of others, he argued, does not require being silent about one's own convictions.

We have already noted that while the liberal mind is essentially reasonable and moderate, it is not without passion. It is certainly not some kind of desiccated calculating machine from which all emotion and sensitivity have been carefully excluded. The fact is that liberalism is open and sympathetic to all aspects of the human personality, physical, emotional, spiritual and the downright irrational just as much as intellectual and rational.

This diversity and breadth of approach comes out clearly in the idea of liberal education, a training for life which is broad, ethical, character forming, which develops the whole personality and which teaches the individual to live in harmony with himself and with the world. This ideal has had few more eloquent or more practical exponents than that remarkable father and son team of Thomas and Matthew Arnold. Between them, they sought to effect a complete diffusion of liberal education throughout Britain, with the son energetically campaigning for the extension by the state to all classes of society of the system for educating the whole man which the father had established at Rugby. Both men deserve a place in the liberal hall of fame.

Some readers, remembering Matthew Arnold's tirades in *Culture and Anarchy* against 'our Liberal practitioners', and particularly against the hapless John Bright, may be surprised to see him thus honoured. Yet as he himself wrote in the introduction to that work, 'I am a Liberal, yet a Liberal tempered by experience, reflection and renouncement'.[5] There were some major aspects of Victorian Liberalism like its Nonconformity and provincialism with which he felt out of sympathy and on which he was excessively hard. But in his insistence that true liberty is to be found not in doing what one likes, but in the application of 'right reason' and the cultivation of one's best self, in his faith in the good sense and responsibility of an educated people, his belief in the free play of minds and plea for 'the spontaneity of consciousness' against the 'strictness of conscience', and perhaps above all in his ideal of human perfection as 'an inward spiritual activity, having for its characters increased sweetness, increased light, increased life, and increased sympathy', he shows an unmistakably liberal spirit.[6]

Matthew Arnold identified three evils in the British education system which continue to worry liberals today: its division along class lines into state and private schools, its excessive reverence for the classics and undervaluing of scientific and technical subjects, and its narrowly academic criteria for assessing success and failure. Comparing British schools with those on the Continent, he was struck by the free intermingling of upper and middle class children across the Channel, and by the high regard in which scientific and technical subjects were held by our major industrial competitors. As a school inspector, he was appalled by the effects of the 'payments by result' system which effectively killed any incentive on the part of teachers to go beyond a narrow and easily examinable timetable based on the three Rs and very little else. It was in order to combat these evils that he spent his life campaigning for a universal system of state secondary schools based on the model that his father had created at Rugby School, for proper recognition and provision of technical and scientific studies, and for a generally broader conception of education as a training for life.

The all-round culture which Arnold extolled was, in fact, a conspicuous feature of many of the great Victorian Liberals. Their breadth of interests and activities makes daunting reading in our more specialised and less energetic age. Mr Gladstone was not just a superb orator and administrator, but also an accomplished academic theologian, classical scholar, singer, hill walker and tree feller who could turn from composing a budget speech to translating Homer and found refreshment from affairs of state in hymn singing or twenty-mile tramps through the Scottish or Welsh hills. He also exemplifies another marked characteristic of the liberal spirit, and of nineteenth-century British Liberals in particular. For all his intellect and his political eminence, he was a man of almost childlike simplicity, directness and earnestness.

These qualities are also evident in a remarkable group of men who were in many ways the last survivors of the heroic age of British Liberalism. I refer to that trio of distinguished historians, remarkable for their longevity, who carried their essentially Victorian principles well into the second half of the twentieth century: Herbert Butterfield, devout Methodist and Regius Professor of Modern History at Cambridge; G. P. Gooch, Liberal MP, president of the Historical Association and crusader for peace; and G. M. Trevelyan, who also held the Regius Chair at Cambridge and whose books have inspired many with a love and a feeling for the past.

In his breadth of interests, his energy and his earnest simplicity of character, Trevelyan, perhaps, came nearest to being the perfect embodiment of the liberal spirit. His mind, in the words of Leonard Woolf, was 'set in the hereditary mould of Victorian Liberalism' – tolerant, open, but with a great sense of the spiritual, of 'something divine, either external to, or immanent in, nature and mankind'.[7] A great hill-walker in the tradition of Mr Gladstone, he was an active supporter of the infant National Trust, securing its first property in the Lake District, and campaigning with his brother Charles for better public access to mountains and moorland. A fervent admirer of John Bright, he showed the same practical pacifism when he commanded the Friends' Ambulance Unit in Italy during the First World War and the same love for the people, and concern for their intellectual elevation, when he helped to found the University Extension movement and taught at the Working Men's College in London.

Trevelyan was never happier than when lecturing to audiences of working men and women. He felt a mission to spread his own enthusiasm and fascination for the past, his pride in the exploits of liberal heroes like Bright and Garibaldi, and his general sympathy and admiration for the humbler achievements and the endurance of ordinary people throughout the ages. The study of history was, of course, his first and greatest love and it was infused by a passionate attachment to liberty. As he told his brother, 'I care *much* more about individual freedom as the precondition of good civilization than about anything else in politics or society'.[8]

As those who still read his work will know, the overriding characteristic of Trevelyan's historical writing is its abiding sense of optimism. So it is with the work of Gooch and Butterfield. These three were the last practitioners of the Whig tradition, the final survivors of that school of historians who saw the past as a story of progress and who stressed the ability of individuals and communities to shape their own destinies in marked contrast to the determinism of the Marxist school and the gloomy metaphysics of conservative historians. In 1963, at the age of ninety, Gooch was received by the Queen and he told her how much the world had changed for the better since Victoria's time. For Butterfield history was a working out of God's plan for the victory of good against evil. For Trevelyan it was 'a series of steps that have been made to ameliorate the human lot', each step the result of individual acts of kindness, courage and enterprise.[9]

The liberal spirit is incurably and eternally optimistic. This is not to say that it is smug and complacent. Liberals do not believe that all is well with the world – far from it: they are restless and impatient for change. But they have faith in the capacity of human beings, for all their weaknesses and frailty, to effect that change and make the world a better place. This chapter has contained several definitions of liberalism. Let me end by quoting one by Michael Howard, the present Regius Professor of Modern History at Oxford, which, I think, brings out this aspect particularly well:

> By liberals I mean in general all those thinkers who believe the
> world to be profoundly other than it should be, and who have faith in
> the power of human reason and human action so to change it that the
> inner potential of all human beings can be more fully realised. This
> excludes on the one hand those conservatives who accept the world as
> it unalterably is and adjust to it with more or less of a good grace; and on
> the other those disciples of Karl Marx and other determinists who see
> men as trapped in predicaments from which they can be rescued only
> by historical processes which they may understand but which they are
> powerless to control. [10]

Faith in mankind and hope for the future shine through the
thoughts and actions of those great figures from the hey-day of
British Liberalism who have been the subject of these early
chapters. It is there in Mill's trust in the 'social feelings of
mankind' and his confident expectation of a new economic
order based on co-operation rather than class conflict; in
Bright's argument that giving people the vote would make
them more responsible and mature citizens and his vision of a
new system of international relations based on the peaceful
resolution of disputes and the promotion of free trade; in
Arnold's belief in the possibility of human perfectibility
through education and the diffusion of sweetness and light; in
Gladstone's faith in the solution of social problems through
individual altruism and voluntary action and his frequent
appeals to the moral conscience of the nation. In the twentieth
century, as we shall see, liberal optimism has been pushed
more and more on to the defensive by the dominance of both
conservatives and Marxists, but it has never quite perished.

PART TWO

THE NEAR-DEATH OF LIBERAL BRITAIN

———————

7

THE POLITICAL ECLIPSE
OF LIBERALISM

The period from around 1850 to 1910 was the golden age of liberalism in Britain. Whatever their professed party affiliations, most Victorians and Edwardians were liberals at heart. They believed in free trade, representative democracy and voluntaryism. Their outlook on life was, broadly speaking, one of earnest, tolerant optimism. They had faith in God, in liberty and in human individuality.

During the next half century these values were displaced by another very different set: cynicism, pessimism, nationalism, protectionism, materialism, corporatism and collectivism – the watchwords of the twentieth century. Liberalism retreated before the onrush of these new and powerful tides and found itself stranded like some near extinct species in the remoter reaches of the British Isles. There, in places like Montgomeryshire, Caithness and Sutherland, and the islands of Orkney and Shetland, it stubbornly refused to die and waited patiently for the illiberal waters that were engulfing the rest of the country to subside.

The theme of the death of liberalism looms large in historical studies of early twentieth-century Britain. Its clearest manifestation, of course, was the dramatic decline in the fortunes of the Liberal Party which plummeted from 400 MPs (and 49 per cent of the total vote) in 1906 to six MPs (and 2.6 per cent of the vote) in 1951. Many books have been written about that decline: nearly all are agreed that it came about as a result of fundamental changes in the political, social, economic and cultural climate of Britain which threatened not just the party of Gladstone and Lloyd George but the continued survival of Liberalism itself.

Historians differ as to the date at which the Liberal Party, and Liberal values, began to falter. Some see the first seeds of destruction as having been sown in the damaging split over Irish Home Rule in the mid-1880s with Chamberlain and the Unionists being the first of a steady stream of pessimists and conservatives to leave the Liberal ship.[1] Others see the resignation and death of Gladstone in the 1890s as marking the end of the era, with the curious coalition which he had kept together by his personal charisma disintegrating into squabbling factions. No one else ever dominated the Liberal Party, nor epitomised Victorian Liberalism, as the Grand Old Man had done – certainly not his immediate successors, the Whiggish Sir William Harcourt and the horse-racing Earl of Rosebery. With Gladstone's departure faith in the values which he had stood for diminished and the distinctly illiberal creeds of imperialism and collectivism began to take hold of many younger Liberal minds.[2]

It was in this period as well that Liberalism first came under serious challenge as the dominant progressive ideology in Britain. The ideas of Karl Marx were slow to spread in his adopted land, and were initially taken up only by a relatively small group of middle-class intellectuals. But with the emergence of unskilled trade unions, socialism, and its peculiarly British cousin, labourism, spread among the working classes. Social and economic historians have related the weakening hold of Liberalism among working people to the long-term decline in the British economy which began in the late 1870s, the emergence of the modern mass-production factory system with its sense of alienation and destruction of individuality, and the growing class consciousness of both workers and employers.

Liberalism was inevitably squeezed out by the rise of aggressive capitalism on the one side and militant labour on the other just as it could only suffer from the weakening of regional identity and provincial pride as Britain became a much more standardised and homogeneous community. This latter phenomenon has been curiously little noticed or studied by historians, an honourable exception being Dr Henry Pelling who has drawn attention to the effects that the influx of English miners into the coalfields of South Wales and of English labourers into the shipbuilding yards of the Clyde had in spreading socialism and diminishing the Celtic consciousness of these former Liberal strongholds. As he puts it, Liberalism suffered from 'the long-term social and economic changes which were simultaneously uniting Britain geographically and dividing her inhabitants in terms of class'.[3]

There is little doubt that the emergence of class consciousness as the main determinant of political allegiance in Britain, replacing religious affiliation, local feeling and broad ideology, was a major blow to Liberalism. The polarisation of the population into employers and workers, trade unionists and bosses, 'us' and 'them' is one of the most striking features of the decades around the turn of the century. Gone was the social harmony that generally characterised the era of Cobden and Bright when manufacturers and labourers lived in the same town, worshipped in the same Nonconformist chapels and attended the same Liberal clubs. A new generation of employers had grown up, educated at public schools and despising the provincialism of their fathers, whose modest houses near the factory gates they had forsaken for secluded suburban villas, just as they had quit the Nonconformist chapel for the socially more respectable religion of Anglicanism. In this process of gentrification they had turned naturally from Liberalism to Toryism. Their workers, meanwhile, were also deserting the chapels and the Liberal clubs for the pleasures of subsidised beer in the working men's club and the cosy collective embrace of trade unionism. For them Nonconformity was giving way to the new creed of secularism, and Liberalism to socialism.

Not all historians, it must be said, have seen the emergence of class-based politics as spelling inevitable doom for Liberalism. In his influential and important study, *Lancashire and the New Liberalism*, Peter Clarke points out that the change to class politics was substantially complete in Britain by 1910. Yet at that time the change from Liberalism to Labour had not really begun. The future seemed to lie with a progressive alliance of New Liberals and Fabian social democrats. It was not, he argues, until after 1910 that Liberalism collapsed.[4]

For George Dangerfield, Liberal England died in the years immediately preceding the outbreak of the First World War, a victim of trade union militancy, the violence of the suffragette movement and the cynical exploitation of the Ulster crisis by the Tories. With these challenges to the rule of law and parliamentary democracy, Britain stood on the brink of a revolution from which it was only saved by the war. In another influential study, however, Trevor Wilson has argued that Liberalism was not terminally sick in 1914. In his view, as in the opinion of many other historians and contemporaries, it was killed suddenly by the shock of the First World War, just as a healthy man might be killed by walking under a bus.[5]

To minds which were naturally tolerant and pacific, which prized personal liberty and voluntary action, the Great War certainly came as a shattering blow. It brought to the fore many of the values which Liberals most abhorred: militarism, protectionism and narrow nationalism in foreign affairs, and coercion, increased governmental power and suppression of liberties at home. To make matters worse, it was a Liberal Government which was banging the jingoistic drum and introducing compulsory conscription and censorship. Argument over the conduct of the war produced the fatal rift between Asquith and Lloyd George which was to split the Liberal Party into two implacable factions for the next fifteen years. It also provoked a string of resignations and defections from the Liberal fold beginning with the departure of John Morley, John Burns and Charles Trevelyan from Asquith's Government in 1914 over the decision to enter the war in the first place and Sir John Simon's resignation the following year over the introduction of conscription, and culminating in the exodus in 1918 of Trevelyan, Norman Angell, E. D. Morel, Arthur Ponsonby, Noel Buxton and Leonard Woolf to join others like J. A. Hobson and H. N. Brailsford who had already defected to Labour.

More than anything else, perhaps, the Great War destroyed

that atmosphere of optimism and faith on which Liberal England was founded. The voices which sounded from the trenches of Flanders spoke in tones of anger and despair. The scale of the suffering perplexed and broke the gentle, humane liberal spirit. Small wonder that when Francis Neilson, MP for Hyde, called in at the office of the party chief whip, Percy Illingworth, a few hours after the declaration of war, 'I found him in tears. He was so shaken that for a minute he could not find speech. Then he muttered, "Liberalism is dead".'[6]

Quite apart from its effect on the national mood, the coming of the First World War, and its prolonged duration, effectively scuppered the prospects of a long list of reforms which were due to be introduced by Asquith's Government. Had it not been for the war, Lloyd George's land programme might well have been implemented, bringing site value rating and the widespread provision of smallholdings; Scotland and Wales would probably have obtained Home Rule and Ireland a less brittle independence, and proportional representation might even have been introduced. As it was, the war brought a level of state control and centralised planning previously unknown in Britain. It also contributed much to the further erosion of regional distinctions and variety. By 1918 the 120 private railway companies of the pre-war era had been reduced to four giant conglomerates. The aftermath of the Second World War was to see these, in turn, reduced to one single nationalised monolith.

Several historians have stressed other factors at work after 1918 which further sapped the strength of the ailing Liberal frame. A recent article in the *English Historical Review* portrays the 1918 Representation of the People Act, which gave the vote to all adult males and women over thirty, as hammering a further nail into the Liberal coffin.[7] Ironically, the party which believed in trusting the people was rejected by the mass electorate which it had helped to create and proved unable to accommodate itself to the new politics of bribes and promises which universal suffrage brought in its wake. In his moving study of the Liberal mind from 1914 to 1929 Michael Bentley shows the enervating effect of the continuing Liberal commitment to the politics of principle in an era increasingly given over to the pursuit of power.[8]

The comments of contemporary Liberals themselves show a similar consensus about the fact of their decline and a similarly broad range of views as to precisely when and why it occurred. John Morley was one of the first to herald the collapse of Liberalism. Predictably he saw it largely as a moral failing on the part of his countrymen:

This is our modern way [he wrote in 1874]: Beware of the high and hold fast to the safe. Dismiss conviction and study general consensus. No zeal, no faith, no intellectual trenchancy . . . Conscience has lost its strong and on-pressing energy, and the sense of personal responsibility lacks sharpness of edge. The native hue of spiritual resolution is sicklied o'er with the pale cast of distracted, wavering, confused thought. The souls of men have become void.[9]

Morley saw one of the main manifestations of this new malaise in the fact that 'at elections, the man of principle has not often a chance against the man of class'.[10] Other Liberals were equally worried about the emergence of class-based politics. The Earl of Rosebery gloomily predicted in 1895 that Britain might be about to witness 'the elimination of Liberalism, leaving the two forces of Socialism and Reaction face to face'.[11] Sixteen years later Hobhouse saw Liberalism as 'a creed that is becoming fossilised as an extinct form, a fossil that occupies, moreover, an awkward position between two very active and energetically moving grindstones – the upper grindstone of plutocratic imperialism, and the nether grindstone of social democracy'.[12]

The First World War, as we have already seen, was regarded by many Liberals as a shattering blow to their creed. Ernest Benn, the publisher, believed that the traditional liberty of England died on 2 August 1914, the day when the Defence of the Realm Act was introduced, giving the Government sweeping powers to censor the press, restrict aliens and ban public meetings. He was later to leave the Liberal Party because of what he regarded as its increasing espousal of collectivism and to found his own Society of Individualists. His brother, William, the father of Tony Benn, by contrast forsook the Liberals for Labour along with others who could not stomach their party's apparent abandonment of its peace-loving and anti-militarist traditions. The departure of these two brothers into opposite camps shows dramatically the polarisation that so fatally weakened the Liberal movement of which they had both for long been devoted adherents.

Early in 1915, horrified by the decision of his erstwhile Cabinet colleagues to introduce compulsory conscription, John Morley wrote to a friend: 'Liberalism, as we have known it, is dead beyond resurrection'.[13] After the war most of those Liberals who wrote about their creed did so in the tones of an obituarist. *Is Liberalism Dead?* was the title of a book written in 1920 by Elliott Dodds, the young editor of the *Huddersfield Examiner*. Wisely, perhaps, he chose not to answer his rhetorical question. Reginald McKenna, former Chancellor of the Exchequer in Asquith's war coalition, had no such hesitation. His autobiography published in 1921 was entitled *The Death of Liberalism*. Twelve years later Ramsay Muir, Professor of Modern History at Liverpool and Manchester universities and perhaps the leading Liberal theorist of the inter-war period, felt compelled to begin a work on *The Faith of a Liberal*: 'Many people think that Liberalism has almost died out in the Western World'.[14]

But if Liberalism had become a corpse, in one respect at least it was a pretty lively one. Sir Ernest Simon might lament as the 1923 election approached: 'What a party! No leaders, no organisation, no policy! Only a summer school!'[15] But that summer school, started in Oxford in 1922 as a result of a meeting in Grasmere the previous year, was at least a sign that the Liberals were still interested in ideas. Leaders they may not have had, but thinkers they had in profusion. Indeed it is no exaggeration to say that in the half century between 1910 and 1960 Liberalism was intellectually the most dynamic and creative force in British politics, producing a stream of good ideas and policies on a wide range of topics.

At the head of this list of thinkers must stand J. M. Keynes and William Beveridge, arguably the two greatest single influences on economic and social policy in twentieth century Britain. Working with them in the summer schools of which Simon had spoken so slightingly, and which he himself had helped to found, and in the preparation of the detailed blueprints for the reconstruction of Britain which Lloyd George commissioned in the 1920s was a formidably talented group of academics and journalists. It included Ramsay Muir, Elliott Dodds, Roy Harrod, Walter Layton, H. A. L. Fisher, J. B. S. Haldane, Gilbert Murray, Seebohm Rowntree, and C. P. Scott and his son Ted.

It is often said that with the decline of the Liberal Party liberal ideas did not die but were taken up by the two other parties that now dominated British politics. At best this is only half-true. As we shall see, when the ideas of Keynes and Beveridge were applied by those who did not share their liberal perspective, it was in a distorted form which produced results very different from those that they had intended. Those who abandoned the Liberal Party abandoned also the traditional liberal concern for a balance between liberty and welfare, and between the rights of the individual and the needs of society as a whole. They brought to their new political homes a perversion of their former faith in the shape either of *laissez-faire* individualism or socialist collectivism. They also abandoned Liberal internationalism for short-sighted nationalism.

Again and again in the twentieth century Conservative and Labour Governments have failed to take up and implement good Liberal ideas. The 1929–31 Labour administration, and the National Government which followed it, largely ignored the bold programme set out in Lloyd George's Yellow Book to increase employment and stimulate the economy. It was left to Franklin Roosevelt to take up many of the Liberal ideas in his New Deal in the United States, while Britain sank further into depression. The 1935 Conservative Government rejected Liberal and Labour pleas to back international action against Mussolini's invasion of Abyssinia, so crippling the League of Nations and initiating the fatal policy of appeasement which was to encourage Hitler to ride roughshod over the smaller nations of Europe. The 1945–51 Labour Government ignored Beveridge's essentially voluntaryist blueprint for a welfare society and created instead a centralised and bureaucratic Welfare State. It also ignored the arguments of Seebohm Rowntree and others for profit-sharing and industrial democracy, preferring to pursue the path of nationalisation. The Conservative administrations of the 1950s showed a similar disregard for Liberal promptings when they failed to respond to the growing movement for political and economic union among our Continental neighbours, so depriving Britain of the chance to be one of the founding fathers of the European Economic Community.

From the Conservatives disregard for Liberal ideas and principles was, perhaps, only to be expected. Liberalism was, after all, their traditional enemy – a more effective enemy, one might add, than socialism. One of the striking features of British politics during the period when Labour has replaced the Liberals as the main party of the left has been the dominance of the Conservatives. In the fifty years between 1868 and 1918, the Conservatives were in power for only 22 years, the Liberals for 28. In the next half century, Conservative and Conservative-dominated governments were in power for 34 years, Labour for only 11.

But what of the party which had risen from the ruins of Liberalism and might have been expected to take on its mantle? Many Liberals had helped to establish the Labour Party as a parliamentary force in the hope that it would be an ally in the battle against reaction, prejudice and narrow sectional interests. It is true that there were many socialists who shared the open-minded, internationalist, radical democratic perspectives of Liberalism. But they were swamped by those who saw Labour first and foremost as a class party, representing a particular sectional interest and indissolubly tied to the trade union movement, and also by the collectivists and state centralists who had little sympathy for Liberal notions of voluntaryism and pluralism. In vain did Keynes ask: 'Why cannot the leaders of the Labour Party face the fact that they are not sectaries of an out-worn creed, mumbling moss-grown demi-semi Fabian Marxism, but the heirs of eternal Liberalism?'[16] The party which might have carried on the Liberal tradition had opted to become the apostle of corporatism and compulsion, the friend of protection and restriction, the defender of restrictive practices, the block vote and the closed shop.

Squeezed between the Conservative and Labour giants, the

small and diminishing band who still called themselves Liberals lost much of the fire and vigour which had characterised their predecessors. With certain honourable exceptions the Liberal Party was happy to swim with the prevailing collectivist tide and to shed its provincial radicalism and Nonconformist zeal in favour of a bland, middle-of-the-road sogginess. Writing in 1927 Alexander MacCallum Scott, a backbench Liberal MP, described a state of affairs that was to persist for at least another thirty years:

The Liberal Party has no creed, no cause. Its ideal is essentially that of a centre party – a do-as-little-as possible party, a carry-on party. It is a pis-aller – a kind of shelter for timid passengers in the middle of a busy street. It rouses no enthusiasm. It enlists no zeal.[17]

8

LOSING FAITH IN THE PEOPLE – THE POLITICS OF BRIBERY AND THE WORSHIP OF ECONOMICS

A nagging doubt lurked at the back of many late Victorian Liberal minds. What if the soon-to-be enfranchised masses turned out not to be good Liberals and to prefer protectionism and state socialism to free trade and individual liberty? The middle-class merchants and manufacturers who got the vote in 1832, the 'respectable' artisans enfranchised in 1867, and even the agricultural workers admitted to the electorate in 1884 were predominantly sober, independent-minded, responsible individuals and many of them happily embraced the Liberal creed. But what would happen to Liberalism when the franchise was extended lower down the social order to those without property or skills, the largely unlettered and not always sober proletariat?

Towards the end of the nineteenth century more and more Liberals came to fear the consequences of the extension of democracy to which they were philosophically committed. Would the advent of a mass electorate, dominated by the unskilled working classes, lead to the abandonment of the politics of ideas and principles and the substitution of a kind of Dutch auction of bribes and promises in which rival parties would shamelessly try to buy the support of the masses? Some, like the distinguished constitutionalist Walter Bagehot and the historians Sir William Lecky and Sir Henry Maine, left the

Liberal fold because they were certain that it would. Others kept their faith in the people and hoped for the best, though not without a certain amount of trepidation.

In fact, the fears of the pessimists were to a large extent confirmed. As the electorate was extended politics became less and less a matter of debate on broad principles and more and more a matter of specific material promises. Asquith noted one aspect of this trend when he deplored in a speech in 1896 'the political fashion which has been in vogue that is equally injurious to both parties of the State, of presenting to the country . . . not a policy but a catalogue'. Such a development, he argued, was the antithesis of the Liberal approach to politics which lay not in the possession at any particular moment of a detailed programme of popular attractions, but rather the possession at all times of an independent mind and a broad attitude of 'hopefulness, of faith, and of confidence'.[1]

The general election of 1906 was arguably the last one to be fought, and won, on broad issues of principle (in this case, the defence of free trade against Tory proposals for tariff reform, moral outrage over the employment of Chinese slave labour in South African gold mines and Nonconformist dislike of the 1902 Education Act). It was also the last election to produce a majority Liberal Government in Britain. Although that Government was to prove the greatest social reforming administration of the twentieth century, it had not gone to the people on a manifesto of promising social benefits. The two elections of 1910, which returned Liberal governments without an overall majority, were partly fought on the issue of the power of the House of Lords, but there were also appeals by both major parties to the material self-interest of both the working and the propertied classes. The 1918 election, the first to be fought on anything approaching a universal franchise (70 per cent of the population had the vote, compared to only 30 per cent in 1910), introduced the lists and counter-lists of specific promises and pledges which have been so marked a feature of elections ever since.

Was the politics of bribery a necessary and inevitable consequence of the achievement of mass democracy? Perhaps it would not have been had the extension of the franchise not coincided with the worsening of Britain's economic decline and the emergence of strong class antagonisms in the country. Perhaps, as the historian Henry Pelling argues, it was simply the case that the people enfranchised in 1918 were characterised by 'political apathy and social conservatism' and dragged down the general level of political life to their lowest common denominator.[2] Or was it rather a sign of the overall collapse of faith in liberal values that politicians responded to the new mass electorate by pandering to their prejudices and offering them material bribes rather than appealing to their hearts and minds and seeking to win them, as Gladstone had, by setting out high ideals and lofty principles?

One of the most striking signs of this retreat from broader issues was the dominance which the single subject of economics came to assume in the minds of both politicians and voters. Statistics and shopping baskets became increasingly vital 'props' in elections as progress was measured more and more in terms of Gross National Product and affluence replaced liberty as the quality to be prized above all others. Politicians were looked upon less as moral leaders and inspirers of the people than as managers elected to get the most efficient performance out of the economy. Voters were encouraged to look upon themselves as consumers, passively registering their wants at election time much as they might do in the supermarket, and not as participators in a vital process of choice and self-determination.[3]

As well as thus draining politics of its moral content, the twentieth century's worship of the great god economics has produced two other damaging heresies. The first is that the answer to any problem is simply to throw money at it, or more specifically at some elaborate bureaucracy specially set up to receive it. The second might be described as the macro-economic heresy – the conviction that because economics is so important it must be dealt with on the largest possible scale, by amalgamations, super-governmental agencies and grandiose national plans, rather than by varied, small-scale localised initiatives.

The man most often blamed for starting this obsession with macro-economics and implanting the doctrine of economic management and the worship of growth in the British body politic is John Maynard Keynes. Seldom has anyone been so misrepresented. Keynes had an abiding Liberal faith in the primacy of the spiritual aspects of life over the material. His own order of priorities was 'Love first, philosophy second, poetry third and politics fourth'.[4] He felt himself compelled to spend more time than he would have liked on the dismal science of economics simply because he felt that his own generation was perplexed by a critical economic problem which stood in the way of the achievement of individual liberty and human fulfilment – the problem of mass unemployment. He sought to tackle this problem so that men might once again be free of mere material concerns, and in his words 'so we shall once more value ends above means and prefer the good above the useful'.[5]

The solution which Keynes devised for the problem of unemployment caused by cyclical slump is well known. He advocated that the Government should run a budget deficit during periods of recession to introduce demand into the economy and that it should specifically stimulate employment by investment in labour intensive schemes of public works. These ideas were fleshed out in the 1928 Liberal Yellow Book *Britain's Industrial Future* and the 1929 Orange Book *We Can Conquer Unemployment* with its plan for public investment in such areas as the renovation of housing stock, the afforestation and reclamation of waste land, and the building of roads, bridges and railways. It is also fair to say that Keynes' ideas laid the foundations for the unprecedented economic stability and prosperity which Britain enjoyed in the thirty years after the Second World War.

Keynes' theory was one of economic management by the government to iron out the ill effects of cyclical depressions. But it was far from being the interventionist and *dirigiste* doctrine preached by so-called Keynesians later in the century. If his work is taken as a whole, Keynes has almost as much claim to be regarded as the apostle of monetarism and the micro-economic approach as he has to be the proponent of macro-economics and state intervention. In many areas he was strongly opposed to government interference: he scorned attempts at price regulation, for example, as ineffective and harmful. He saw the answer to excessive inflation as 'a swift and severe dose of dear money'. The whole purpose of his great treatise *The General Theory of Employment, Interest and Money* was to preserve the capitalist free market system, not to replace it with state socialism. By inclination he was a pragmatist, by conviction a voluntaryist. 'The important thing for Government', he told the 1925 Liberal Summer School, 'is not to do things which individuals are doing already, and to do them a little better or a little worse, but to do those things which are at present not done at all'.[6]

Keynes' ideas have suffered immense distortion at the hands of his supposed disciples. He himself would be appalled at what has been put forward since his death in the name of Keynesianism: the continuing worship of growth, the faith in government intervention and the failure to find new wisdom for a new age in a world vastly changed from that in which he lived and thought. He would have been even more appalled, perhaps, at the way in which economists have been erected into a new priesthood before whose wisdom and authority politicians and people together bow. 'If economists could manage to get themselves thought of as humble, competent people, on a level with dentists', he once wrote, 'that would be splendid.'[7]

The rule of economists is, of course, just one aspect of a general trend in the twentieth century towards government by experts. For this paternalistic and undemocratic invention we have to thank the Fabian social democrats of the turn of the century. It was one of the key features which distinguished their essentially mechanical approach to reform from the moral reformism of the New Liberals. In the words of Hobhouse, there was 'all the difference between benevolent officialdom setting the world in order from above, and democratic collectivism which seeks not to restrict liberty but to fulfil it'.[8] There were many socialists who shared the democratic, decentralist, participatory perspectives of the Liberals, but it was not their trust in the people which gained ascendancy in the Labour Party but rather the Fabian view that the gentleman in Whitehall knows best. 'As the "expert" comes to the front, and "efficiency" becomes the watchword of administration',

Hobhouse noted in 1905, 'all that was human in socialism vanishes out of it'.[9]

The Labour Party may have been the most enthusiastic proponent of government by experts and the rule of the bureaucratic mind that is so perfectly summed up in Herbert Morrison's definition of socialism as 'the achievement of tidiness'.[10] But the Conservatives have not been far behind for most of the twentieth century. Indeed, as we shall see in more detail in Chapter Twelve, it was during the Conservative Government of 1970–74 that the notion of government as an exercise in management by planners and experts reached its zenith.

It was not only in the field of politics and administration that the liberal principle of trust in the people broke down in the face of the growing obsession with economics and efficiency. Something similar happened in the world of work. The sorry story of industrial relations in twentieth-century Britain is too well known to need re-telling in detail here. Indeed the very use of that phrase indicates the cold formality and the institutionalised mistrust that characterises the relationship between the two sides of industry (another tell-tale British phrase). It is easy to be starry-eyed about the relations between employers and workers in the golden age of liberalism. Of course there was oppression and exploitation on the one side and bitterness and frustration on the other. But there was also much co-operation and much sharing of mutual aims and aspirations – an overall atmosphere altogether more like that which prevails, say, in West Germany today.

Many of the reasons for the breakdown of this trust in the early years of this century have already been mentioned in the last chapter. Britain's worsening economic decline squeezed both profits and wages and led both sides in industry towards aggressive collectivist action to protect their own interests. As we have seen, workers and their bosses were moving physically, politically and spiritually further apart as they deserted the common ground of the factory town, Liberalism and Nonconformity, the former for socialism, secularism and trade union membership, the latter for the suburbs, Anglicanism and villa-Toryism. Major changes in the organisation of industry were also producing a greater polarisation and alienation on both sides. New techniques of mass production herded workers together in large and anonymous factories, removing them further away from the bosses whom they had often previously worked alongside and making them feel like cogs in some vast relentless machine. At the same time the trend towards the amalgamation of small businesses into large corporations removed the old owner-managers who had often been close to their workforce and substituted a new class of salaried managers who in many ways felt as anonymous as the men on the factory floor.

The most obvious manifestation of these new tensions at work was, of course, the growth of militant trade unionism. Trade union membership soared in the early twentieth century from less than two million in 1900 to well over eight million in 1920. So also did the number of days lost through strikes, up from three million in 1900 to forty-one million in 1912. No longer did the unions see themselves primarily as friendly societies offering mutual aid and insurance to their members. They now saw their main role as being to take on employers with every weapon at their disposal to force up the level of wages.

As they became more militant and powerful the unions also established themselves as being above the rule of law. The curbs on picketing imposed by Gladstone's Government in 1871 had been removed by the Conservatives four years later and the 1906 Trades Disputes Act, passed by Campbell-Bannerman's Government in response to pressure from the infant Labour Party, removed the unions' liability for acts committed by their members or agents and established their total immunity from civil actions for damages. An increasing number of unions imposed the closed shop, thereby creating a monopoly position just as privileged and protected as that of the closed trading and manufacturing companies of the mercantilist era which seventeenth century liberals had opened to the healthy air of competition. Small wonder that in 1926, the year of the General Strike, Keynes described trade unionists as 'once the oppressed, now the tyrants, whose selfish and sectional pretensions need to be bravely opposed'.[11]

It would be very wrong, of course, to portray the trade union movement in the twentieth century as a wholly illiberal phenomenon. There has been a high-minded, profoundly democratic side to trade unionism, particularly evident in the early part of the century. Certain unions, like the mineworkers, took over some of the functions previously fulfilled by Nonconformist chapels and mechanics' institutes and gave working men a cultural identity, a chance to educate themselves and an opportunity to take part in democratic decision making. But all too often the decision making was very undemocratic, based on the right of the majority to coerce the minority, or even worse the right of the vocal minority to coerce the silent, apathetic majority.

Nor was it just the working classes who departed from the liberal principles of trust, tolerance and democracy. The period which saw the rise of militant trade unionism also saw the formation of employers' federations and cartels, wage-cutting, lockouts and the tearing up of contracts and agreements. Goaded on by an increasingly class-conscious Conservative Party, aggressive capitalism mounted its headlong challenge against organised labour.

There were some employers who refused to join in this battle and instead stuck to the traditional liberal principles of trust and co-operation. They included three well-known names in British commerce. In 1909 William Hesketh Lever introduced a co-partnership scheme at Port Sunlight, the model factory community into which he had already poured most of the profits of the soap making business he had started there twenty years earlier. Seven years later Seebohm Rowntree established an elected works council in the almond paste department of his confectionery works just outside York. He later extended the councils to the entire factory and introduced profit-sharing, a shorter working week, a works psychologist and a special scheme of unemployment insurance which helped those made redundant to set up their own businesses. In 1929 John Spedan Lewis set up the retail co-partnership which still bears his name, based on profit-sharing and an elaborate system of participatory democracy which gave every employee a say as well as a stake in its running and made every manager fully accountable to the workforce through a procedure modelled on Parliamentary question time.

Altogether it has been estimated that 635 profit-sharing schemes were implemented between 1865 and 1929. Those behind them, who included such other well-known business names as Cadbury, Brunner and Mond, hoped to show to their fellow-employers that treating workers as responsible individuals was not incompatible with profitable business enterprise. In 1921 Rowntree wrote an important book, *The Human Factor in Business*, in which he argued for legislation to establish works councils in all factories and the encouragement of profit-sharing schemes by various measures, including the provision of a national minimum wage. Both these demands were incorporated in the Yellow Book of 1928 and in successive Liberal Party manifestos, but they fell on deaf ears in both the Labour and Conservative parties. Nor, it must be said, did the principle of co-partnership find much support on either side of industry. Many of those schemes started before 1929 lasted only for a short time before they were killed off, often by trade union opposition, and very few new ones were started after the slump of that year. Co-operation had apparently died with the passing of Liberal England.

The fact was, of course, that it suited the new mood of both employers and unions to regard workers not as individuals but as a commodity called labour. In vain did Rowntree protest 'There is no such thing as "Labour". The working force is made up of a number of individuals each having a personality different from the rest.'[12] He might just as well, and just as vainly, have protested about the concept of 'management' which was equally impersonal and dehumanising, or about the prevailing view of the electorate as a mass consumer market to be won by bribery and manipulation. Such liberal sensitivity about the worth of the individual human personality was out of keeping with the spirit of the age.

9

THE SERVILE STATE –
THE ABANDONMENT OF
VOLUNTARYISM

In liberal thought and action concern for welfare and for liberty have traditionally gone together. With the eclipse of liberalism, they got out of step. Instead of operating on the voluntaryist principle, governments went for highly centralised all-embracing public provision of social welfare which left little room for voluntary action or individual or community choice. With the best possible intentions, structures were created in the name of universality and equality which were highly illiberal, over-bureaucratic and de-humanising. The result was the creation of a Welfare State seen, in Jo Grimond's graphic words, as 'positively malevolent' by many of those it was specifically designed to help. [1]

Just as some Liberals feared that the advent of mass democracy might herald the end of the politics of principle so others worried that the social reforms introduced by the 1906–16 Liberal government signalled a potentially dangerous departure down the collectivist road. In 1912 the writer, poet and former Liberal MP, Hilaire Belloc, published a book entitled *The Servile State* in which he expressed the fear that the increasing protection being extended by the state to the less well off might turn to suffocation and produce a large passive, dependent, benefit-receiving class in society. He predicted 'a future in which subsistence and security shall be guaranteed for the Proletariat, but shall be guaranteed at the expense of the old political freedom and by the establishment of that Proletariat in a status really, though not nominally, servile'.[2] The working classes would, indeed, become slaves twice over, both to their employers in the increasingly harsh climate of industrial relations and to the inspectors and administrators of the new Welfare State.

The alternative course which Belloc and others proposed for promoting the general welfare, the pursuit of distributism, is another of the good Liberal ideas which has been largely lost in the twentieth century. Distributism was not a doctrine of *laissez-faire*. It called for vigorous action by the state to distribute property more widely through society, via profit-sharing and co-ownership in industry, the creation of small-holdings and allotments along the lines proposed in Lloyd George's land programme, and redistributive taxation, particularly on inherited wealth. Through the implementation of such measures, instead of becoming dependent clients of the state, the working classes would become independent owners and proprietors.

For a brief period during and after the First World War it looked as though the ideas of the distributists might be taken up by the Labour Party. Belloc's arguments had attracted much interest among the Guild Socialists and two of that group, S. G. Hobson and G. D. H. Cole, tried to swing the Labour Party as a whole behind the distributist cause. They were defeated, however, by what Hobson dubbed 'the Fabian attitude to democracy – an arrogant and supercilious attitude – largely due to the reliance which it places upon the bureaucracy to administer social reforms from above; it cannot conceive wage slavery doing it for itself'.[3]

If the Labour Party's failure to take up distributism in the early 1920s was a clear indication that the political eclipse of Liberalism spelt the end of voluntaryism, the creation of the post-war Welfare State on the basis of ideas proposed by William Beveridge shows the almost complete take-over by a collectivist mentality on the part of both Labour and the Conservatives. Like Keynes, Beveridge nowadays tends to be regarded as one of the prime architects of the modern collectivist state, the friend of bureaucracy and control and the enemy of personal initiative and voluntary action. The reality is very different. Although he had certain collectivist tendencies he was a voluntaryist at heart. Unfortunately this aspect of his thinking, which was fundamental to his proposed scheme of comprehensive social welfare, was almost completely ignored by those who created the Welfare State.

Like Keynes, Beveridge was rooted in the traditions of British liberalism. In her recent biography José Harris has pointed to his strong belief in the force of moral ideas, his underlying commitment to the free market and free trade and his essential pragmatism and lack of doctrinaire rigidity on the question of the proper balance between the rights of the individual and the power of the state. His commitment to social welfare was based on his attachment to the Liberal ideal of liberty as the fulfilment of human potential. 'Liberty', he wrote, showing himself to be a true disciple of T. H. Green, 'means more than freedom from the arbitrary power of Government. It means freedom from economic servitude to want and squalor and other social evils; it means freedom from arbitrary power in any form. A starving man is not free because till he is fed, he cannot have a thought for anything but how to meet his urgent physical needs; he is reduced from a man to an animal'.[4]

With intellectual and civil liberty largely achieved, Beveridge saw British Liberals in the twentieth century being called on to fight for three particular freedoms: freedom from want and fear of want, freedom from idleness enforced by unemployment and freedom from war and fear of war. It is, of course, with the campaigns for the first two of those freedoms that Beveridge is particularly associated through his authorship of the highly influential reports on *Social Insurance and Allied Services* (1942) and *Full Employment in a Free Society* (1944).

Beveridge's overall aim was the creation of a comprehensive scheme of social welfare which would provide for everyone, from the cradle to the grave, the physical and material security without which they could not be truly free. As a first step towards achieving this, he advocated in his first report a single system of national insurance which would pay a basic subsistence income to the sick, the elderly and the unemployed. A basic precondition for the successful operation of such a scheme would, he recognised, be the maintenance of full employment, without which the demand for benefits would exceed the amount of contributions. In his second report he advocated an approach to this question which was broadly the same as that of Keynes, involving regulation of demand in the economy by the government and the use of public investment to create employment in times of recession.

These proposals, it will be noticed, are wholly in accord with the traditional British liberal approach to social welfare. Like the Liberal social reformers at the beginning of the twentieth century, Beveridge took insurance rather than taxation as the basis of his scheme. There was, of course, a substantial element of redistribution involved, with the contributions of those who enjoyed good health and regular work going to help the chronically sick and unemployed, but the principle was one of self-help and mutual aid rather than state hand-outs. In his own words, 'Benefit in return for contributions, rather than free allowances from the state is what the people of Britain desire'.[5] His ideas on the promotion of full employment show a similar attachment to traditional liberal principles, rejecting both the harshness of unrestrained capitalism and the rigidity of whole-sale socialism in favour of a mixed economy of private enterprise and public investment.

To a considerable extent Beveridge's reports laid the basis for the unparalleled period of rising living standards and full employment enjoyed by Britain in the thirty years following the Second World War. Yet the author was deeply unhappy about some of the results which their implementation brought about, as indeed must be any liberal. These unfortunate and unforeseen consequences can largely be attributed to the fact that of two key principles on which Beveridge based his scheme one, as he himself later admitted, was fallacious and the other was largely ignored by those responsible for translating his reports into action.

Beveridge's great mistake was to insist in his social insurance scheme on the principle of universality with benefits going to everyone regardless of their means. This misplaced egalitarianism, understandable in the climate of 1942 when the whole nation was engaged in a common sacrifice, was to prove very expensive and very unjust. A universal system of benefits was impossible to finance out of insurance contributions alone and required considerable increases in taxation, including of the lower paid. Benefits went to many people who did not need them while at the same time a growing number of people were caught in the 'poverty trap', having to pay in taxation more than they received back in benefits. The means-tested national assistance programme, which Beveridge envisaged as a temporary state-funded back-up to the main insurance scheme, became a permanent feature and assumed more and more importance, while a whole range of other special benefits, requiring a small army of officials to administer them, had to be introduced, and financed from taxation. On his last appearance at a Liberal Assembly in 1960 Beveridge admitted that the universality principle had been a mistake. He had never envisaged the state paying out substantial benefits to those who did not need them while those who were suffering hardship found their taxes going up.

The second key principle which underlay Beveridge's proposals was that social well-being would only be achieved through a partnership between state and voluntary action. Echoing Mill, he declared his purpose as being 'to propose for the State only those things which the State alone can do or which it can do better than any local authority or than private citizens either singly or in association, and to leave to those other agencies that which, if they will, they can do as well or better than the State'.[6] The state had a duty to ensure that everybody had a minimum subsistence level of income, but provision beyond that level should come from individual saving, mutual aid and philanthropy. In words which echo Churchill's description of the philosophy underlying the work of the 1906 Government, Beveridge's 1942 Report declared:

Social security must be achieved by co-operation between the State and the individual . . . The State, in organising security, should not stifle incentive, opportunity, responsibility, in establishing a national minimum it should leave room and encouragement for voluntary action by each individual to provide more than the minimum for himself and his family.[7]

Beveridge developed this argument further in the third and least known of his reports on social welfare, *Voluntary Action*, published in 1948. 'The theme of this report', he wrote, 'is that the State cannot see to the rendering of all the services that are needed to making a good society'.[8] Nor did he believe that it should:

The State is, or can be master of money, but in a free society it is master of very little else. The making of a good society depends not on the State but on the citizens, acting individually or in free association with one another, acting on motives of various kinds, some selfish, others unselfish, some narrow and material, others inspired by love of man and God. The happiness or unhappiness of the society in which we live depends upon ourselves as citizens, not on the instrument of political power which we call the State.[9]

In his reports and in speeches during his brief period in the House of Commons as Liberal MP for Berwick-on-Tweed, Beveridge made numerous specific suggestions as to how a welfare society involving a partnership between state and voluntary action could be built up. He argued, for example, in favour of allowing better-off workers to opt out of the state pension scheme and of handing over the administration of sickness benefit to friendly societies to introduce a more 'humanising and personalising' element into national insurance. None of these voluntaryist ideas was taken up by either Churchill's or Attlee's Government. (Nor, it might be added, were many of the ideas in Beveridge's report on full employment, like the call for a minimum national wage, compulsory arbitration and the fostering of a more co-operative spirit in industry.) Both Labour and Conservative leaders preferred the administratively easier and tidier option of concentrating everything on the state.

The creation of the National Health Service provides another example of the distortion of a Liberal idea. The establishment of a comprehensive national service for the prevention and treatment of disease and disability was one of the prerequisites for a welfare society which Beveridge listed in his 1942 report. But he was far from advocating the monolithic, centralised structure created by the Labour Government in 1946. A

Liberal Party report, *Health for the People*, linked to the 1942 Beveridge Report, had called for a partnership between the state and existing voluntary institutions on the model of the 1870 Education Act and subsequent Liberal welfare legislation. It argued, for example, that voluntary hospitals should retain their independence and local management and that both public and private money should go into a new national health service. However, the Labour planners who set up the National Health Service rejected this decentralised and pluralistic scheme in favour of one which better fitted their Fabian instincts for uniformity and tidiness.

It is all too easy to carp at the failings of the Welfare State. In many respects it is something to be proud of – a comprehensive system of care based on need rather than ability to pay which compares favourably with the welfare services of other countries. There is no doubting that overall standards of health, housing and material prosperity have risen considerably in the last forty years. But it is equally clear that something is wrong. Despite swallowing up more and more public money, the benefits system has not eliminated poverty – indeed studies show the number of people falling below official minimum levels to have increased. It is the better-off who tend to have done best out of the National Health Service, the state education system and even the jungle of benefits. Those whom the Welfare State was specifically designed to help, the poorer, the weaker and the less articulate, have all too often had their dignity and independence reduced, sometimes without any significant improvement in their material circumstances. The security which Beveridge sought does not seem to have been achieved for them as much as for the officials who run the increasingly complex system. To some extent Belloc's Servile State has, indeed, arrived.

How has this come about? Largely, I think, because those responsible for creating and running the post-war welfare system have approached their task with an essentially collectivist outlook rather than in the voluntaryist spirit of the Liberal pioneers. Instead of basing their system on the principle of redistribution and income transference, like the Liberal social reformers of 1906–16, and thereby encouraging maximum

100

individual liberty and choice, they have preferred to set up
nationalised services to provide such services as health,
education and housing on a near-monopoly basis. Instead of
seeing the prime function of the social services as being to
ensure that no one is in want, they have conceived them rather
as instruments for the transformation of society, and specifically
for the attainment of social equality. As a result the goal in
welfare provision has become uniform standards rather than
the minimum standards advocated by the New Liberals and
Beveridge.

Perhaps the most damaging result of this take-over by a
collectivist mentality has been the almost total dismissal of the
value and importance of voluntary action. Liberals from Mill to
Beveridge have, as we have seen, traditionally viewed the
welfare of the people as a matter for joint action by voluntary
effort and public power, with the latter being used to supplement and complement the former. Those responsible for social
welfare policy and provision in the last forty years have
operated from a very different viewpoint. Their justification for
the centralised state system which they created is that it is
founded on the principle of public service rather than that of
private gain. Better, they argue, to have welfare provided by
bureaucracy, cumbersome and unwieldy as it may be, than to
leave it in the hands of rapacious profit-seekers. But this
argument totally overlooks a third powerful human impulse at
work in the field of social welfare, what Beveridge identified as
the mutual aid and philanthropic motives.

Both these motives have continued to flourish in the era of
state-provided welfare, inspiring substantial giving to charitable causes, large-scale participation in voluntary organisations
and countless individual actions of spontaneous kindness and
generosity. But they can hardly be said to have been given
much official encouragement. There are some striking examples of the successful integration of the altruistic motive into the
state system – perhaps the most impressive is the National
Blood Transfusion Service which provides hospitals with what
is arguably their most essential raw material entirely on the
basis of voluntary donation. But in general those responsible for
the organisation of welfare have preferred the certainty and

uniformity of publicly provided services to the spontaneity and variety of voluntary action. This attitude has spread. Voluntary organisations themselves have become increasingly bureaucratised, dependent on public funding and reliant on full-time paid professional staff and suspicious of volunteers. There is a general assumption that the state should provide and that social problems are better solved by paid officials and experts than through the direct intervention of individuals, families and communities. As Jo Grimond has said, 'to many people voluntary action, good deeds done for no material reward, are positively wrong'.[10]

The devaluing of the natural human instinct to help both oneself and others has, perhaps, been the most unfortunate consequence of post-war developments in the field of social welfare. The Labour and Conservative Governments which created the modern Welfare State were motivated by a deep concern for the well-being of the community. But they lacked the Liberal vision of a welfare society, an organic, interdependent relationship between individuals, communities, voluntary organisations and the state. They were, to repeat the distinction which we have made before, mechanical rather than moral reformers, inclined to put too much faith in structures and not enough in human beings. They also lacked the liberal perspective that the end of social welfare is the spiritual liberation of humanity. Beveridge summed up this perspective in an article which he wrote in 1945 explaining why he had joined the Liberal Party:

In many practical measures for improving the material conditions and the security of the masses of the people, Liberal and Labour men will go together, as with them will go many Tory Reformers. But as distinct from Labour, Liberals will always have more consciously in mind as their aim, not material progress but spiritual liberty; they will emphasise the importance of the individual and the need to let each man develop on his own line, so long as he does not harm others.[11]

It is, perhaps, neglect of this aim more than any other single factor which lies at the root of the failings in the Welfare State.

10

THE RETREAT FROM
INTERNATIONALISM

In a century which has hardly been distinguished by a commitment to peace and internationalism Britain has remained truer than many other countries to liberal principles in foreign policy. We have carried the standard of liberty in two world wars and fought, at times, it seemed, almost alone, against aggression and fascism. We have divested ourselves of our empire and given self-government to former colonies in an orderly and honourable way. There have been some splendid exemplars of liberal internationalism in the likes of Sir George Schuster, successively involved in the founding of the United Nations, Voluntary Service Overseas and the United World Colleges, and Guy and Molly Clutton-Brock, who for twenty years courageously ran a multiracial community in Rhodesia until they were thrown out for the offence of 'turning yes-men slaves into independent human beings'.[1] But although Britain may have avoided the nationalism, the boastful militarism and the ugly racialism that has infected much of the world in the twentieth century, there has been a perceptible retreat from the open-minded, forward-looking internationalism of the Liberal hey-day.

As with other aspects of the decline of liberalism the first signs of this retreat can be seen in the closing decade of the nineteenth century. In the face of Britain's loss of industrial supremacy and the challenge of cheap imports from the United States and Germany there was a growing call for the abandonment of free trade. Enthusiasm for imperial conquest and adventure was also gaining popularity, even among Liberals, many of whom supported the Boer War. The desire to match the growing military might of Germany prompted a rapid escalation of defence spending, provoking the resignation of Gladstone who was appalled by the rising tide of militarism. As the nineteenth century gave way to the twentieth, Hobhouse gloomily observed that 'efforts at internationalism have yielded to a revival of national exclusiveness, seen in the growth of armaments, the revival of aggravation and protectionism, the growth of anti-alien legislation. The doctrine of democratic rights has been replaced by the demand for efficiency, or by the unadorned gospel of blood and iron'.[2]

The culmination of these illiberal forces gathering strength across Europe was, of course, to be the Great War of 1914–18. The shattering effects of the war on Liberalism in Britain have already been noted. In the particular sphere of foreign affairs it seemed to embody everything that the Liberals most abhorred: secret diplomacy, the settlement of disputes by force of arms rather than by negotiation and arbitration and the flag-waving jingoism of military adventure. The war had been entered by a Liberal Government on the Gladstonian principle of defending the rights of small nations. Yet after all the terrible slaughter and devastation, it had not really ended in a victory for Liberal principles. The peoples of central and south-eastern Europe were not liberated in 1918 but simply left to the doubtful mercies of bigger states. The victorious nations did not cut down on military spending. In the words of Charles Trevelyan, one of the many who quit the Liberal fold in revulsion at the useless carnage: 'The Liberal "war to end war" has closed with an imperialist peace to perpetuate national injustice and armaments'.[3]

One of the many casualties of the war was the policy of free trade. The 33 per cent tariff on so-called 'luxury' goods (including tea and coffee) imposed by Reginald McKenna, the Liberal Chancellor of the Exchequer, in 1915 represented the first clear departure from the policy of free trade on the part of a

British Government for more than seventy years. During the war many traditional British markets had been lost to foreign competitors and after it was over the demand for a permanent policy of protection grew louder and louder. The McKenna duties were retained in a modified form and in 1921 the Safeguarding of Industries Act was passed to protect industries launched during the war to produce goods which had previously been imported from Germany.

Liberals held out against the growing clamour for restrictions on trade. Indeed, defence of free trade was the issue which finally reconciled Asquith and Lloyd George and produced a united Liberal front against Balfour's call for the adoption of protectionism in the 1923 election. Beveridge and other leading Liberal economists took up the cudgels on behalf of free trade and argued that as a trading nation Britain could only suffer from the retaliation and overall drop in international commercial activity which would follow the adoption of protectionism. Although the free traders won the argument in the 1920s, they were unable to defeat the clamour for protection that followed the slump of 1929–31. In 1932 Neville Chamberlain introduced a 10 per cent duty on all manufactured imports. Preferential arrangements were later negotiated with the Commonwealth and some duties were raised as high as 33 per cent.

The abandonment of free trade did little, if anything, to help the British economy. Dr Forrest Capie has demonstrated in his recent book, *Depression and Protectionism* (1983), that those industries most protected in the 1930s made least contribution to the recovery from the depression. It was new, unprotected industries and the least protected of the old ones, iron, steel and construction, which led Britain out of the slump. The main effects of protectionism, he argues, were to provoke retaliation from other countries, depress the level of world trade generally and positively hinder Britain's economic recovery by encouraging resources to shift to the least dynamic sectors of industry.

If Liberalism suffered a major blow with the abandonment of free trade in the aftermath of the First World War, it looked briefly at least as though another long-held liberal ideal might

105

actually be brought to fruition as a result of the events of 1914–18. The setting up in 1919 of the League of Nations seemed to offer at last the prospect of settling disputes between nations on the basis of arbitration and creating the international moral order of which Gladstone and others had dreamed.

As we have seen, the notion of a League of Nations had first been put forward by Victorian Liberals like John Morley and W. T. Stead in the latter years of the nineteenth century. During the war the idea had been taken up by dissident Liberals and socialists in the Union of Democratic Control and by a group set up by the Liberal elder statesman, Lord Bryce, which became the League of Nations Society. In many ways the League was a classic creation of British Liberalism. It is true that its chief architects, Viscount Cecil of Chelwood, Lord Grey of Falloden, Jan Christian Smuts and President Woodrow Wilson, were neither all Liberals nor all from Britain. But they shared the open-minded internationalism, the pacific idealism and the abiding optimism which distinguish the liberal mind.

Not the least attraction of the League for Liberals was the opportunity which it offered for resolving their long-standing dilemma between the principles of non-intervention and positive assistance to those struggling for freedom. The League made possible a new kind of response towards aggression or oppression based on concerted action and involving international sanctions, including, in the last resort, the deployment of a multinational force. To idealistic liberal minds it offered much else as well. E. D. Morel, the leading light in the Union of Democratic Control, looked forward to the eventual disappearance of standing armies and navies and the establishment of a federal Europe. Professor Gilbert Murray, a key figure in the League of Nations Union, dared to predict that wars might cease as the suspicion engendered by secret diplomacy gave way to frank, open discussion. Ramsay Muir spoke for all Liberals when he demanded that 'belief in the League of Nations as a substitute for swollen armaments and rival alliances should henceforth be the pivot of British foreign policy'.[4]

Initially, it seemed that Britain would indeed lead the world in its determination to make the League work. As Prime

Minister from 1918 to 1922, Lloyd George, who had himself played an important role at Versailles in establishing the League, insisted on referring important political and legal disputes, such as that over Upper Silesia, either to the Council of the League or to the Permanent International Court of Justice. He also sent leading Cabinet ministers to the discussions in Geneva on international disarmament.

Successive Conservative and Labour premiers did not show the same commitment to the League and its aims, however. Stanley Baldwin stood aloof from it and in 1925 his Government refused to ratify the Geneva Protocol which embodied the three principles of collective security, all-round disarmament and compulsory arbitration. Despite the considerable enthusiasm of the Labour Party as a whole for the League, Ramsay MacDonald showed a similar lack of interest and in 1932 his National administration effectively killed President Hoover's bold and imaginative plan for all-round reductions in armaments.

In November 1935 Baldwin came to power again at the head of a National Government which promised to make support for the League of Nations the keystone of its foreign policy and specifically pledged itself to back the League's use of sanctions against aggressors in Europe. This policy of collective security had been endorsed by more than 90 per cent of the 11½ million people who had been polled in a nationwide peace ballot by the League of Nations Union. Yet within a few weeks of the election news leaked out of a secret pact signed by the British Foreign Secretary, Sir Samuel Hoare, and his opposite number in France, Pierre Laval, which effectively promised one of the greatest aggressors in Europe, Benito Mussolini, that no sanctions would be taken against him over his invasion of Abyssinia. Baldwin's Government opposed the League's demand for sanctions against Mussolini and so scuppered what Lloyd George described as 'the greatest chance in the history of the world of arraying the whole of the nations behind the cause of international right'.[5]

The failure to use the collective power of the League of Nations against Mussolini in late 1935, for which Britain must take a major share of the responsibility, had disastrous consequences for the future of Europe. There is no doubt that Hitler took the Hoare-Laval pact as a green light for aggression and abandoned his earlier hesitation about invading the Rhineland. It may be too much to argue, as some historians have done, that firm collective action over the invasion of Abyssinia would have prevented the chain of events that led to the Second World War. But it is indisputable that the British failure to back sanctions fatally weakened the League of Nations and marked the first decisive victory for the disastrous policy of appease-ment. That policy, which was to be promoted by both Conservative and Labour leaders in the later 1930s, was vigorously opposed by Liberals. In the House of Commons Sir Archibald Sinclair, the Liberal leader, denounced the failure to stand up collectively to the aggressors. J. L. Hammond, in more mystical vein, prayed that the spirit of Gladstone might descend and fire Europe with a collective moral will to fight for the principles of liberty and justice.

If the Second World War appears to have inflicted less of a body blow to Liberalism than the First, then that is largely because that body was already well on the way to becoming a corpse. Those who still remained true to the liberal faith regarded with horror the second round of mass slaughter in a single generation, the Nazis' systematic elimination of the Jews and the chilling events at Hiroshima and Nagasaki. But they refused to abandon hope for the future. In a powerful and moving lecture delivered in Oxford in 1943 in memory of the Liberal statesman and diplomat James Bryce, Gilbert Murray set out to persuade his audience that the terrible events through which they were living provided 'no warrant for rejecting our own ideals of progress, humanity and justice'.[6] After all long wars, he pointed out, there was an abundance of good-will and idealism, a strong conviction that such carnage must never be allowed to happen again. What was needed was the creation of organisations strong enough to put those feelings into permanent effect.

Post-war reconstruction was, indeed, carried out in a spirit of liberal internationalism. The establishment of the International Monetary Fund and the World Bank, the General Agreement on Tariffs and Trade, and the creation in the United Nations of an international peace-keeping and development agency with stronger executive powers than the League, showed a general determination to break with nationalism and protectionism. But somehow Britain's commitment to this aim seemed rather half-hearted. Delusions of grandeur from our imperial past and an unwillingness to adjust our foreign policy to suit our reduced economic circumstances combined to produce a slightly pathetic jingoism which showed itself in the debacle of the Suez affair and involvement in costly missile projects, more than one of which had to be cancelled before it had reached completion. We backed the United Nations, yet we failed to take the leading role which many had expected of us in the Security Council and General Assembly. We joined NATO yet developed at the same time our own independent nuclear deterrent.

Perhaps the clearest expression of this insular and backward-looking stance was our attitude towards our neighbours in Europe. To quote Sir Nicholas Henderson's valedictory dispatch as British Ambassador in Paris: 'We had every western European government ready to eat out of our hand in the aftermath of the war. For several years our prestige and influence were paramount and we could have stamped Europe as we wished'.[7] Yet post-war Labour and Conservative Governments took virtually no interest in Europe and rejected the overtures of those like Jean Monnet who wished to see Britain as the nucleus of a political and economic union which would fulfil Gladstone's dream of a Concert of Europe.

The attitude of British Liberals was very different. In 1948 the Party Assembly passed a motion calling for 'the establishment in West Europe of a political association conceived on broad and imaginative lines . . . a political union strong enough to save democracy and the values of Western civilisation'.[8] Alone among British political leaders, the Liberal Clement Davies welcomed Monnet's proposals. He also pressed strongly for Britain to join the European Coal and Steel Community, the Franco-German union established by the Schumann Plan, once it had become clear that Monnet's original hope of a Franco-British union was not to be. Attlee's Government, by contrast, could hardly have shown greater indifference to the whole subject. The decision not to join the new community was taken at a ministerial meeting from which the Prime Minister, the Foreign Secretary, the Chancellor of the Exchequer and the Lord Chancellor were all absent. The Conservative governments of the 1950s scarcely showed any more interest in the growing pressure on the Continent for closer economic and political integration. The Liberals were alone in 1956 in calling for active British participation in the moves being made to set up a European Economic Community. The following year the Treaty of Rome was signed without Britain.

The failure of successive Labour and Conservative Governments to embrace the principle of European union is surely the sorriest aspect of post-war British foreign policy. When we did eventually apply for membership of the Community in 1961, after more than a decade of total indifference and indeed of attempts to wreck efforts at European union, it was hardly surprising that our application was vetoed. And when we did at last join the Community, a reluctant and uncertain recruit, more than ten years later, it was hardly surprising that we found that many of its institutions and arrangements were not as we would have wished. Had Britain been among its founding fathers, and the ideas of its Liberal supporters been put into practice, the Common Market might well have been a less bureaucratic, less protectionist and altogether more vigorous body than it became without us.

— 11 —

THE ASSAULT ON
THE LIBERAL SPIRIT

———————

Contemplating the beginnings of the demise of liberalism in Britain in the mid-1870s, John Morley had little doubt as to the root cause. 'The most penetrating of all the influences that are impairing the moral and intellectual nerve of our generation', he wrote in his essay *On Compromise*, 'are the immense increase of material prosperity . . . and the immense decline of sincerity of spiritual interest'.[1]

Many of those who have since chronicled the decline of Liberal Britain have agreed that it is not so much a political or social phenomenon as, to use Dangerfield's graphic description, 'a brief but complete phase in the spiritual life of the nation'.[2] A sense of outrage and despair at the crushing of the spiritual basis of liberalism by the forces of materialism echoes through the writings of Liberals over the last hundred years. It is the major theme of the *Essays in Liberalism* written by a group of Oxford graduates in 1897 to show that 'the Liberal Party has been beaten because it has attempted to meet the collectivist on his own ground – because it has tried to compete with him in materialist programmes and promises of increased comfort'.[3] It underlies the frequent invocations of the concept of 'spirit' which Michael Bentley identifies as one of the most marked features of the liberal mind between 1914 and 1929.[4] It is the recurring cry of the great exponents of liberal values in

111

the twentieth century from Ramsay Muir and Gilbert Murray to Donald Wade and Jo Grimond.

It is even present in the writings of those liberals who might be thought to have predominantly material concerns. Keynes, as we have seen, had a strong sense of the primacy of the spiritual and deplored the worship of economics. Seebohm Rowntree, after fifty years of researching social and economic conditions in Britain, turned in the early 1950s to an investigation of the nation's spiritual state because he felt that it was there that the real barriers to social progress lay. Beveridge concluded his third and last report on social welfare by expressing the hope that a return to voluntary action on the Victorian scale might come 'through one spirit breathing again through many men'.[5] Explaining this remark, he added:

In former days there was a great alternative to the pursuit of gain as the guiding force in society; there was a force for good inspired by religious belief and based on membership of a Christian community. Now this religious force for good is less widely influential than it was in the nineteenth century. It must either be revived or be replaced by some equally good alternative, if that can be found. Perhaps it must be both in part revived and in part replaced.[6]

The decline of religious belief has, of course, been the dominant feature of Britain's spiritual life in the twentieth century. It has also been the most destructive of traditional liberalism, bringing in its wake a loss of respect for the sanctity of the human personality, a retreat from voluntary action and participation in the community and the growth of a cynical, pessimistic materialism. The decline of Nonconformity, the special ally of British Liberalism, was particularly quick and dramatic. There was a brief revival at the beginning of the century which helped to secure the return of around 200 Nonconformists to Parliament in the 1906 election. But in the 1910s the desertion from the chapels gathered pace again and all the denominations saw their already depleted congregations falling by more than half in the next fifty years.

Nonconformity had been more than the backbone of the Liberal Party. The chapels, temperance societies, Sunday Schools and literary institutes of Victorian Britain provided a culture and a way of life based on participation, self-improvement and wholesome enjoyment. The decline of these institutions produced a sense of emptiness and aimlessness among the working class and lower middle class communities in which they had been a central feature. The cultural transformation of the South Wales valleys in the first half of the twentieth century shows dramatically the effects of the decline of chapel culture. In the 1920s, despite unemployment rates of up to 80 per cent, virtually the entire adult population of the Rhondda valley were engaged in adult education courses, choirs, and other community activities. Thirty years later, with much greater material prosperity and little unemployment, the chapels were virtually empty, the miners' libraries sold, and most of the population only ventured out of their homes in the evenings to drink or play bingo. As the journalist Jeremy Seabrook commented after a recent visit to the valleys:

> If the young have, for the most part, been released from the joyless disciplines of chapel and pit, they have also been disinherited from the other half of that life: a sense of secure identity, anchored in a tradition of music and singing, of mutual improvement societies, penny readings, drama and oratorios, a world in which it was possible to be an intellectual and a working man.[7]

There are those who explain this transformation, which affected many parts of Britain, in terms of the innate weakness and dullness of humanity. On this argument the sobriety, activity and thirst for self-improvement of the Victorian era was a strange and temporary aberration. Given political emancipation and material wealth, people reverted to their natural condition, passive, pleasure-seeking and philistine. The truth, I think, is rather different. It was not a natural and spontaneous process which turned the grandchildren of those who had walked for miles and queued for hours to hear Gladstone's complex oratory into dulled gazers at television soap operas. Rather the spirit of participation, individual discovery and individual development had been steadily and remorselessly eroded by the brutalising pressures of collectivism and commercialism and the enervating and dehumanising influence of the mass media.

In an interesting book published in the first year of the twentieth century, *The Heart of the Empire*, a group of young Liberals, which included G. M. Trevelyan, G. P. Gooch and C. F. G. Masterman, expressed their fears about the growth of an urban proletariat cut off from all intellectual and spiritual influences and fed on a diet of trash papers and magazines. Just under half a century later George Orwell made the 'prolerisation' of the people by the mass media one of the main themes of his admonitory novel *1984*. In his moving study of changes in popular culture, *The Uses of Literacy*, first published in 1957, Richard Hoggart showed that this was exactly what was happening. Decent, personal, local, communal working-class culture was being destroyed by the pervasive influence of papers, magazines and novels which offered an unvaried diet of sensation without commitment 'likely to render its consumers less capable of responding openly and responsibly to life . . . and to induce an underlying sense of purposelessness in existence'. The mass media were, in fact, turning people into a race of 'irresponsible obedients'.[8]

Perhaps the most striking aspect of this whole sad development was the decline of the British popular press from its high-minded, Liberal, provincial, Nonconformist origins into the sensational, meretricious tabloid rubbish with which we are all too familiar today. At the root of this decline was the dominance of purely commercial values. The editor-proprietors of the nineteenth century, as we have seen, felt a sense of mission to inform, educate and elevate their readers and to involve them in campaigns for the great righteous causes of the day. The press barons of the twentieth century have had a rather different outlook. Under the influence of the profit-motive the 'New Journalism', so brilliantly used by Stead to assist his crusades against evil, was perverted into easily digested sensationalism. Campaigning journalism took second place to the competitions and free gifts which were introduced to boost circulation. Hobhouse noted sadly in 1909, 'The Press, more and more the monopoly of a few rich men, from being the organ of democracy, has become rather the sounding-board for whatever ideas commend themselves to great material interests'.[9] Nor was it just on the owners' side that collectivist and materialist values replaced the passion for truth and the campaigning spirit. Trade union attitudes entered the editorial process with the founding of the National Union of Journalists in 1907. When Kennedy Jones, assistant to Alfred Harmsworth and one of the leading representatives of the new order, met John Morley, one of the last survivors of the old, in 1919, he told him: 'You left journalism a profession, we have made it a branch of commerce'.[10]

One of the most dramatic effects of these growing commercial pressures and of the increasing concentration of ownership was the demise of many of the provincial daily papers which had been the bastions of Victorian Liberalism and Nonconformity. In 1900 there were over 40 provincial dailies. Forty years later there were less than 20, only a handful of which were locally owned, the rest being part of large nationwide conglomerates. The new 'popular' papers were almost aggressively metropolitan, like Harmsworth's *Daily Mail*, launched in 1896 with the aim of building up a national readership 'centering on London and looking to London for its news and opinions'.[11] In the face of competition from papers like the *Mail* and its downmarket stablemate, the *Daily Mirror*, started in 1903, the more staid Liberal papers found their circulation falling. The *Daily Chronicle* had already compromised with the times and started publishing betting odds in 1894, much to the disgust of its Nonconformist editor, A. E. Fletcher, who resigned declaring, 'I regard this as the curse and shame of journalism'.[12] The other leading Liberal London morning paper, the *Daily News*, owned by the teetotal George Cadbury, held to its high-minded Nonconformist principles until the 1920s, when it reluctantly introduced advertisements from bookmakers and brewers. This decade also saw the demise of the two leading Liberal London evening papers, the *Pall Mall Gazette* and the *Westminster Gazette*. In 1930 the *Daily News* and the *Daily Chronicle* were forced to combine to form the *News Chronicle*, while outside London only the *Huddersfield Examiner* and the *Manchester Guardian* were left to represent the fierce provincial radicalism and the 'readable righteousness' which had once distinguished so much of the British press. Even that small remnant of Liberal journalism was not to remain unscathed.

The *News Chronicle* folded in 1960, the same year that saw the *Guardian* move its editorial offices to London and remove 'Manchester' from its title.

The values of the new mass papers and magazines were profoundly illiberal. In the words of Richard Hoggart, they promoted an outlook in which 'liberty equals licence to provide what will best increase sales; tolerance is equated with the lack of any standards other than those which are so trite and vague as to be almost wholly incantatory and of little practical use; any defence of any value is an instance of authoritarianism and hypocrisy'.[13] This spiritual shallowness and intellectual doublespeak was not the only undesirable feature of the new popular press. It also pulled the nation apart socially as it united it geographically. The provincial papers of Victorian Britain had been classless – as likely to be read by the mill-owner as by one of his labourers. The new metropolitan papers were carefully tailored to particular social groups, designed to meet the advertisers' demand for a good 'profile' and to achieve near-saturation coverage of a particular consumer market.

In the increasingly tough commercial battle between proprietors, the middle classes were just as much victims as the working classes. If the *Daily Mirror* dulled the senses of its blue-collar readers with its unceasing sensationalism, then the *Daily Mail* narrowed the minds of city clerks and suburban housewives with its sanctimonious smugness. It encouraged them to feel superior to the working classes, to despise foreigners and to resist change and reform. It was, indeed, the mouthpiece of the new culture of suburbanism, characterised by John Carvel Williams, a Congregationalist and Liberal MP, as standing for 'respectability, which is incompatible with enthusiasm, great apathy, and sometimes downright snobbishness, and a recantation of principles firmly held in days gone by'.[14] Secure and private behind their privet hedges and their lace curtains, the middle classes retreated from involvement in the voluntary organisations and political activities which they had for so long kept alive. On a visit to Liverpool in the 1890s Beatrice Webb lamented that the Liberal Nonconformist generation which had dominated the city's social, cultural and political life was dying out and that 'the sons are not worthy of the fathers . . . The present generation of rich folks want to enjoy themselves, find nothing to resist, no class or creed interest to fight for, so that they have ceased to consider anything but their pleasures'.[15] A few years later, recognising the implications of this change of outlook among its readers, the leading middle-class paper, the *Daily Telegraph*, switched its political stance from Liberal to Conservative.

The forces of centralisation, concentration and standardisation which so changed the nature of the British press were at work in many other areas of cultural life. They lie behind the determined campaigns in the early years of this century to stamp out the Welsh and Gaelic languages in schools, the nationalised and homogenised system of broadcasting introduced with the establishment of the BBC in 1926, and the erosion of the broad principles of liberal education by increasing academic specialisation. Intellectuals have been on the retreat in the twentieth century as much as anyone else. The independent man of letters has given way to the salaried academic attached to a university or research institute, and the wide-ranging, eclectic reviews of the nineteenth century have been replaced by narrow periodicals read by a handful of experts. The cultural climate which produced the diversity of interests and the marriage of the practical and the speculative mind of a Gladstone or an Arnold is no more. Professional academics find themselves barely able to communicate with colleagues in other disciplines, let alone with those outside universities, while those in public life find their time increasingly taken up with the boring paraphernalia of bureaucracy.

New intellectual currents washed over the shores left dry by the receding tide of liberalism. Freudian psycho-analysis suggested that man was not governed by conscience and reason but by blind prejudice and cultural conditioning. Marxist determinism excluded the possibility of progress through individual or community action and preached rather that man was in the iron grip of economic forces. The increasing hold of the scientific explanation meant that more and more things were viewed in purely material terms. Novelists from Thomas Hardy onwards turned from celebrating character and individuality to an obsession with fate and the overpowering forces which turn people into virtual prisoners. Overall, the twentieth century has seen the ascendancy of the reductionist values which John Morley had first noted in 1874 when he wrote that 'Character is considered less and less with reference to its absolute qualities than as an interesting scene strewn with scattered rudiments, survivals, inherited predispositions. Opinions are counted rather as phenomena to be explained than as matters of truth and falsehood'.[16]

This assault on the liberal spirit was not just confined to the world of ideas, of course. It came also, as we have seen, from a new style of politics in which the electorate was seen as a mass market to be won by bribes and promises, from changes in the organisation of industry and business which made both workers and managers feel less personal identity and more like cogs in a machine, from the development of a bureaucratic Welfare State which treated people as dependent clients and impersonal statistics, and from the rise of mass media geared to producing a uniformity of taste in the interests of maximising profits. In the twentieth century it has increasingly been the category rather than the individual that has counted. The importance of people lies in the label that can be attached to them – be it trade unionist, unmarried mother, recipient of supplementary benefit, breakfast-time television viewer, or member of the C1 group of consumers – rather than in what they are in themselves.

What particularly disturbed those who still clung to liberal values about these developments was the readiness with which the vast majority of people gave in to collectivist and materialist pressures. In the words of Morley, 'They have ceased either to trust or distrust liberty and have come to the mind that it matters little either way. Men are disenchanted. They have got what they wanted in the days of their youth, yet what of it, they ask'.[17] An uncharacteristic mixture of self-doubt and pessimism overtook the minds of many Liberals towards the middle of the twentieth century. It can be seen in the nostalgic, backward-looking glances cast by Hammond and G. M. Trevelyan towards the golden age of Gladstone and Bright, in Sir Ernest Simon's statement in 1939 that it was doubtful whether a revival of liberalism was feasible 'with the world in its present state of mind', and in the gloomy observation of Seebohm Rowntree three years later that 'it is time Liberals seriously considered whether the philosophy on which Liberalism has been based in the past still holds good'.[18]

Those who retained some faith in the enduring power of the liberal spirit increasingly pinned their hopes for the future on the existence of a small élite who might stand out against the vulgarity, the commercialism and the mass uniformity of the age. In 1939 E. M. Forster, one of the most eloquent exponents of liberal values in the twentieth century, wrote: 'I believe in aristocracy . . . Not an aristocracy of power based upon rank and influence, but an aristocracy of the sensitive, the considerate and the plucky. Its members are to be found in all nations and classes, and all through the ages, and there is a secret understanding between them when they meet. They represent the true human tradition, the one permanent victory of our queer race over cruelty and chaos.'[19] Four years later Gilbert Murray drew the attention of an audience in Oxford to the fact that 'the common man is to be the dominant power of the coming age' and to 'the constant pressure to lower all our standards to what is easy, to what pays, to what suits the momentary taste of great majorities'. He went on to outline the responsibility facing those who still clung to liberal values:

Living, as we do, so largely outside the struggle for material ends, among the great thoughts and achievements of the spirit of Man during these last few thousand years of his pilgrimage, let it be ours to recognise that which is higher than ourselves, to love, to understand, to revere; and to keep alive in the world those things of beauty and high value which are always in peril because they are difficult and can be reached only by few.[20]

__ 12 __

THE NADIR OF LIBERALISM

The years from 1945 to the mid-1970s saw the nadir of liberalism in Britain. It is difficult to identify exactly when it reached its lowest ebb: perhaps in the gloomy years of state socialism which followed the Second World War; perhaps in the 1950s, that decade of material plenty and spiritual poverty which saw the coming of television and tower blocks; perhaps in the 'swinging' sixties with their devotion to the strangely twinned gods of planning and permissiveness; or in the early 1970s when the power of militant trade unionism and managerial conservatism combined to produce that ugly and illiberal Leviathan, the Corporate State.

Many readers may be surprised to see the post-war period described in these terms. Was not this the era of the Butskellite consensus, that enlightened, rational, progressive approach which eschewed narrow dogmatism and extremism, united Labour and Conservative governments and gave Britain three decades of general prosperity, full employment and increasing social welfare? It is true that there were some notable liberal reforms in this period and the achievements of the post-war governments should not be belittled. But as we have already observed in the distortion of the views of Beveridge and Keynes, there was a general retreat from liberal principles on the part of politicians and administrators. Increasingly faith was placed in experts and planners rather than the people, material goals were put before spiritual values and uniformity and equality were preferred to diversity and liberty. In this gradual retreat from liberalism Butskellism played a subtle but significant role.

The bible of Butskellism was, I suppose, Anthony Crosland's *The Future of Socialism*, published in 1956. This was, in fact, a much more humane work than both its reputation and its influence would suggest. Crosland himself had much sympathy for the liberal, decentralist strain in the British Labour tradition epitomised by such movements as Guild Socialism. But the overall theme of his book is unmistakably materialist. It set as the ultimate political goal the pursuit of equality to be achieved through the means of economic growth and state action. In a rather cruder form than that proposed by Crosland, this was the basic philosophy of successive Labour and Conservative governments in the thirty years following the war. Their approach was characterised by an almost blind faith in the statistics of economic output and productivity and in the beneficial effects of interventionist government. It was not really socialism at all – Crosland's own term 'statism' is a much better description. Certainly one of the most conspicuous features of the Butskellite years was a steady and inexorable growth in the power and size of both central and local government and public authorities.[1]

The Labour Government elected immediately after the Second World War established one of the main elements of this new statism in its wide-ranging programme of nationalisation. Public ownership of industry had long been championed by the Fabians in the 1890s and it had been enshrined in the Labour Party constitution since 1918, but it was only with the election of Attlee's administration that it was put into practice. Nationalisation was applied to a wide range of industries and utilities, including coal, iron and steel, the railways, telecommunications, electricity, gas and civil aviation, with the result that by 1951, to quote Crosland, 'Britain had, in all essentials, ceased to be a capitalist country'.[2]

Nationalisation was, for the most part, passively accepted by both Conservatives and Liberals with only a few dissenting voices, like that of Seebohm Rowntree, questioning whether it would do anything to improve either economic efficiency or industrial relations. It turned out in practice to be a highly illiberal form of industrial organisation, monopolistic in tendency and failing to give workers in the industries involved any more say or stake in their running. Despite its manifest weaknesses and unpopularity it took on the status of a tribal totem within the Labour Party, as Hugh Gaitskell discovered to his cost when he dared to question its central place in the party's constitution in 1959. At a time when other progressive socialist parties in Europe were shedding their commitment to public ownership, Britain's major party of the left remained wedded to a doctrine which was at best out-dated and irrelevant to the needs of an advanced industrial society.

The Conservative Governments of the 1950s and early 1960s did little to reverse the tide of statism. Although they were initially elected on a promise to 'set the people free', their conception of freedom proved to be very different from that of traditional British liberalism. Another slogan from the 1951 election, 'More red meat', sums up the essential materialism which underlay the Tories' electoral appeal during their thirteen uninterrupted years of power. These were not entirely wasted years, as Labour's subsequent propaganda was to suggest. Harold Macmillan's policy towards Africa, for example, was in many ways a model of just and orderly disengagement from imperial commitments and went some way towards atoning for the jingoistic folly of the Suez invasion and the insular attitude adopted towards the emerging European Economic Community. But the overall atmosphere was one of complacency and conspicuous consumption, well summed up in Macmillan's oft-quoted phrase, 'Most of our people have never had it so good'.

Culturally the Macmillan years were dominated by the growing influence of television. In assessing the impact of this most pervasive and powerful mass medium it is difficult to improve on the initial verdict of the redoubtable C. P. Scott: 'The word is half Latin and half Greek. No good can come of it'. Television contributed powerfully to the general retreat from participation, involvement and self-development noted in the last chapter. By the end of the 1950s the average Briton was spending a total of twenty hours a week (the equivalent of nine years in the average lifetime) slumped in front of the screen passively receiving a diet composed largely of the trivial and the mildly sensational. Finding it difficult to handle ideas, television, particularly in its early days, generally preferred subjects that lent themselves better to pictorial representation. Elections were covered like horse races, with most of the interest being concentrated on who was going to win rather than on the issues at stake. The essentially materialist bias of the medium was reinforced by the equation of happiness with possessions in the ubiquitous quiz games, soap operas and commercials.

By its nature television, at least until the advent of cable and low-cost technology, has tended to be a centralised and authoritarian medium. A very small number of people effectively control what vast numbers will watch. In Britain this powerful new priesthood of pundits and producers has been drawn from a very narrow social and geographical background, being predominantly made up of middle-class, London based university graduates. It has also tended to subscribe to a rather exclusive set of social and political values which is perhaps best labelled 'trendy permissive'. The overall attitude of the new cultural establishment which television has created is often characterised as liberal. This is a serious misuse of the word. The cynical, secular, metropolitan outlook of most media folk is the antithesis of liberalism as it has traditionally been understood in Britain.

The other major cultural development of the 1950s and early 1960s, the emergence of a distinct youth culture based on pop music and rapidly changing styles of fashion and behaviour, was another distinctly illiberal phenomenon. To only a very limited extent, if indeed at all, did it bring liberation and fulfilment to young people. Rather they tended to become the slaves of powerful commercial interests, pressurised into buying more and more records and clothes, drinking more alcohol and taking more drugs, and feeling that happiness lay in instant gratification and the acquisition of material possessions. Far more than the citizens of mid-Victorian Britain, indeed, modern teenagers live under an overwhelming pressure to conform – and to a much greater extent than when Mill protested against the despotism of custom and convention in his essay *On Liberty*, those pressures are now exerted by powerful commercial operators. It is small wonder that some of the youngsters who are daily bombarded by messages and images which treat people as objects, and which extol violence and material success, themselves turn to anti-social behaviour.

The values promoted by television and the pop culture – admiration for the new and the flashy and reduction of people into the role of passive consumers – spread also into the political sphere. Increasingly Governments were elected on the promise of doing bigger and better things than their predecessors, much as a new washing powder might be chosen for its dazzle and brightness. Image and style became all-important as politicians discovered the delights, and the advantages, of projecting themselves as television stars. Big but empty words like 'dynamism' became the common currency of Westminster and Whitehall as politicians and administrators set themselves grand goals and embarked on elaborate and expensive prestige projects. Experts and planners were given their head and encouraged to indulge in large-scale efforts at social engineering which abandoned the limited objective favoured by liberal reformers of securing certain minimum standards of welfare, in favour of the much grander aim of establishing a uniformity of provision and creating an equal society.

The 1960s and 1970s were full of these misguided schemes which were conceived with the best of paternalist intentions but almost always without the involvement of those who were most directly affected. Many of them ended up by diminishing the freedom of those they were designed to help. Slum clearance and urban re-development schemes, which looked splendid on planners' drawing boards, destroyed the cheerful, communal chaos of back-to-back terraces and replaced it with the soul-destroying anonymity of the tower block. Urban motorways, designed to speed traffic flow and promote mechanical mobility, were driven through residential and commercial areas, bisecting communities and turning parts of many cities into virtual no-go areas reached only by tunnels and overhead walkways. Large comprehensive schools, designed to end divisiveness in education, too often simply transferred the 11+ failures from the old selective system to the bottom of the pile in vast, remote communities where they often had less chance of attaining responsibility or finding fulfilment. The reorganisation of local government and the health service undertaken between 1970 and 1974 in the interests of rationalisation and efficiency took the control of services further away from those who used them. In a similar way the professionalisation of social work produced a new managerial mentality in which people in need of help and advice became 'clients'.

Similarly unfortunate, and largely unforeseen, results were produced from the several attempts at protective legislation which were made during this period. Rent Acts designed to give tenants protection against landlords had the effect of severely reducing the amount of furnished accommodation available for letting and made life more difficult for those with limited means who were searching for somewhere to live. Employment protection legislation designed to prevent unfair dismissals had the effect of lessening the number of jobs on offer, particularly in small firms. Legislation controlling agricultural tenancies virtually closed the opportunity to enter farming to all but those with very substantial amounts of capital. Planning regulations too often inhibited individuals from setting up businesses. Far from liberating people and making Britain more dynamic, this paternalist and protectionist approach was having a smothering effect. The servile state had well and truly arrived.

The ultimate expression of the planning and paternalist mentality of the 1960s and 1970s was the creation of the so-called Corporate State. In 1962 Harold Macmillan set up the National Economic Development Council, or Neddy as it came to be known, as a forum for industrialists, trade unionists and government to work out the nation's economic strategy. Three years later Harold Wilson launched his famous National Plan with an array of detailed targets worthy of the Soviet system. Although the plan was soon discreetly abandoned, the mentality which had produced it continued to dominate Whitehall and Westminster for the next ten years or so. Increasingly, the direction of the nation's economic policy, and of a sizeable part of its social welfare policy too, became a matter not so much for Parliament and public opinion, nor even for the elected Government, as for a small group of favoured corporate interests which were effectively co-opted into the governing process and allowed to dictate their own terms in return for a commitment to control their members.

The most powerful of these favoured interests was, perhaps, the trade union movement. During the era of prices and incomes policies and social contracts the trade unions managed to squeeze substantial concessions out of successive governments and to feel that they had a special role in the running of the country. The catalogue of these concessions, which began with the Wilson Government's climb-down in 1969 over the 'In Place of Strife' proposals for union reform and ended with the Callaghan Government's legalisation of the closed shop in 1976, makes depressing reading. They were for the most part won not through the open processes of democracy but by largely covert bargaining. By 1977, with nearly a quarter of the country's entire workforce in legally protected closed shops, enjoying total immunity from civil actions and freedom to picket and engage in other intimidatory and obstructive behaviour, trade unions occupied a uniquely and unjustifiably privileged position in British life.

But it was not just the unions which throve in the Corporate State. So also did the giants on the other side of industry, the conglomerates formed out of amalgamations and take-overs, and the large new public bureaucracies. To be big was indeed to be beautiful in the eyes of the authorities. To be small was to be a nuisance, an obstacle to efficiency and rationalisation to be swept away as quickly as possible like the branch lines which Dr Beeching had so enthusiastically axed in the mid-1960s. This was the era of the fusing of government departments to create jumbo ministries like the Department of Economic Affairs, the Department of Health and Social Security and the Department of Trade and Industry. Meanwhile all around the country cottage hospitals and village post offices were being closed down. Those who lost out were the groups not represented by powerful corporate bodies – the elderly and the unemployed, the self-employed and small businesses. In 1971 the Bolton

Committee reported that Britain had a smaller proportion of its workforce employed in small firms than any other industrialised country in Europe. The nation of shopkeepers and small workshops had become the land of mergers and multinationals.

Many Liberals, it has to be said, seemed happy to ride with this new corporatist current. It is true that the Liberal Party stood out against some of the more illiberal trends of the 1960s. It took a courageous and consistent stand, for example, against the racial discrimination displayed in some of the legislation of the period, like the 1968 Commonwealth Immigration Act which aimed to stop the entry into Britain of Asians fleeing from persecution in Kenya, and which was so vigorously opposed by David Steel. There was also some Liberal agitation, led by two MPs, Donald Wade and Emlyn Hooson, for a Bill of Rights which would outlaw the closed shop and protect individual liberties against increasing encroachments by the state. But many Liberals seemed happy enough to espouse Butskellism and quietly drop their historic commitment to free trade, voluntaryism and the primacy of personal liberty.

It would, of course, be quite wrong to portray the whole political and cultural climate of Britain in the 1960s and 1970s as illiberal. Tolerance and open-mindedness still prevailed in many areas of life. As we shall see in the next chapter, the spirit of liberalism was far from dormant and was, indeed, stirring in exciting and often surprising ways. There was also much important reforming legislation which brought a significant increase in personal liberty for many people. It included the abolition of capital punishment in 1965, the Race Relations Acts of 1965 and 1968, the establishment of the Parliamentary Commissioner, or 'Ombudsman', in 1967, the creation of the Open University in 1969, the Equal Pay Act of 1970 and the trio of measures in 1967 which legalised homosexual acts between consenting adults, widened the grounds for abortion and made divorce easier.

But it is undeniable that powerful political and cultural forces were combining to assault traditional liberal values. At the same time, and perhaps in a way even more disturbingly, the idea of liberty was perceptibly changing. The so-called permissive society, which the last three measures mentioned above played a part in helping to create, is often spoken of as a liberal movement. In so far as it brought greater tolerance and greater possibilities of fulfilment for those who had previously been the victims of prejudice, that is certainly a fair description. But in other ways the permissive society was, and indeed still is, very illiberal, being based on the false equation of liberty with licence. Certainly many of its proponents have taken a cynical and materialistic view of life which is in almost total opposition to traditional liberal concern with spiritual values and the sanctity of the human personality. The same could be said of some of those groups who have spoken most stridently about 'rights' but who have shown little regard for the sense of responsibility and little of the tolerance towards the views of others which are equally part of the liberal tradition.

I began this chapter by saying that it was impossible to pinpoint the exact time when liberalism reached its lowest ebb in Britain. But one can perhaps identify the mid-1970s as the period when the various illiberal forces which had been welling up throughout the post-war years came to a head. The creeping corporatism and statism of the Butskellite era seemed to reach its apogee in the Wilson-Callaghan Government of 1974 to 1979. The boredom and despair engendered among the young by unemployment, the mass media and the commercial pop culture found its ultimate expression in the wholly nihilistic punk movement and in the ugly racism of the National Front and the British Movement, whose brief but significant upsurge of support provoked some scarcely less intolerant demonstrations of left-wing extremism. Militant trade unionism seemed to reach a new level of violence and disruptiveness. Some observers seriously began to predict that Britain, racked as it was by economic crisis and consumed by self-doubt, might be on the verge of succumbing to anarchy and extremism.

In the midst of this troubled period, Alexander Solzhenitsyn, the Soviet dissident, posed a series of questions on BBC Radio Three about the state of Britain. Why was it, he asked, that the birthplace of western liberalism was now experiencing the sapping of its strength and will to a greater degree than any other country in the world? How had it come about that 'those

128

who soar unhampered over the peaks of freedom suddenly lose the taste of freedom, lose the will to defend it, and hopelessly confused and lost, almost begin to crave slavery again'? Why did a society 'with access to every kind of information suddenly plunge into lethargy, into a kind of mass blindness, a kind of voluntary self-deception'? He concluded:

We have become hopelessly enmeshed in our slavish worship of all that is pleasant, all that is comfortable, all that is material – we worship things, we worship products. Will we ever succeed in shaking off this burden, in giving free rein to the spirit that was breathed into us at birth, that spirit that distinguishes us from the animal world?[3]

Even as he spoke, this last question was being answered in the affirmative. A strange new movement was afoot in Britain, a heightening of spiritual awareness, a new heeding of the call to conscience, a growing attachment to diversity and variety, a renewed commitment to voluntaryism and decentralised democracy, a new internationalism, an increased consciousness of individual and communal development. At the very time that it perhaps seemed nearest to extinction, liberalism was being reborn.

PART THREE

THE STRANGE REBIRTH OF LIBERAL BRITAIN

———————

13

STRANGE STIRRINGS IN
THE SIXTIES & SEVENTIES

Powerful though they undoubtedly were, the forces of corporatism and commercialism did not go unchallenged in Britain in the 1960s and 1970s. Under the surface a growing number of people were beginning to question their validity and to reassert the counter-values of diversity, voluntaryism and moral principle. These stirrings of the liberal spirit were not immediately obvious. They tended to receive little attention from commentators in the media. Yet small-scale and even insignificant as they may have seemed individually, taken together they heralded an important change in the national mood – a rebirth, indeed, of the Liberal Britain which had apparently died at the beginning of the century.

One interesting sign of this new mood was the renewed interest shown in the idea of liberty itself following the long period in which it had largely been taken for granted. As we shall see in the next chapter a much greater sense of the importance and value of freedom overtook both those on the political left and those on the right. Movements and events abroad undoubtedly provided much of the impetus for this change. From the United States of America came both the hippies' search for personal fulfilment and enlightenment which made 'liberation' one of the in-words of the sixties and

also the radical ideas of the 'New Right' which made libertarianism one of the main intellectual themes of the seventies. The
revelations of Russian dissidents about the extent and the
effects of totalitarianism in the Soviet Union played a part in
strengthening the West's commitment to liberty and human
rights, as did events in Czechoslovakia, Poland and Afghanistan.

In Britain, as in other countries, the emergence and growth
of the women's movement has been one of the strongest
expressions of this new-found interest in liberty. Admittedly in
some of its more strident and militant manifestations it is
difficult to fit modern feminism into the tolerant and gentle
traditions of British liberalism. But then there is every reason
for women to feel passionate and angry about a society in which
they are oppressed and exploited and in which male values
predominate. The feminist movement has helped to bring
about far greater opportunities and more equality of treatment
for women in many areas of life, even if there is still a long way
to go. Just as important, through groups like the Greenham
Common Peace Women, it has promoted some of the feminine
values which are sorely needed in a world where there is
altogether too much masculine machismo at the helm. The
exclusivity and sectarianism of some of these groups may be
unattractive to the liberally-minded, but overall there can be
no doubt of the key role that the women's movement has played
in the rebirth of Liberal Britain.

The same is true of those other movements which took off in
the 1960s and 1970s for gay liberation and black civil rights.
Once again a certain stridency and exclusivity has sometimes
been evident in these movements, but this is understandable, if
not, perhaps, wholly excusable, when set against the prejudice
and harassment to which homosexuals and black people are
subjected. The changes both in the law and in social attitudes
which have been brought about in the last twenty years or so in
respect of these and other minority groups in Britain represent
an important victory for liberal principles.

The introduction of anti-discrimination legislation is only one
way in which the cause of liberty has been promoted through
the law in the last two decades. In a rather different vein the

134

trenchant and sometimes idiosyncratic judgements of Lord Denning as Master of the Rolls from 1962 to 1982 re-asserted the best traditions of British liberalism by powerfully upholding the rights of the individual against entrenched corporate interests like public authorities and the trade unions. Overall, the defence of liberty seemed to assume a greater importance in the eyes of lawyers. One sign of this was the growing campaign for a Bill of Rights which attracted the support of such eminent legal figures as Lord Hailsham, Lord Gardiner and Lord Scarman.

Another indication of the liberal reawakening in the 1960s and 1970s was the growing importance which issues of conscience assumed, particularly among the young. The outcry against nuclear weapons is perhaps the outstanding example of this. The Campaign for Nuclear Disarmament, set up in 1958, brought back into British public life the passionate anti-militarism and crusading moral spirit of John Bright and the Victorian Nonconformists. It may no longer be possible to talk of a Nonconformist Conscience, or even perhaps a specifically Christian conscience in modern Britain, but there can be no denying that the cause of nuclear disarmament has become an important moral focus for many people in this country and has, indeed, almost attained the status of a religious crusade. It is perhaps significant that one of the first leaders of the Campaign for Nuclear Disarmament, Canon John Collins, should have been an Anglican clergyman, its 'guru', E. P. Thompson, the son of a Methodist missionary, and the man who presided over its recent revival, Bruce Kent, a Roman Catholic priest.

Many consciences were also stirred by the plight of those living in the Third World. The new medium of television probably played an important and positive role here by bringing pictures of horrific disease and malnutrition into nearly every living room in the land. The response to these scenes of suffering was generous and widespread. Donations to relief agencies like Oxfam and War on Want increased dramatically. Organisations like Voluntary Service Overseas and International Voluntary Service were set up to send young people out to help directly in development work. On a political level, pressure groups like the Haslemere Group, Third World

First, the World Development Movement and the United Nations Association secured considerable support for campaigns urging the Government to increase the level of overseas aid and take more account of the needs of the developing world. The Brandt Report, urging a more equitable distribution of the world's resources between rich and poor nations, became a minor best-seller.

Closely related to this re-awakening of internationalism was the widespread concern about the environment and ecological matters which began to show itself in Britain, as in other industrialised countries, in the 1960s. Pressure groups like Friends of the Earth alerted many people to the destructive nature of the modern throw-away society and began to change public attitudes to favour conservation and recycling of the earth's resources. There was growing unease about the ethical and nutritional effects of factory farming and the use of chemicals in food production and many people began to echo Mill's plea for the preservation of the world's wildernesses and wild places for the sake of man's sanity and spiritual peace.

The brutalising and de-humanising aspects of the mass media and the permissive society were also coming under increasing attack. The best-known campaigner in this field has been Mrs Mary Whitehouse who started her Clean Up TV Campaign (later the National Viewers and Listeners Association) in 1964. It has been fashionable for self-styled 'liberals' to sneer at the efforts of Mrs Whitehouse and her supporters to stop dirty words from intruding into the drawing-room. It is true that their campaign has had a narrow-minded and illiberal side. But at the same time it cannot be denied that in crusading against the trivialisation and exploitation of sex and violence they stand to some extent at least in the British liberal tradition, which, as we have seen, has always upheld the dignity and integrity of the human personality and firmly resisted attempts to reduce and debase it.

Voluntaryism is another liberal value which has been redis-covered in the last twenty-five years. The coming of the Welfare State after the war may temporarily have weakened the British tradition of voluntary service, but it was not long before that tradition was revived again to complement and supplement the contribution of the new statutory services. An early example was the establishment of leagues of hospital friends to continue in the new National Health Service the close links that the old voluntary hospitals had with their local community. The 1960s and 1970s saw a mushrooming of voluntary activity. A committee set up under the chairmanship of Lord Wolfenden in 1977 estimated that more than five million people were regularly involved in voluntary work, quite apart from the many millions more who cared informally for relatives and friends. It also found that there were three voluntary organisations to every thousand people. To established old-stagers like the Red Cross and the Women's Royal Voluntary Service, there had been added a host of new groups covering just about every imaginable human need.

These new voluntary organisations fall into three distinct categories. Firstly, there are those most directly inspired by what Beveridge termed the philanthropic motive and providing help to people in need. Particularly worthy of mention in this group are the trio of national organisations set up in the 1960s to channel the altruism of young people into practical community service, Community Service Volunteers, Task Force and the Young Volunteer Force Foundation. As well as directly giving thousands of youngsters experience of voluntary action, they have also helped to inspire what has surely been one of the most exciting educational developments in the last two decades, the introduction of community service as a regular and popular activity in many schools and colleges.

Then there are the organisations which, while often also involved in direct philanthropic work, are first and foremost pressure groups campaigning for changes in the law or in public attitudes. Among the best known are Shelter, the national campaign for the homeless, the Child Poverty Action Group, set up in 1965 to promote the interests of the many families living below the official poverty line, the Disablement Income Group and MIND, the National Association for Mental Health. The former Labour Prime Minister Lord Wilson pointed out in a famous observation that these organisations had captured the energies and enthusiasms of the 1960s generation in a way that conventional political parties failed to do – and, one might add, in a way that revived the best traditions of British Liberalism. It had, after all, been the emergence of pressure groups cast in a similar radical crusading mould in the middle of the nineteenth century that had given birth to the Liberal Party.

The third and largest group of new voluntary organisations is made up of those animated by what Beveridge called the mutual aid motive. It includes such diverse bodies as the Pre-School Playgroups Association, set up in 1961 and now co-ordinating the activities of more than 7000 playgroups run by mothers around the country, Release, the round-the-clock help and information service for drug addicts established in 1967, and Gingerbread, the organisation for single-parent families founded in 1970. Many self-help groups have been set up by sufferers from particular diseases or by their relatives, like the Multiple Sclerosis Society and the National Society for Autistic Children. Then there are the numerous tenants associations which have been formed in both publicly and privately rented housing estates, the co-operative shops, car sharing schemes and community bus schemes which have been established in an effort to revive rural life, and the many self-help schemes which have been started in inner-city areas like the enterprising Network Project in Liverpool which enables people to swap their time and skills as an alternative to conventional employment.

This great expansion of voluntary activity prompted a re-adoption of voluntaryist policies on the part of both central and local government. Public money was increasingly made available to voluntary bodies. Volunteer bureaux and councils of social service were set up to stimulate voluntary action at local level, full-time voluntary help organisers were appointed in many hospitals and community workers were recruited to encourage and support self-help groups and co-operative ventures in both urban and rural areas. The principle of community service was also applied with notable success in the field of penal policy. In 1973 community service orders were introduced as an alternative to custodial sentences or fines. More than 150,000 offenders have now undertaken a wide range of unpaid tasks of social benefit and this constructive and highly liberal form of punishment has been taken up in France,

Denmark, Norway and the Netherlands.

Needless to say government encouragement of voluntary action has involved an increase in bureaucracy. There are now three publicly funded bodies (the National Council of Voluntary Organisations, the Volunteer Centre and the Voluntary Services Unit of the Home Office) all supposedly co-ordinating and directing the activities of the voluntary sector and treading on each other's toes as a result. These organisations seem to spend much of their time churning out lengthy reports and research papers. But there has also been some action as well, particularly at the local level. Over the last few years in particular there have been several interesting experiments in establishing new patterns of care for the disadvantaged based on a partnership between public authorities and voluntary effort. Under the innovative direction of Nicolas Stacey, Kent Social Services Department has successfully fostered with families disturbed children who would otherwise have languished in impersonal and expensive institutions. It has also paid neighbours to do chores for old people who might otherwise have had to occupy a hospital bed or a place in a residential home. Other local authorities have experimented with similar schemes to 'foster' old people with families and in several inner-city areas Good Neighbour Schemes have considerably improved the lot of the elderly and housebound. An interesting recent initiative in this area is the emergency alarm system for the elderly introduced at the end of 1983 by the Oxfordshire Council of Voluntary Service and linked to the county's ambulance service which alerts volunteers when a bleeper is activated.

While these practical schemes have been developed at the local level, the whole principle of voluntaryism, or welfare pluralism as it is now more often called, has found an increasing number of champions in what might be termed the 'welfare establishment'. An important statement of that principle is contained in *Voluntary Action in a Changing World*, a study by Francis Gladstone commissioned by the National Council of Voluntary Organisations and published in 1979. As befits his name, Mr Gladstone makes a powerful call for the re-adoption of the traditional liberal approach to welfare, with the Government laying down minimum rather than uniform standards and then leaving the field open for local initiatives and experiments. His book is a plea for decentralisation, diversity and freedom of choice. It is also a plea to trust the people. As he remarks in his final paragraph, 'Faith in the latent ability of "ordinary people" to help themselves and to help each other, given adequate support, will need to become much more prevalent among experts and professionals, planners and managers, administrators and politicians if voluntary action is to be fostered where it is most needed'.[1]

Voluntaryism was not the only traditional liberal value to enjoy a renaissance in the 1960s and 1970s. There was also a revival of provincial consciousness and Celtic radicalism. The most conspicuous manifestation of this was perhaps the dramatic upsurge in the electoral fortunes of the Scottish and Welsh Nationalist parties which reached a highpoint in the two elections of 1974. But the resurgence of Celtic nationalism was just one aspect of a more general revolt against the dominance of metropolitan values which showed itself in the development of local radio and regional television to challenge the London monopoly of broadcasting, the revival of interest in local folk customs and the establishment of movements like the Campaign for the North and Pennine Heritage. The long-standing trend which had centred more and more activities on the metropolis was reversed as offices were relocated in the country and people began to discover the pleasures of living outside the South-East corner of Britain. At the same time those remoter regions which had for so long been ignored or despised began to find themselves the object of new interest and admiration, praised by sociologists and eulogised in television documentaries for the strength of their community values and the integrity of their way of life.

This increasing interest in lifestyle and community was part of a more general rediscovery of spiritual values. This showed itself not so much in a revival of Christianity – although certain churches, particularly those associated with the charismatic and Pentecostalist movements, did experience a significant increase in membership – but rather in a growing interest in mysticism, meditation and other aspects of Eastern religion and philosophy. It would, of course, be quite wrong to see all the religious and philosophical movements of the 1960s and 1970s as essentially liberal phenomena. There was an undeniable element of pure escapism about some of them and several of the cults which sprang up were decidedly illiberal in their dogmatism and intolerance towards outsiders. But for all their Californian chicness, the hippies' slogans of 'flower power' and 'all you need is love', like the technique of transcendental meditation taught by the Maharishi Mahesh Yoga and the speaking in tongues practised by the Charismatics, represented a search for direct spiritual experience and a rejection of the secular materialism that had been gaining ground so steadily through the previous half century or more.

Another major twentieth-century shibboleth came under attack with the questioning of the gospel of economic growth. Influenced by such works as Fred Hirsch's *The Social Limits of Growth* (1977) and by general unease about the effects of industrialisation on man and his planet, more and more people began to wonder whether the pursuit of material wealth was not, in fact, a misguided policy the effect of which was to worsen the general quality of life. There was growing unease about the equation of progress with the Gross National Product, an economists' construct which counted as wealth the results of the labours of cigarette and drinks manufacturers but not of doctors, housewives or teachers. Some were moved to opt out altogether from the rat race and lead simple lives of self-sufficiency on a smallholding in the country. John Stuart Mill's call for a stationary, or steady-state economy seemed to many to have a new relevance and a new urgency.

An interesting and important indication of this disenchantment with the gospel of growth was the interest in so-called alternative technology shown by certain sections of the trade union movement. In 1974, in the face of a likely collapse of the aerospace industry, the Lucas Aerospace Combine Shop Stewards Committee sent a questionnaire to all the company's employees inviting their suggestions for alternative products which would avoid the necessity for large-scale redundancies. As a result of the replies received the committee was able to draw up a plan proposing that the firm diversify into the manufacture of a wide range of socially useful and environment-ally desirable products including heat pumps and a combined road-rail bus. Similar strategies, involving the development of recycling technologies and renewable energy sources, were drawn up by the Vickers Shop Stewards Combine Committee in 1974, the Power Engineers Industry Trade Union Committee in 1977 and the shop stewards at Dunlop's Speke factory in 1979.[2]

These proposals were just one element in the development of a comprehensive alternative to the high-growth, high-consumption society which Britain had become. The 1970s was the decade of 'alternatives', many of them publicised and explored in the column with that title which Harford Thomas contributed to the *Guardian*. The rise of the Ecology Party brought an alternative voice into politics, interest grew in alternative medicine and alternative education, and a small but not insignificant number of people began experimenting with 'alternative' lifestyles in various types of community. Organisa-tional expression and focus was given to these various inter-related impulses not through the creation of formal and centralised bureaucracies but through the development of loose networks, like Turning Point, set up in 1975 by James Robertson, a former civil servant in the Cabinet Office. Robertson brought together much of the thinking behind these new movements in his book, *The Sane Alternative*, published in 1978. Significantly, this important work was printed privately by the author after he failed to find a commercial publisher. The cultural establishment as yet had little time for ideas that it regarded at best as distinctly fringe and at worst as positively loony.

The powers that be were not wholly indifferent to the new liberal ideas which were bubbling up around the land, however. They showed some sympathy, for example, with the growing attack on the worship of size. The phrase coined by E. F. Schumacher in 1973, 'small is beautiful', became a major rallying cry for many groups who sought to turn the tide of corporatism and centralisation. But it was also being heard increasingly at Whitehall and Westminster and in the boardrooms of large companies. Amalgamation and concentration were no longer necessarily the order of the day. The benefits of corner shops, cottage hospitals and small businesses were rediscovered and efforts were made to break down industrial giants like British Leyland into smaller units. Despite the Government's shelving of the Bullock Report in 1977, many companies were showing a growing interest in industrial democracy and were setting up works councils. A survey by the British Institute of Management in 1981 found that 93 per cent of responding firms had either recently established or were in the process of establishing schemes for worker participation. An independent survey the following year of employees in 413 major companies found that more than half felt that their managements had become less secretive and more inclined to consultation.

The paternalistic rule of experts and planners was also being assailed by those in authority as well as from below. The cancellation of motorway box schemes and the blowing up of tower blocks in the early 1970s signalled the end of the era of dictation from the drawing board. In 1976 Peter Shore, the Secretary of State for the Environment, proudly told an international conference that Britain had 'pensioned off the bulldozer'. There were to be no more wholesale demolition and rebuilding schemes – instead the accent would be on conservation and rehabilitation. This dramatic conversion came too late to save many cities, but it was welcome nonetheless. Equally significant was the conversion of Professor David Donnison, for long a leading advocate of the Fabian-style paternalistic Welfare State, who announced in 1979 that 'Governments will have to take more seriously the capacity of ordinary people to do things for themselves with a little training and support. We need not just more nursery schools, but more mothers running their own playgroups, not just more legal aid and advice, but more "bare-foot" conveyancing'.[3]

An important aspect of this return to the principle of trusting the people was a growing revolt against the over-professionalisation of society. The leading theorist of this revolt was, of course, Ivan Illich, who argued in his books *Deschooling Society* (1971), *Medical Nemesis* (1975) and *Disabling Professions* (1977) that important areas of life had been taken over by professionals with narrow perspectives and an excessive regard for institutions and technology. Illich's ideas were taken up in the movement for more natural forms of medicine, spear-headed by such organisations as the Natural Childbirth Trust, and by those who set up 'alternative' schools which sought to avoid the rigid rules and institutionalisation of conventional education. More generally, there was a growing demand that experts and professionals should become less remote and be stripped of some of their mystique.

One of the most successful examples of 'de-professionalisation' has been the adoption in certain parts of the country of community policing. During the 1950s and 1960s the police became increasingly remote from the communities which they were supposed to serve. Taken off the beat, they were put into fast cars and equipped with the latest in high technology equipment. In the early 1970s John Alderson, Chief Constable of Devon and Cornwall, decided to reverse this trend. Instead of reactive policing, where officers cruised around in cars waiting to rush to trouble spots, he proposed a return to community policing, where they spent most of their time walking the beat and getting to know people in the neighbourhood. Consultative groups were set up which brought together teams of policemen and representatives of the local community. Commander David Webb introduced a similar style of policing in the Handsworth district of Birmingham with dramatic results in terms of improved race relations. More recently the Metropolitan Police have put more constables back on the beat and involved Londoners in neighbourhood watch schemes which have produced significant falls in crime figures.

Sadly, the principle of community policing has also met with some setbacks. Commander Webb felt obliged to resign from the West Midlands force out of frustration at the lack of progress in implementing the idea more generally. More recently the police have found themselves used in the miners' strike in a reactive and even at times in a provocative way with consequent damage to their reputation and standing in mining communities which may take a long time to repair. There are disturbing signs that we are moving towards the creation of a national police force with less local identification and control. Despite these setbacks, however, the manifest success of community policing experiments where they have been carried out gives one grounds for hoping that this positive and liberal trend may continue.

Standardisation and uniformity, those other great idols of the twentieth century, have not escaped unscathed from the revival of liberal values. The Welsh and Gaelic languages are undergoing a renaissance and are being taught in schools more widely than at almost any other time this century – there is even a Welsh language television channel. Diversity and variety is coming back into our lives, not least into the important business of eating and drinking. There has been a welcome proliferation of regional specialities, vegetarian and wholefood shops and restaurants and ethnic eating places. And when historians of the future come to chronicle the strange story of the rebirth of Liberal Britain I hope they will not overlook the importance of the victory which has been won by the Campaign for Real Ale against the might of the big brewers and the monstrosity of fizzy keg beer.

All the movements which have been mentioned in this chapter involve participation, commitment and a sense of the worth of individual action. These are the common factors which link the anti-nuclear protestors, the real ale campaigners, the enthusiasts for recycling and alternative technology, the crusaders against pornography, and the practitioners of transcendental meditation. The near-death of Liberal Britain was accompanied, as we have seen, by a retreat into passive apathy and pessimism. Its rebirth has been heralded by a return to activism, belief and optimism about the potential of the human spirit.

Even television, for so long a major force for passivity, has contributed to this revival. Its use as a catalyst for voluntary action and involvement in the community has been one of the most exciting and encouraging cultural developments in the last decade. When in May 1974 Granada Television's 'World In Action' programme broadcast an appeal to families to adopt children, more than 6,000 people rang in, of whom over 200 subsequently became foster parents. So impressed was the company with this response that the following summer it introduced a weekly fifteen minute slot in its local news magazine programme appealing for volunteers for various projects. In the autumn of 1975 this was extended to a weekly half-hour programme called 'Reports Action' which in its first season raised 11,000 potential kidney donors, 2,000 visitors for mental hospitals, 550 domestic appliances to give to people who needed them and over 400 derelict plots of land for use as allotments. 'Reports Action' has subsequently been shown nationally on the ITV network, with telephones manned by volunteers in all major cities to take the thousands of offers of help which followed each item. Other independent television companies have broadcast similar programmes in their own regions. There has also been much use of local radio as a medium for stimulating community action and involvement while a further spur to participation and activity has been provided by a popular BBC television programme for children with the admirable title 'Why Don't You Switch Off Your Set and Do Something More Interesting Instead?'[4]

It is, of course, possible to exaggerate the extent of these new stirrings of the liberal spirit. But it is also easy, and quite fallacious, to dismiss them, as some have done, as being confined to a small element of the population, namely the *Guardian* reading progressive middle classes. It is true that the *Guardian* has been one of the very few news media to take serious notice of these new trends and movements and to understand their importance. Indeed the impressive rise in the circulation of that paper over the last decade represents a small but indicative sign of the rebirth of Liberal Britain. It is also true that those who first espoused some of the more off-beat aspects of that rebirth, like communes or alternative medicine, were drawn predominantly from the middle classes, although there are signs that this is no longer the case. But it has not just been the middle classes who have responded to Reports Action's appeals for kidney donors and hospital visitors, who have seen the benefits of alternative technology and become worried about the over-use of insecticides and factory farming, and who have joined tenants associations and inner-city co-operatives. And it has certainly not just been *Guardian* readers who have rejoiced at the re-appearance of draught beer. The death of Liberal Britain was a complex episode which had many different and even contradictory facets and ramifications. Its rebirth three-quarters of a century later is proving a similarly far-reaching and strange phenomenon.

___ 14 ___

THE NEW LEFT
AND THE NEW RIGHT

As we have already observed, neither Labour nor the Conservatives moved very far into the territory which was vacated by the retreating Liberal Party in the first half of this century. They preferred rather to move with the prevailing tide in the direction of greater materialism, managerialism and nationalism. But in the last ten years or so there has been a dramatic change. Both the major parties have undergone ideological transformations which have in several important respects, though not in all, brought them closer to the British liberal tradition. The emergence of the so-called New Left and New Right has, indeed, been one of the most significant, and certainly one of the strangest aspects of the rebirth of liberalism in contemporary Britain.

Both these new movements have sprung from a common rejection of the corporatist, centralist social democracy of the post-war era. The origins of the New Left can perhaps best be traced to 1960, the year of the launching of the influential *New Left Review* and of the publication of E. P. Thompson's book *Out of Apathy* which attacked the centralised statism of Crosland and other Labour revisionists and called for a new democratic, decentralised radicalism in which the state would simply provide the circumstances to enable people to 'build their own, organic community in their own way'.[1] Another founding father of the movement was Raymond Williams whose book *The Long Revolution*, published in 1961, argued for the application of the co-operative principle in social and economic policy and for the creation of 'a participatory democracy, in which the ways and means of involving people much more closely in the process of self-government can be learned and extended'.[2]

The New Right was born at much the same time. Its intellectual power house, the Institute of Economic Affairs, was founded in 1957 and has since produced a steady stream of publications arguing the case for the free market and questioning the wisdom of universal and monopoly state welfare services. The leading theorist of the New Right has almost certainly been Friedrich von Hayek whose book *The Constitution of Liberty*, published in 1960, is a powerful restatement of the liberal principles of free moral choice, voluntaryism and maximum individual liberty in a society 'in which a man is not subject to coercion by the arbitrary will of another or others'.[3] Another key text of the New Right is Michael Oakeshott's *Rationalism in Politics*, published in 1962, which attacked the rationalist, managerial style of politics in the Butskellite era.

Both of these groups of thinkers stress the central importance of liberty. In many ways, indeed, those socialists who have taken up the decentralised, participatory democracy espoused by Williams and Thompson and those Conservatives who have adopted the radical libertarianism of Hayek and Oakeshott are much closer to each other than they are to the more conservative and paternalist members of their own parties who are so often and so mistakenly dubbed as liberals. On several issues it is the libertarians generally found on the so-called right wing of the Conservative Party, rather than the 'wets' and others who cling to traditional Tory paternalism, who deserve the description of liberal, just as it is often those on the so-called left wing of the Labour Party who come closest to representing liberal values in socialism. Samuel Brittan, that perceptive and sympathetic observer of the rebirth of Liberal Britain, identified the close affinity of the two groups when he wrote in 1973 that 'The time is ripe for a re-alignment in which the more thoughtful members of the New Left and the more radical advocates of competitive free enterprise realise that they have a common interest in opposing the corporate industrial state'.[4]

Such a re-alignment has yet to take place. But what has happened, to an extent that would have been hard to predict fifteen years ago, has been the assimilation of these new liberal ideologies by both the major political parties. In the case of Labour, the ideas of the New Left gradually gained adherents at grassroots level. Alongside the crude Marxist rhetoric issuing from the universities and polytechnics and the bully-boy tactics of some militant groups, there has been a genuine resurgence of interest within the Labour movement in democracy, co-operation and the long neglected doctrines of guild socialism and distributism. A significant step was taken in 1968 with the formation of the Institute for Workers Control which rejected the goal of nationalisation in favour of more decentralised industrial democracy and co-operatives. In 1978 an inquiry into state intervention in industry by the trades councils of Coventry, Newcastle, Liverpool and North Tyneside argued that the way to humanise and improve industry lay not through state intervention but by working people getting together at local level to shape their own futures. The workers' plans drawn up by shop stewards' combines and mentioned in the last chapter provided a concrete expression of these aspirations.

A similar approach has also been taken up by several Labour local authorities. In 1979 Glasgow District Council launched an alternative housing strategy to give its thousands of tenants a greater say and control in the management of their homes. More than 10,000 tenants in the city's inter-war estates have modernised their homes themselves with the aid of council grants and nine tenant co-operatives have been set up to manage external improvements. The council has also freed land for private housing development and is now planning to sell some of its estates to housing co-operatives. In Sheffield the city council, under the dynamic leadership of David Blunkett, has devised a strategy to promote economic and social welfare by setting up co-operatives and stimulating local people into action to help themselves rather than relying on provision from the Government. Other authorities have adopted similar decentralist and community-based policies which are much closer to

149

Joseph Chamberlain's municipal radicalism than to Fabian-style authoritarian direction.

This new liberal thinking among trade unions and local councils found little reflection in the ideas or actions of the Labour Governments which ruled Britain from 1974 to 1979. They remained wedded to a corporatist approach which was well demonstrated in the establishment of a National Enterprise Board in 1975. Although a Royal Commission under Lord Bullock was set up the following year to advise on how best to achieve industrial democracy, nothing was done to follow up its recommendations, which were themselves indicative of the prevailing corporatist mentality in the central role which they accorded to trade unions. A similar timid conservatism characterised the Government's response to the Layfield Report of 1976 which urged the serious consideration of a system of local income tax to give more autonomy to local authorities and reduce their dependence on central government. Of the few positive liberal steps which were taken by the Government during this period the most significant was, perhaps, the setting up of a Co-Operative Development Agency in 1978, which was largely the result of pressure from the Liberals.

One member of the Labour Governments of the mid-1970s did try to implement the ideas of the New Left. As Secretary of State for Industry, Tony Benn invited the Institute for Workers Control to submit plans for industrial democracy and launched workers co-operatives at the Meriden motorcycle factory, Kirkby Manufacturing and Engineering and the *Scottish Daily News*. He also championed the democratisation of the Labour Party, making it less élitist and authoritarian and more responsive to the wishes of the rank-and-file members. Since 1979 he has become the leading spokesman and the focal figure not just for the New Left in the Labour Party but also for several of those liberal groups whose emergence and growth we noted in the last chapter, notably the peace movement and the women's movement.

Tony Benn is, of course, first and foremost a socialist rather than a liberal. Some of his ideas, such as his advocacy of economic protectionism and planning and his faith in trade union collectivism, are, indeed, the very antithesis of liberalism. But there is no doubt that in other respects, not least in his strong commitment to both political and industrial democracy, his manifest trust in the people, his opposition to militarism, his fierce moral radicalism and his crusade against the materialistic and trivialising influence of the mass media, he stands in the tradition of John Bright, C. P. Scott and other great Liberal Nonconformists of the past. The so-called Bennite left of the Labour Party is, I would venture to suggest, in several respects a good deal more liberal in its ideas and approach, though not always in its behaviour, than the media would have us believe – and, indeed, than are certain other sections of the Labour movement.

This is not to say that liberal influences within the higher levels of the Labour Party over the last few years have only come from Tony Benn and his associates. Since the party's defeat in 1979 some other Labour politicians have become noticeably more liberal in their thinking. A notable example is Frank Field, the MP for Birkenhead and former director of the Child Poverty Action Group, whose book *Inequality in Britain* (1981) attempted to shift the goal of socialism from equality to freedom. Another important recent book, *The Democratic Alternative* (1983) by Peter Hain, a former Liberal and now one of the leading exponents of the ideas of the New Left, also makes much of the central importance of individual liberty as an objective for socialists. Overall, however, the leaders of the Labour Party at national level, like the leaders of the trade union movement, have so far preferred to cling to statism and corporatism and have not moved far down the more liberal road that is being trod by an increasing number of their members at local level.

In the case of the Conservatives new more liberal ideas have come not from the grassroots but rather from the leadership. Like Tony Benn, Margaret Thatcher is a child of Liberal parents deeply imbued with the Nonconformist Conscience. She has never, as far as I know, described herself as a liberal but she has been thus described by some of her supporters. Sir John Nott, while a member of her Cabinet in 1982, declared, 'I am a nineteenth century Liberal. So is Mrs Thatcher. That is what this Government is all about.'[5] Professor Milton Friedman, high priest of monetarism, put it equally emphatically: 'The thing that most people do not recognise is that Margaret Thatcher is not in terms of belief a Tory. She is a nineteenth century Liberal'.[6]

An examination of one of Mrs Thatcher's most important and interesting speeches makes clear the extent to which she is, in fact, cast in the Victorian Liberal mould. It is her Iain Macleod Memorial Lecture, delivered in July 1977 and entitled, somewhat ironically, 'Dimensions of Conservatism'. The starting point of this address is a Christian, and distinctly Protestant, argument which draws significantly on the doctrines of the Puritan fathers of the seventeenth century:

> Our religion teaches us that every human being is unique and must play his part in working out his own salvation. So whereas socialists begin with society, and how people can be fitted in, we start with Man, whose social and economic relationships are just part of his wider existence. Because we see man as a spiritual being, we utterly reject the Marxist view which gives pride of place to economics.[7]

The lecture goes on to stress the value of choice in a free society:

> Morality lies in choosing between feasible alternatives. A moral being is one who exercises his own judgment in choice, on matters great and small, bearing in mind their moral dimension, i.e. right and wrong. Insofar as his right and duty to choose is taken away by the state, the party or the union, his moral faculties, i.e. his capacity for choice, atrophy and he becomes a moral cripple in the same way as we should lose the faculty of walking, reading, seeing, if we were prevented from using them over the years.[8]

This argument leads Mrs Thatcher on to attack the all-embracing Welfare State for crushing the opportunities for exercising morality and producing two classes, the bureaucratic élite and the manipulated masses. She calls for the creation of a market economy where people are free to give their money and time to good causes. This leads to a great commendation of Victorian voluntaryism and of the enduring legacy of nineteenth-century philanthropy as represented by such institutions as the National Society for the Prevention of Cruelty to Children, the Royal National Lifeboat Institution and the St

John's Ambulance Brigade. The lecture ends with a burst of optimism in which post-Keynesian faith in economics and demand management is replaced by a more fundamental faith in people and in the belief that 'men can still shape history'.[9]

I have quoted from this speech at some length because it gives a particularly good indication of the extent of Mrs Thatcher's liberalism. It establishes her as a believer in liberty, as a voluntaryist and as a radical rather than a conservative, seeking not to preserve the consensus but to transform society. It also establishes her as a moral rather than a mechanical reformer, seeing the key to progress as lying not so much in the proper management of the economy or in correct social engineering but in the liberation of human energy and potential and the restoration of the moral values of self-discipline and responsibility.

To that extent Mrs Thatcher belongs to the British liberal tradition. But there are other attributes which disqualify her and her colleagues from being described as liberals and which certainly rule out the claim that she is heir to the spirit of Victorian Liberalism. A government which has sought to define British nationality in racial terms, which has aligned itself with the interests of landlords and big business and which is the friend of centralised control and the enemy of local government cannot be said to be following in the footsteps of Mr Gladstone. There is a distinctly illiberal materialism about much of Mrs Thatcher's ideology and her vision of the future. For all her attack on Marxists for giving pride of place to economics, she herself shows an excessive interest in the dismal science and adopts an almost reverential attitude towards monetary targets and output figures. Her ultimate goals appear to be the narrowly economic ones of bringing down inflation and reducing personal taxation. Like others on the New Right she is inclined to be over-obsessed with the idea of the market and with a view of man as a consumer or producer rather than as a rounded human being with emotions and needs outside the economic sphere. This tends to produce a somewhat doctrinaire adherence to the principle of *laissez-faire* and a rather selfish individualism, neither of which, as we have seen, has ever been part of the British liberal tradition. There is altogether too much stress on material success and aggressive go-getting and not enough on compassion and redistribution in her view of the good society. In foreign affairs she behaves much more in the traditions of jingoistic Conservatism than in the spirit of Liberal internationalism.

These major limitations on her liberalism can be seen in practice when Mrs Thatcher's rhetoric is compared to the reality of her achievements in Government since 1979. In her Iain Macleod lecture she set herself six targets: 'how to revive the economy, how to enlarge our liberties, how to restore the balance between trade unions and the community, how to further our European partnership while protecting legitimate British interests, how to simplify the welfare maze which often baffles those who most deserve help, and how to regain an underlying sense of nationhood and purpose'. [10] It is interesting to examine how well, and how liberally, her Governments have performed in meeting these aims.

It is difficult to pass a verdict at this stage on the overall effects of the Thatcherite experiment in reviving the economy. Inflation has certainly fallen but in many other respects the economic life of the nation is more sluggish and depressed now than it was six years ago. For all the talk about the virtues of the free market, Mrs Thatcher's Governments have proved disappointingly conservative and even protectionist in their approach to many economic issues. In the words of Peter Riddell, the perceptive political editor of the *Financial Times*, in his book on the first Thatcher Government, 'Competition has taken second place to mercantilism. Any Government which is as assiduous in protecting both subsidies to owner occupiers and special interests (like the Stock Exchange) as Mrs Thatcher's has been is unlikely to win many plaudits from free-market economists'. [11] It is true that some important steps have been taken to stimulate competition, like the ending of the National Bus Company's monopoly on long-distance coach travel and the abolition of the solicitors' monopoly on conveyancing. There have been some useful and positive Government initiatives to help and stimulate small business like the notably successful enterprise allowance scheme. The privatisation of nationalised industries has also brought some significant gains like the creation of the management-workforce co-operative which has taken over the British Freight Consortium and the widening of share ownership through the sale of British Telecom. But too often privatisation has simply meant the substitution of a public monopoly by a private one and has led to no real increase in competition. Large corporate institutions like pension funds and insurance companies have been allowed to keep their dominant position in the world of finance and there has not been as much spreading of wealth and ownership throughout the community as there could and should have been. After six years of Thatcherism, the British economy still remains too corporatist, too centralised and too regulated.

Has Thatcherism enlarged our liberties? Once again, the record is a somewhat mixed one. There has certainly been a reduction in red tape – bureaucracy has been cut and some restrictions eased. Several groups of people have achieved a new freedom and independence in Thatcherite Britain, like the 750,000 or more council house tenants who have bought their own homes. But for others, and particularly for immigrants, the unemployed and the poor in general, there has been a net reduction in personal liberty springing both from economic circumstances and Government policy. The Nationality Act of 1981 was a particularly illiberal piece of legislation. Mrs Thatcher's Governments have been curiously timid about taking up measures which might increase freedom and choice, even on a small-scale experimental basis. An example of this is their failure to try out the education voucher. In their assault on local government autonomy through the device of rate capping, their attachment to more centralised control over education and their stubborn refusal to change the voting system, they have also shown themselves to be no great friends of the democratic principle.

Their approach to the trade unions has displayed a similar mixture of liberal and illiberal impulses. By refusing to treat them as a privileged estate of the realm and by legislating against the coercive practices of secondary picketing and the closed shop, Mrs Thatcher's Governments have at least begun to restore the proper balance between trade unions and the community as a whole. If anything, indeed, they have not gone far enough in this respect. But at the same time there have been some rather heavy-handed and autocratic attempts to bludgeon the unions, like the wholly unjustifiable ultimatum delivered to the employees of the Government Communications Head-quarters at Cheltenham in 1984.

The problems besetting the European Community are so enormous that it would be unfair to blame the British Government for the lack of progress in this sphere. Mrs Thatcher can, perhaps, be fairly criticised, however, for a tendency to display that insularity which has, indeed, been characteristic of most Labour and Conservative politicians in their dealings with Britain's partners in the European Community. But this said, she has at least made a bold start, which must be welcomed by all liberals, at reforming the protectionist common agricultural policy and curbing some of the bureaucracy with which the EEC seems to be particularly laden.

There has been some equally welcome encouragement of voluntaryism in the sphere of social welfare. Government funding for the voluntary sector as a whole has been increased and useful schemes have been introduced like the Manpower Services Commission's Voluntary Projects Programme and the Opportunities for Volunteering project. But the Government seems to have been frightened by fears of media reaction and trade union opposition and by the conservatism of its own supporters from developing more radical plans to turn the Welfare State into a welfare society. It is true that it has had the courage to launch a full-scale inquiry into the whole benefits system but there is little sign that this will lead to radical reforms of the kind long advocated by Liberals to merge the taxation and social security systems into a single tax credit scheme. Despite the ending of some tax privileges for the better-off, like the relief on life insurance premiums, the Thatcher Governments have done nothing to redistribute wealth and have on balance left the poor poorer and the well-off richer and better protected.

It has to be said that the 'wetness' of Liberal MPs, along with Labour members and not a few Conservative backbenchers, has been one of the main barriers to a more radical and liberal approach in this area. Sir Keith Joseph's plan to abolish minimum grants for students and make better-off parents pay something towards the tuition fees of their children at university was a bold and reasonable attempt to end one of the many state subsidies which are provided for the middle classes. No doubt if the present Government were ever courageous enough to propose the abolition of income tax relief on mortgage interest payments it would be howled down by a similarly conservative coalition masquerading as liberals.

The last target which Mrs Thatcher set herself in her Iain Macleod lecture, that of regaining an underlying sense of nationhood and purpose, is perhaps the one which she has been least successful at achieving. Britain is more divided and polarised now, between haves and have-nots, North and South, extreme right and extreme left, employed and unemployed, than it was when this Government first came into office. There is an apparent lack of compassion and narrowness of vision on the part of the Government towards the weak, the less successful and the unemployed which makes these members of society feel guilty and unproductive. A sense of national unity and purpose seems to be precisely what is lacking. Some have claimed that it was rekindled during the war with Argentina over the Falklands Islands in 1982, but if that unpleasant spirit of jingoism and xenophobia is what Mrs Thatcher means to foster as an expression of a new sense of national purpose, then liberals will want nothing whatever to do with it.

Perhaps the overwhelming lesson to be learned from the Thatcher experiment has been that the capacity of governments to effect significant changes in a society as complex as ours is very limited. This is in its way, I suppose, a very liberal lesson showing as it does the inadequacies of mere mechanical reforms. To some extent, of course, it has been a deliberate message. Instead of the Government being regarded as the universal provider and the body which will solve all the nation's problems, the onus and responsibility has been shifted back on to the people. But one suspects that the last six years have shown up the basic impotence of government more even than Mrs Thatcher had really bargained for. The two Conservative Governments elected since 1979 have been less gripped by a paralysis of will and more committed to a bold and radical transformation of Britain than any of the others elected in the last thirty years. Yet they have found themselves constrained and frustrated at every step by external forces, by the power of vested interests like big business, the agricultural lobby and the Whitehall machine, and by the powerful force of inertia and the sheer complexity of modern society. A Labour Government committed to the radical policies of the Bennite left would probably encounter similar problems and also find itself severely constrained in what it could do.

That said, it cannot be denied that in certain respects Mrs Thatcher's two premierships have had the effect of pushing Britain in a more liberal direction. They have helped to create a mood in the country which is more hostile to corporatism and collectivism and more favourable to individual responsibility and moral choice than it has been for many years. Of course, Thatcherism has produced illiberal effects as well, but this overall change of mood may well prove to be very important in creating the willingness for experimentation and initiative on which the continuing rebirth of Liberal Britain partly depends. In a curious and not altogether different way, Tony Benn has also contributed to creating this new mood by turning the minds of many on the left away from corporatist and statist solutions and towards more direct action and involvement. Both politicians, it might be added, have also made a welcome and long overdue departure from the politics of bribery, basing their appeal to voters not so much on specific promises and pledges as on broad ideological arguments of the kind favoured in the heyday of Liberal Britain.

This is not to say that either Margaret Thatcher or Tony Benn should be hailed as the modern embodiment of the British liberal tradition. There is in both of them, and much more in some of their followers, a distinctly illiberal shrillness and stridency, a preference for confrontation and conflict and a lack of those broad and humane sympathies which distinguish the true liberal temper. Indeed, as we have seen, neither of them ultimately qualifies to be described as a liberal in the fullest sense of the word. But it is equally wrong to dismiss them as wholly illiberal ogres, as certain sections of the press, and many Liberals, are wont to do. Their ascendancy in their respective parties over the last ten years or so is a sign, albeit a strange one, of the resurgence of liberal ideas in British politics. Theirs is not a phoney battle – there are major issues of policy which divide them from each other and, indeed, which divide them both from Liberals. But in certain important respects they do stand together as representatives of the new ideology of liberty which is replacing the old orthodoxy of Butskellite statism and centralised social democracy. As Jo Grimond has written:

The present battle is not between a Conservative Government ruthlessly and unnecessarily applying the conventional wisdom and an alternative championing the underdog. The battle on which the ultimate victory will depend is not between the Conservative and Labour parties at all. It is between the new, to some extent libertarian thought and the old entrenched corporatist thought and interests, dominant in all parties for the last thirty years and still lying behind its main (but by no means only) mouthpiece, the Labour Party.[12]

___ 15 ___

THE LIBERAL PARTY
AND THE SOCIAL DEMOCRATS

How much has the Liberal Party had to do with the rebirth of Liberal Britain? At first sight this may seem a rather unnecessary question to ask. Surely the most important indicator of the revival of liberalism in Britain in the last thirty years has been the dramatic improvement in the electoral fortunes of the Liberals, up from 2.7 per cent of the total votes cast and only 6 MPs in the 1955 election to 19.3 per cent of the vote and 14 MPs in February 1974 and, in partnership with the new Social Democratic Party in 1983, to 25.4 per cent of the vote and 23 MPs, 17 of them Liberals, representing the party's largest grouping in Parliament since 1935?

It is true that the revival of the Liberal Party has been a very important aspect of the rebirth of Liberal Britain. But these psephological statistics of which modern Liberals are so fond (perhaps, dare one say, too fond) need to be interpreted with some care. Many of the votes which have been cast for Liberal candidates in recent times are not in truth votes for liberalism at all, but rather expressions of protest against the other two parties or indications of the personal popularity of the three men who have had the difficult and largely thankless task of leading the Liberal Party over the last thirty years. Under Jo Grimond, Jeremy Thorpe and David Steel, the Liberals have stood firmly for the pre-eminence of conscience and moral

principle in politics, for the defence and extension of democratic values and for the support of minorities subjected to
prejudice and harassment. But it has to be said at the same time
that they have also seemed curiously timid and conservative in
other areas, preferring to cling to the Butskellite consensus
rather than to develop radical new approaches to the economy
and to social welfare in keeping with the traditions of British
liberalism. The Liberal Party, in short, has not always been the
force for liberal revival that it could and should have been.

The early years of the party's post-war revival did bring a real
renaissance in liberal thinking in Britain. This was almost
entirely due to Jo Grimond, elected leader of the party in 1956.
Grimond gave political Liberalism in Britain a new direction
and purpose, based on a re-assertion of the traditional liberal
insistence that ideas and principles were more important than
interests, a rejection of class-based politics and of the lingering
imperialism of the post-war era, and a belief in the possibility of
a re-alignment in British politics to reflect the real division
between progressives and conservatives. He made Liberalism
exciting, attractive and appealing. It is scarcely an exaggeration
to say that the Liberal Party has been living off the capital
created in the Grimond years ever since.

Jo Grimond's contribution goes well beyond the confines of
the Liberal Party. He has been one of the main exponents of
liberal ideas in the last thirty years. His books, *The Liberal
Future* (1959), *The Liberal Challenge* (1963), *The Common
Welfare* (1978) and *A Personal Manifesto* (1983), have applied
to the problems of the modern age traditional liberal principles
of liberty, voluntaryism and trust of the people. They draw
heavily on the robust values of the island communities of
Orkney and Shetland which he represented in Parliament for
thirty-three years and which remained for longer than most of
the United Kingdom immune from the twentieth century tides
of secular materialism and passive conformity. They are also
rooted in a fundamentally spiritual outlook on life. Grimond
takes as his starting point the general conclusion of G. E. Moore
in his *Principia Ethica*: 'By far the most valuable things which
we know or can imagine are certain states of consciousness
which may roughly be described as the pleasures of human

intercourse and the enjoyment of beautiful objects'.[1] This is the central conviction which underlies the recurrent themes of his writings and speeches – the development of a welfare society based on voluntaryist principles, the building of democratic and co-operative values in politics and industry, the attack on corporatism and the bureaucratic outlook, and the championship of nonconformity, variety and individuality.

Grimond also encouraged others to think and write about liberalism. Under his influence a significant revival in liberal thinking took place in the late 1950s. An important forum for much of this thinking was the Unservile State Group, which had been set up in Oxford in 1953 and which included among its members, in addition to Grimond himself, Elliott Dodds, Nathaniel Micklem, George Watson, Alan Peacock, Peter Wiles, Richard Wainwright and Nancy Seear. In 1957 the group produced what they rightly claimed to be 'the first full-scale book on the attitudes and policies of British Liberalism since *Britain's Industrial Future* in 1928'.[2] *The Unservile State* restated the traditional Liberal approach to the constitution, to industry, to foreign affairs and, perhaps most importantly, to social welfare where it called for increasing use of private enterprise and voluntary effort, and a greater harnessing of both the philanthropic and the mutual aid motive.

The Unservile State Papers produced by the group in the early 1960s contain many radical proposals which directly challenged the prevailing Butskellite consensus. In a pamphlet published in 1961 and entitled *The Welfare Society*, for example, Alan Peacock called into question the view that all social services must be free, universal and uniform. 'The custodians of "conventional wisdom" in Britain', he wrote, 'may be said to be those who unquestioningly assume that any new social or economic problem requires a new government department . . . The true object of the Welfare State, for the Liberal, is to teach people how to do without it'.[3] Among the reforms which he proposed were the extension of home ownership by enabling council tenants to buy their houses, the introduction of loans rather than grants for students, charges in the health service, for example for the 'hotel' costs of hospital, and an element of fees in state schools, perhaps allied to a voucher system. Nearly a quarter of a century later the Conservatives are beginning cautiously to tip-toe around some of these ideas.

The Liberal Party as a whole proved curiously reluctant to take up the radical ideas of the Unservile State Group, and Grimond himself showed much less interest in them when he was leader and in a strong position to influence the development of party policy than he did after vacating the driving seat. It is true that the Liberals did take up and develop several important and radical policies in advance of both Labour and the Tories, such as British membership of the emerging European Economic Community, the scrapping of the British independent nuclear deterrent, and the ending of our military presence East of Suez. But in general they were content to cling to trusted old friends like co-ownership in industry, constitutional reform and international co-operation. The party fought shy of radical ideas in the field of economic and social policy and even came close to abandoning its traditional commitment to free trade. Although the 1958 Assembly carried a resolution re-affirming the Liberals' support for the principle of unilateral free trade, it narrowly passed another which supported protection for agriculture.

During the 1960s the Liberals became what Jo Grimond had hoped they would not become – a party of the centre associated in the public mind not with progressive radicalism but with a rather woolly middle-of-the-road approach and offering a convenient temporary resting place for those wishing to register a protest vote against the other two parties. The famous by-election victory in Orpington in 1962, heralded as a sign of a great Liberal revival, was probably an early example of this rather depressing trend. Labour's return to power in 1964 after thirteen years of opposition dashed Grimond's hopes of a realignment on the left and he quitted the Liberal leadership three years later depressed and disillusioned. Thereafter the party seemed more interested in short-term electoral tactics and opportunism than in developing a long-term identity based on the assertion and development of liberal principles.

While in the Grimond years much of the impetus for new thinking in the Liberal Party had come from the top, since then it has come overwhelmingly from the grassroots. During the late 1960s a group of young activists in the party developed a new style of liberalism which was radical, practical and highly relevant to the needs of the modern age, while at the same time remaining faithful to the fundamental principles of liberalism. At the 1970 annual assembly they succeeded in persuading the party as a whole to commit itself to their new classless, locally based, participatory approach to politics and to redefine its role as being 'to help people in communities to take and use power'. This idea of community politics, as it came to be called, has been the starting point of most of the new thinking that has gone on in the Liberal Party in the last fifteen years. Its gradual spread and its practical application in many different parts of the country must be counted as one of the more important and exciting features of the rebirth of Liberal Britain.

The original development of the idea of community politics was closely tied to the emergence of the New Left and the campaigning pressure groups and voluntary organisations of the 1960s. The main architects of the new Liberal approach, Peter Hain, Gordon Lishman and Tony Greaves, were all involved in these campaigning movements and felt a greater affinity with the kind of direct-action politics which they represented than with the more remote Westminster variety. For them community politics provided a way of resisting the dehumanising authority of bureaucracy and new technology by re-asserting the values of community, voluntaryism and trust in the people. They took as their texts Mill's essay *On Liberty* and Joseph Chamberlain's assertion of 'the principle, which should be at the bottom of all Liberalism, that the best security for good government is not to be found in *ex-cathedra* legislation by the upper classes for the lower, but in consulting those chiefly concerned and giving shape to their aspirations wherever they are not manifestly unfair to others'.[4] In his book, *Radical Regeneration* (1975), Peter Hain took up and extended this fundamental liberal principle:

Community politics is a style of political action through which people gain the confidence to mobilise for their rights and the ability to control their lives. It involves cultivating in each individual a habit of participation. It also involves a willingness to take direct action . . .

The aim is to create a society with an infinity of centres of power, expressing the principles of mutual aid and co-operation, rather than competition and authoritarianism.[5]

Despite its endorsement at the 1970 Assembly, community politics has never found much favour with the Liberal Party leadership. This is a great pity. It is true that it can degenerate into crude populism and opportunistic vote-catching with expectations being raised which cannot be fulfilled. There is also a danger that local politicians can descend to the politics of bribery with a promise that a vote for them will mean the dustbins being emptied more often or the cracked paving stones being replaced. But this is a perversion of genuine community politics which has in several places brought people more control over their environments and a much greater sense of involvement in the decisions which affect their lives.

One of the places where community politics has worked in this way is the city of Liverpool. Liberal rule over the city council there, which began in 1973 and continued, albeit with a lack of overall control, for most of the next ten years, was marked by a determined attempt to put the principles of community politics into practice. All meetings of the council and its committees were opened to the public and the press, with half an hour being set aside before each policy meeting for the presentation of citizens' petitions. Schools in the city were opened to the community with parents being encouraged to come in and use the facilities and classrooms for adult education. There was also an attempt to set up democratically elected community councils but this had to be abandoned in the face of combined Labour and Tory opposition.

It was in the field of housing that Liverpool's Liberal councillors pursued community politics with most dramatic effect. When they took over 38,000 homes in the city were scheduled to be demolished and replaced by tower blocks or new estates. The Liberals found that 30,000 of these houses were in good basic condition and could be restored. They instituted a policy to ensure that no bulldozer would be applied to a house unless it was structurally unsound. Instead, tenants were provided with the wherewithal to refurbish their homes and given the opportunity to decide for themselves on schemes of redecoration and improvement.

The council actively encouraged the development of co-operatives and self-management schemes among tenants of both publicly and privately rented accommodation. In the private sector, eleven co-operatives were set up to manage more than 1,000 properties. Several of these co-operatives purchased streets of terraced houses from private landlords, refurbished them and took over their management. Tenants' co-operatives proved much more difficult to set up in the municipal housing estates because they were resisted by the Labour Party and the trade unions who feared that jobs would be at risk among council workmen if tenants got control of their repairs. But several successful co-operatives were formed by residents in those properties which were scheduled for demolition. The council sold them land and provided money for them to employ architects whom they were encouraged to consult. Thus for the first time in Britain council tenants were given a say in the design of their homes. At the same time the council initiated a building for sale scheme which aimed to break down the division between council and private estates by providing low cost homes. There was also a vigorous policy of selling council houses to tenants. Overall, the level of home ownership in Liverpool was raised from 35 to 43 per cent and the number of properties lacking inside toilets, running hot water or bathrooms was cut from 50 to 15 per cent.

Somewhat shunned by the party establishment, several of the leading lights in the community politics movement have responded by distancing themselves from the official Liberal Party machine. Peter Hain, undoubtedly the movement's leading theorist, left the Liberals altogether in 1977 to join the Bennite wing of the Labour Party. Tony Greaves has since 1976 presided over a kind of Liberal Party in exile, the Association of Liberal Councillors, which has had a fairly frosty relationship with the party leadership. He claims with some justice that it is the Association's 2,000-odd members, the great majority of whom are elected Liberal local councillors practising community politics all over the country, rather than the handful of Liberal MPs and party officials in London, who represent the real Liberal Party. Certainly the atmosphere at the group's headquarters, a converted Baptist Chapel high in the Pennines, where the bearded Greaves and his earnest colleagues sit almost submerged under piles of Focus newsletters breathing provincial defiance and northern fervour, does in some ways seem rather closer to the spirit and traditions of British Liberalism than the metropolitan smoothness, and media-oriented style which sometimes seems to characterise the Liberal Party's dealings at national level.

To some extent, indeed, two quite distinct Liberal parties have developed in the last fifteen years or so. There is the one which people see on television news and discussion programmes, and on Liberal Party political broadcasts, which is predominantly made up of well-groomed men committed to moderation and macro-politics, and there is another quite different one which they encounter in their own communities, and from whom they receive a steady stream of Focus newsletters, which is made up of generally rather more scruffy individuals committed to the micro-politics of radical local campaigning. Standing somewhere between these two groups are the representatives of what is almost a third Liberal party, made up of those splendid survivors of old-style Liberalism, often Nonconformist in religion, strongly individualistic in temperament and stubbornly standing out against the secular materialism of the twentieth century. There are forums which bring all three elements together, most notably the annual assembly where leading members of the party establishment can be found in packed fringe meetings and singing Nonconformist hymns far into the night, but to a considerable extent they have kept their distance and gone their separate ways.

The radical voice from the grassroots often heard at the annual party assemblies speaks in the language of those campaigning movements which were discussed in Chapter Thirteen. The 1978 Assembly passed a motion, for example, expressing 'fundamental opposition to an economy based primarily on material objectives' and pointing out that 'contentment is not the product of material well-being alone' and that 'economic and social policies of maximum consumption are having a disastrous effect'. The following year the assembly went even further and declared that 'sustained economic growth as conventionally measured is neither achievable nor desirable'. Decentralist, environmentalist themes have also found their way into statements of party policy. *Foundations for the Future*, the draft programme presented to the 1981 Assembly, castigated both Labour and the Conservatives for being obsessed with materialism and fighting a mechanistic battle over the control of the economy and went on:

> Liberals disagree vigorously with such a narrow view of British politics. The roots of Britain's problems do not lie essentially in economics. Indeed, one of our problems is that we have allowed economists to dictate the terms of political debate. Political principles are too important to be left to economists.
>
> One of the problems with conventional economics is that it only deals with what can be measured. Thus sales of choc ices add to GNP, whereas better-educated or happier children do not. Sales of whisky are evidence of wealth-creation, while clean air and peaceful streets are not. Liberals judge economic growth, not just by statistics, but by its contribution to a human society living in harmony with nature.[6]

This radical challenge to the conventional wisdom of twentieth-century politics was never fully taken up by the party as a whole, however. The Liberal leadership, and a good many rank-and-file party members, still thought in Croslandite terms about the importance of economic growth and clung to the notion of incomes policies and other instruments of macroeconomic management. Radical ideas on economic and social policy, of the kind put forward by Alan Peacock in his Unservile State Group pamphlet, by Jo Grimond in his books and articles, and in the lively and radical magazine *New Outlook* founded by Tim Beaumont and edited by Gordon Lishman, were cold-shouldered. Any questioning of the structure of the Welfare State or the post-Keynesian economic system seemed to be regarded by many Liberals as virtually heretical. The party stood for good sense and moderation, not unimportant values in the increasingly confrontational atmosphere of British politics and industry, but it seemed to lack the distinctive radicalism and conscience of the British liberal tradition. Even its commitment to long-held principles like devolution and decentralisation was characterised by a mechanical rather than a moral reformer's approach. Elaborate 'machinery of government' panels were set up and complex proposals for constitutional reform produced which involved adding yet more layers of administration.

The new Social Democratic Party (SDP) launched in 1981, with whom the Liberals entered into electoral alliance, looked at first as though it would be even less radical in its approach. Its very name suggested adherence to the corporatist and centralist creed which had guided the Labour and Tory governments of the 1960s and 1970s. Its founders, the so-called Gang of Four, had served in prominent positions in the Labour administrations of this period which had hardly been conspicuous for their attachment to liberal principles. In setting up a new party, they insisted that they were not signalling a recantation of former principles and a change of political direction. Rather they argued that it was the Labour Party which had changed while they had remained loyal to the social democratic consensus. They took with them into the new party some of the most conservative and right-wing elements in the Labour Party whose attitude on a whole range of questions from immigration to European integration was the antithesis of the British liberal tradition of tolerance and internationalism.

The organisation and style of the SDP in its early days hardly suggested that it was going to play a major part in reviving the traditional principles of liberalism. Run from the top, its ethos was managerial rather than campaigning. It appealed strongly to many in the London cultural establishment and was highly media-conscious, as its razzmatazz launch in the West End of London showed. There was a distinct lack of provincial radicalism or moral passion about its early gatherings which had rather the quality of university seminars. One left-wing historian was moved to suggest that the SDP was, perhaps, Britain's first post-Christian party, conceiving politics 'in temporal rather than spiritual terms, as a pursuit of the arts of government rather than as a struggle between darkness and light.'[7]

Not surprisingly those within the Liberal Party who were particularly concerned about the radical traditions of British liberalism gave their new allies a somewhat cool reception.

Michael Meadowcroft, a leading community politician from Leeds, wrote a pamphlet entitled *Social Democracy – Barrier or Bridge?* in which he pointed out that 'the SDP is at one and the same time the greatest opportunity and the greatest danger to Liberalism for thirty years'.[8] Tony Greaves of the Association of Liberal Councillors took a similarly equivocal view. Roger Pincham, who in 1973 had founded the Gladstone Club as a forum for those concerned with preserving and restating the traditional values of liberalism, sounded a note of caution in an editorial in the Club's newsletter, *Liberal Clarion*:

The revival of the Liberal Party has been based upon a deep commitment to a style of politics which gives pride of place to the value of local communities and local determination. Perhaps the most powerful expression of our devotion to liberty has been the resolve to return power to the people. By contrast, the leaders of Social Democracy look back to years of power, often exercised by central diktat with little regard for the views of the people in receipt of a torrent of legislation.[9]

Several Social Democrats, for their part, were somewhat dismissive of traditional liberalism. They were particularly inclined to poke fun at the crankiness of Liberal grassroots campaigners, characterised by one Social Democrat MP as 'chewing celery and wearing open-toed sandals'.[10] The SDP's Manchester organiser expressed a commonly-held perception of the gulf that separated the members of the two parties:

The Liberals are steeped in tradition and I think have many more eccentrics than we have. If I want to go to another part of the country, I could imagine me going by train and the Liberal going on horseback or by bicycle. I think that they're a completely different group of people to us. We've got more so-called establishment people, business people, not steeped in the radical traditions of the Liberal Party – and to go back to my word, not a lot of the charming eccentrics that the Liberals gathered.[11]

But if one goes beyond this rhetoric and examines some of the writings of the founders of the SDP there is evidence of a much greater respect for liberal values. In several areas, indeed, the Social Democrats emerge as arguably more liberal in their approach than many Liberals. It is true that some of them retain a vestigial Fabian authoritarianism, an egalitarianism which produces a demand for a strong state, and a preference for mechanical rather than moral reform, but there is also a powerful cry for decentralisation, for voluntaryism and for internationalism.

Two of the most important statements of this new liberal social democracy were, in fact, made before the founding of the new party. In a book which he wrote while he was still Labour MP for Oxford, and published in 1979 with the title *Socialism Without the State*, and in a Fabian Society pamphlet *Socialism at the Grassroots*, which appeared the following year, Evan Luard argued that the Labour Party in general, and Social Democrats in particular, had become excessively preoccupied with the state, macroeconomics and the pursuit of equality. 'Our policies', he wrote, 'appear to involve the continuing proliferation of bureaucracy, a continuing deference to the pressures from powerful trade unions, a continuing necessity for high taxation, a continuing enhancement of the power of the state'.[12] He proposed a radically new agenda for social democracy, 'organising individual communities rather than building up ever more centralised nation states', enhancing the consciousness of individuals and giving more sense of self-direction by encouraging community councils and industrial co-operatives.[13] This new decentralist emphasis was taken up and developed by David Marquand, former Labour MP for Ashfield and aide to Roy Jenkins, in his 1980 Rita Hinden Memorial Lecture, *Taming Leviathan: Social Democracy and Decentralisation*. The policies of post-war social democracy had rested, he argued, on an over-optimistic view of the possibility of changing society by acting through the state. Social democracy had become a system of social engineering rather than a movement for personal liberation. It had created a new Leviathan, the centralised corporate state. This beast could only be tamed by adopting an aggressively decentralist strategy, involving the devolution of power and the strengthening of the micro-economy of small firms, self-employment, profit sharing and co-operatives.

The most interesting, and the most liberal, of the books written by the founders of the SDP is undoubtedly David

Owen's *Face the Future*. It is strongly internationalist, democratic and voluntaryist in tone while taking a pragmatic and flexible approach to economic and industrial policy, avoiding both the narrow rigidity of total state control and the harshness of doctrinaire *laissez-faire*. The themes of decentralisation and distributism loom large – there are bold and radical suggestions for reducing the power of Whitehall, reviving local government on the basis of a local income tax and encouraging the spread of wealth through tax reform and the development of profit sharing schemes and co-operatives. Significantly, Owen sees the Social Democrats as the heirs of both the Guild Socialists and the New Liberals, by no means an unreasonable claim when it is remembered that Hobson and Hobhouse often described themselves as social democrats.

There is one particularly interesting feature about Owen's book. When it first appeared as a 550 page hardback in January 1981 it was an ostensibly socialist work. The first chapter was, indeed, entitled 'The Values of Socialism'. But when it was reissued as a slimmed down paperback later that year it had been subtly but significantly transformed. The first chapter was now entitled 'Social Democratic Values' and a seventy-two page section on 'The Pursuit of Equality' had been removed. Altogether there was less emphasis on mechanical and institutional reform and more on moral reform, and specifically on harnessing human altruism to the service of the Welfare State, so turning it into a welfare society. A new final chapter, entitled 'The Enabling State', ended with a statement that could have come from the pen of any Liberal:

> Government can and should provide a framework for the society in which the citizen lives. It can encourage specific values in society to develop, specific policies to be introduced, but its power to enable is more important than its power to control. It is in the enabling power of government that the strength of social democracy lies.[14]

The rewriting of *Face the Future* marked the beginning of a process of 'liberalisation' for the Social Democrats, and for David Owen in particular. There were other early manifestations of liberal thinking in the new party. Like the Liberals under Grimond the SDP in its early days attracted a considerable number of intellectuals who were encouraged to develop radical new ideas. Their writings, which generally appeared under the imprint of the new party's 'think tank', the Tawney Society, were highly liberal, as their titles suggest. Among the Society's early pamphlets were *Inflation, Unemployment and the Remoralisation of Society* and *Bigness is the Enemy of Humanity*, both by Michael Young, *The Springs of Co-Operative Wealth* by Mark Goyder and *Plain, Russet Coated Captains* in which David Marquand sought to place the Social Democrats in the tradition of Cromwell's Puritan soldiers. Most radical, and most liberal, of all these early Tawney Society pamphlets was *The Middle of the Night* (1982), written by a group of Social Democrats, which powerfully asserts the rights of the individual against collective interests and stresses free choice, distributive justice, decentralisation and global independence. It is also, despite its title, a work of shining and inspiring optimism.

Little of this radical thinking found its way into the SDP's official policy statements, and still less into its policy agreements with the Liberals. The joint document which the two parties produced in June 1981, *A Fresh Start for Britain*, was bland and uninspiring. In the words of Jo Grimond, 'It leaves open the question as to whether its authors are searching for a middle ground – a reformed and diluted variety of statism, a mixed economy where the mix is to be much as now, or whether they intend to strike out for a new highly decentralised political economy with drastic changes in our methods of running industry, competition, workers' ownership, and so on; in fact a total alternative to state socialism.'[15]

For the first two years of the Alliance's existence it seemed to be the first of these two options that its leaders favoured. The policies which it developed were highly reminiscent of those of the Butskellite era – corporatist, statist and heavily dependent on incomes policy and demand management. Commenting on the report of a joint SDP-Liberal Commission on industrial strategy a leading article in *The Times*, entitled 'Back Where We Were', observed that it took Britain 'back to the consensus that had presided over the nation's comfortable decline in the 1960s and early 70s'.[16] The *Financial Times* remarked, with equal justification, that to read the Alliance's 1983 general election manifesto was to 'suffer something very like nostalgia'. Certainly it was the most conservative of the alternatives put forward by the major parties in that election, a pallid and uninspiring programme indeed compared with those put forward in the publications of the Tawney Society and the Association of Liberal Councillors, or with the *Personal Manifesto* which Jo Grimond published on the eve of the election campaign.

The result of the 1983 election caused the Alliance to rethink its approach. Mrs Thatcher's second resounding victory, at a time of rising unemployment, signalled the electorate's rejection of corporatist social democracy with its promise of 'a better yesterday'. In an article in *The Times* David Marquand drew the lesson for the Alliance:

> The last thing the British people want now is consolidation. They applaud Mrs Thatcher's determination to have done with the apologetic and arthritic corporatism of the 1960s and 1970s . . . The Alliance must belong as unmistakably to the new, post-collectivist epoch as Mrs Thatcher does . . . The Alliance should be more determined to strengthen competition, widen choice and break up monopolies than she is, not less. [17]

David Owen, who took over as leader of the Social Democrats shortly after the election, was quick to take up this theme and spell out its policy implications. In his first speech to the party's annual conference, and in an important article in the October 1983 number of the Institute of Economic Affairs' journal *Economic Affairs*, he proclaimed his faith in what he called the social market economy. This, he explained, meant neither doctrinaire *laissez-faire*, nor avoidance of the disciplines of the market, but the promotion of a decentralised society based on the principles of choice and diversity. He called specifically for a full-blooded competition policy, more attention to the micro- and less to the macro-economy, the promotion of industrial democracy through profit-sharing, works councils and co-operatives, the privatisation and franchising of parts of public industries and services, an assault on the monopoly bargaining power of certain trade unions, and a move from a universal to a selective approach in the sphere of social welfare.

The change in both the policies and style of the Social Democrats which has come about since 1983 under Owen's leadership has been interpreted by many commentators as a shift to the right. It would be much more accurate to describe it as a move towards liberalism. Those within the new party who espouse radical and libertarian ideas seem to be winning the ideological battle over the proponents of a better yesterday. The fact is that in many respects the SDP is now more liberal in its outlook than the Liberal Party, more sceptical of mechanical reforms like incomes policies and demand management, more alive to the essential illiberalism of monopoly trade union power and so-called employment protection legislation, more committed to redistribute wealth and spread the ownership of capital and more ready to apply a voluntaryist and pluralist approach in the sphere of social welfare.

Although it now appears in many ways to be the more conservative partner in the Alliance, the Liberal Party has shown some signs of becoming more liberal in the last couple of years. Among those who became Liberal MPs in 1983 were two leading practitioners of community politics, Michael Meadowcroft and Paddy Ashdown. They have brought both to parliamentary debates and to television discussions a powerful reassertion of the traditional liberal stress on the importance of moral and human values and a condemnation of purely material goals. A similar perspective has been introduced into the pages of the party newspaper, *Liberal News*, not least through the writings of Charles Stainsby who has boldly exposed the essential illiberalism of such supposedly 'liberal' phenomena as the media establishment and the permissive society. The party at national level is beginning to adopt something of the campaigning style and crusading vigour of the Association of Liberal Councillors. David Steel has taken up such issues as the Falklands War, overseas aid and freedom of information which allow him to express his own innate radicalism and deep attachment to the politics of conscience and moral principle.

Overall, however, it has to be said that in its policies and thinking at the national level, although not so much in its local campaigning, the Liberal Party today wears a distinctly conservative face which is out of keeping with the radical traditions of British liberalism. In the important area of economic policy its stance is backward-looking and *dirigiste* as evidenced in both the title and content of the pamphlet produced by the Treasury Affairs Panel and adopted by the 1984 Assembly, *Managing the Economy*, which advocates demand management and the implementation of an incomes policy. In common with their counterparts in the other major parties, leading Liberals remain committed to the outmoded and unrealistic concept of full employment and lack the imagination or the courage to embrace the post-work society which is already springing up around us. A similar conservatism is evident when it comes to discussions of future developments in the field of social welfare. It is, indeed, hard to avoid the conclusion that the Liberal Party has itself been affected by rather more than it has contributed to those recent stirrings which I have suggested may herald a rebirth of Liberal Britain. But then perhaps that is how it should be. Liberalism, after all, is not something manufactured by political parties, but rather an expression of the creativity, the initiative and the free spirit of individuals and communities. That is where the real source of the strange phenomenon which is the subject of this book really lies.

— 16 —

WHERE WE ARE NOW

At first sight contemporary Britain may seem a curious place to describe as being in the throes of a revival of liberal values. Unemployment is high and likely to remain so. Class feeling is strong and industrial life dominated by bitter clashes between unions and management and bloody battles between strikers and the police. Inner city areas, long neglected and run down, are festering with discontent. The spectres of violent crime and public disorder haunt the streets. New technology is creating an alienated and bored populace which finds relief in drinking, glue-sniffing and watching video nasties.

Such is the depressing picture of our land which is portrayed by the media, and there is some truth in it. But it shows only one side of an overall picture which is both much more complex and much more encouraging. Britain in the mid-1980s is a society in the midst of enormous change and upheaval, much of it very painful and disruptive in the short-term but potentially liberating in its long-term effects. The present high level of unemployment is an aspect of the structural change from an industrial to a post-industrial economy and from a society based narrowly on work to one which is likely to offer people the possibility of spending their lives in a much broader range of activities. There is a sense in which the class bitterness and confrontation demonstrated in the prolonged miners' strike represent the death throes of the old economy, the last desperate writhings of a dinosaur which is doomed. A new economy is growing up, based on self-employment and small-scale units of production, which offers the prospect of a much more co-operative atmosphere and a more classless society.

There are, in fact, plenty of signs of the health and strength of liberalism in Britain today for those who have eyes to see them and who do not allow themselves to be misled by the pessimism and gloom which tends to prevail in the media. One is the way in which we have over the last twenty years or so become a multiracial and multicultural society. Of course there has been prejudice and bad feeling on the part of both immigrant groups and the indigenous white community but there has also been an enormous amount of tolerance and positive good will on both sides. The spread of Chinese takeaways to become even more ubiquitous than fish and chip shops, the new uses found for redundant Anglican and Nonconformist churches as Hindu temples and meeting places for black Pentecostalists, the proliferation of Asian owned shops open late into the evening, the involvement of ethnic minorities in local government and cultural life – these are all signs of the rich diversity of contemporary British society, a diversity which has been broadly welcomed by many people.

Of course our inner cities wear a depressed and shabby face, the product of decades of neglect and decline. Granted too that we live in an age of violence and widespread crime. But if it is tempting in these circumstances to ignore the grim reality and delude ourselves with false hopes, it is even more tempting, perhaps, to become alarmist and frightened. The ugly urban riots which occurred in the summer of 1981 look increasingly like a once-only experience, the final on-rush of a tide that has now turned rather than the first portent of a total collapse into anarchy and lawlessness. Already there is evidence of a fall in the incidence of several categories of crime and of an improvement in community relations in those areas most affected by the riots. For every one person watching video nasties there are many more taking part in voluntary community work or finding fulfilment in other creative activities. It is worth taking a more detailed look at what exactly is happening to contemporary

Britain, not in a mood of fear and despair but with a cool analytical eye enlivened by just a glimmer of natural liberal optimism.

The structural changes which are affecting the economy have four major aspects. There is a shift from manufacturing to the service sector; the proportion of the population who work for themselves rather than for others is increasing; new technology is changing patterns of work; and there is an overall decline in the amount of work that is available (or more accurately of work as it has conventionally been defined) and therefore a shortage of jobs. All these changes, which are normally spoken of in tones of alarm and despondency, have profoundly liberal implications.

The shift from a manufacturing to a service base has, perhaps, been the dominant feature of the British economy over the last twenty-five years. There has been a steady decline in the number of people employed in heavy industries like iron and steel, shipbuilding, coal-mining and heavy engineering and a rise in the number working in the professions, administration, finance and commerce, science and technology and the leisure industry. There are now twice as many people employed in professional and scientific services as in engineering and four times as many in banking, insurance and finance as in mining and quarrying. This shift of employment has radically altered the balance between manual and non-manual workers in the country. The former have declined from 62.5 to 49.7 per cent as a proportion of the total workforce since 1961, while the latter have increased from 37.5 to 50.3 per cent.

Now it would be ridiculous to suggest that those working in service industries are necessarily more liberal than those in manufacturing, or indeed that non-manual workers are by definition more liberal than manual ones. But there are certain grounds for suggesting that a service-based economy, with a higher proportion of the population employed in 'white-collar' jobs, is likely to produce a more liberal society than one based on manufacturing. In general, services are more personal than manufacturing, more concerned with peo; le and less with things. They are also likely to be more decentralised and small-scale. The old-style heavy industries which we are now shedding tended to produce among those who worked in them a sense of alienation and anonymity and a strongly collectivist mentality. They brought large numbers of people into factories to perform repetitive jobs which were often dirty, noisy and unpleasant. Is it being excessively rash to predict that as fewer people work in those jobs and more are engaged in interesting and varied occupations which involve greater contact with people liberal values will spread?

The second significant trend in the pattern of economic activity in contemporary Britain, the growth in the number of people who work for themselves, is closely related to the shift from manufacturing to services. In the two years from 1979 to 1981 alone, the number of self-employed jumped by twelve per cent, or 215,000 people, the great majority of whom were working in the service sector. There has also been an increase in the last few years in the number of people working in co-operatives, stimulated partly by the Co-Operative Development Agency set up in 1978. More worker co-operatives were established in the first quarter of 1983 than in the first three quarters of the twentieth century. There are now well over 700, ranging from the large and old-established John Lewis Partnership, with more than 27,000 working members, to the new co-operative set up by former council dustmen in Birmingham which won the contract against other bidders when the city's refuse collection service was privatised, and which now operates a highly successful service with old restrictive practices abolished and staff morale high.

Another interesting and related trend in the last few years has been management buy-outs of firms in which they have previously been salaried employees. Among the 500 or so companies where managers have become owners in this way are Tyne Ship Repair, Stone International, the specialist supplier of railway air-conditioning equipment, and the Bishop Auckland Precast Concrete Company which was formed out of the ashes of the Atcost group when it went into receivership in 1983. Taken together, the increase in self-employment, the growth of co-operatives and the rise in managerial buy-outs constitute a significant social trend which cannot but help the liberalisation of Britain. The fact that fewer people are in the position of being 'wage slaves' and more and more are working for themselves is bound to promote attitudes of independence and personal fulfilment. So, one might add, is another significant current social trend, the dramatic rise in home ownership.

Technological advances in the fields of computing and microelectronics have similarly liberal implications. They are systematically removing boring and repetitive jobs and bringing about more flexible working arrangements. The ubiquitous microchip is likely to prove a powerful decentralising force, enabling many people to work from home if they choose and avoid the need to commute into an office or factory. It can also be an agent for promoting individuality by putting into people's hands the capacity to process information which has, until now, remained the exclusive domain of large organisations and by enabling them, on their own initiative and at their own pace, to pursue and develop hobbies, skills and business interests. The much-vaunted new technology which is so often seen as a threat to our culture and creativity does, in fact, have the potential to be tremendously liberating and enriching of the human spirit.[1]

But what of those who lose their jobs to machines and who are thrown out of work by the collapse of manufacturing industry? What of those without go-getting drive and initiative? Are they the inevitable casualties of a new society which brings benefits to others? Are the unskilled and the semi-skilled, those made redundant and the school leavers who cannot find work doomed to a life of failure, of inactivity and of comparative poverty? Such an outcome would be wholly unacceptable in any society which dared call itself liberal.

It is impossible to generalise about the lives and condition of those who are at present unemployed. Many are suffering poverty, boredom and a terrible sense of pointlessness and emptiness. But although they lack jobs in the formal economy, there is evidence of considerable activity among the unemployed in the so-called informal economy. This is an umbrella term which covers three distinct areas – the black economy of jobs done for rewards in cash or kind which are not declared to the tax man and so do not appear in official statistics, but which everyone agrees represent a significant and growing element in the nation's economic life; the household economy which embraces unpaid domestic work, like cooking, cleaning, car maintenance, do-it-yourself and gardening; and the voluntary or gift economy which includes all the work which goes on, both through formal organisations and at an informal level, in caring for the sick, the elderly, children and others in need in either the community or the family.[2] Studies by Professor Ray Pahl of the University of Kent and Dr Jonathon Gershuny of the University of Sussex, suggest that many unemployed people are very actively engaged in doing odd jobs for friends and neighbours, growing their own fruit and vegetables, making and repairing things around the house and involved in a variety of voluntary work and leisure activities. Certainly a varied lifestyle of this kind seems to be emerging in the former steel town of Consett in north-west Durham where the unemployment rate is around 25 per cent. There sport and music making are flourishing and small-scale co-operatives and community ventures are being set up by those out of work.[3]

This kind of lifestyle is likely to become the norm for a growing number of people in the coming years. It may well be that we are running out of work in the sense of conventional nine to five jobs in an office or factory but there is no shortage of work to be done, or activities to be engaged in, in the various areas of life which make up the informal economy. Several steps need to be taken if we are to equip ourselves properly for the new kind of society which is already emerging and to ensure that it will be fair and liberal. One of the most important will be to devise a means of distributing the nation's wealth other than through paid employment – probably by an overhaul of the taxation and social security system to ensure that there is a guaranteed national minimum income for every individual, regardless of whether he or she is working or not. Another will be the sharing out more widely of what conventional employment is available and the spreading of work and activity more evenly throughout the population. A third and no less important priority is to rid ourselves of the old work ethic and the social connotations that go with it and to see education much less as a training for jobs and much more as a preparation for life in all its aspects. If we can achieve the change of outlook and emphasis that will make these reforms possible, then the prospect opens up of a future in which all of us will have greater control over our lives and the possibility at least of finding more personal fulfilment and satisfaction.

The political and social implications of moving from the old, traditional work-based economy to a much more diversified activity-based society are considerable. To a large extent both *laissez-faire* capitalism and state socialism are creatures of the old dying industrial economy which will have less and less relevance in the future. The Thatcherite ethic of a competitive, go-getting society in which those without jobs are made to feel guilty and the Bennite commitment to full employment and the right to work which involves trying to provide jobs where there are no jobs to be done are both equally inappropriate to the kind of society that is already clearly beginning to emerge. A decentralised and pluralistic liberalism seems a much more natural and relevant expression of the political mood of the coming age.

The strong class feelings which have for so long dominated British politics and given both the Labour and Conservative parties much of their identity and *raison d'être* are also likely to weaken. Social class is, after all, based to a large extent on income and occupation. As we move into an age where conventional paid employment is no longer the sole, or even, perhaps, the main source of income and status that it is now, so the importance of class will diminish. Already there is considerable evidence of the weakening hold of class and class-based loyalties in social and political behaviour. The Conservatives won the last two elections by picking up a very substantial vote among those conventionally seen as working class. On the other side of the political spectrum, the agenda of the left is increasingly defined by cross-class campaigns like feminism and the peace movement. Some people have seen the recent miners' strike as an indication of the continuing strength of class feeling in Britain. Yet in reality it demonstrated the extent to which class-based politics has already collapsed in this country. The miners failed to enlist the support of the working classes or of organised labour as a whole. Their struggle took on the character of a sectional dispute rather than the broad class struggle which their leaders had hoped that it would become. In the words of Michael Ignatieff, author of a highly perceptive analysis of the strike in the *New Statesman* (14 December 1984), 'the miners' strike is not the vindication of class politics, but its death throes'.

For all our current troubles, Britain is, in fact, better placed than many other countries to accomplish the transition to a post-industrial and more classless society. We have never been particularly wedded to the work ethic or to a material-istic view of life. There is a deep anti-industrial strain in our make-up, perceptively traced by Martin Weiner in his recent book *English Culture and the Decline of the Industrial Spirit*. Opinion polls consistently show that we are less concerned about becoming rich and more prepared to trade money for leisure than our Continental neighbours.[4] The British tradi-tion of voluntary service should also help us to adapt to a society based on a much wider range of activities than conventional work. The proliferation of voluntary organ-isations, pressure groups and informal community networks which make up what is sometimes called the market society bodes well for the future social welfare of the country in an era when economic constraints and other factors are likely to have limited the ability of public services to meet ever-increasing demands.

These strongpoints have been noted by two perceptive foreigners who håve both observed the rebirth of Liberal Britain over the last few years and appreciated its significance rather more sharply than many domestic commentators. In his book *Britain, A Future that Works* (1978), Bernard Nossiter, London correspondent of the *Washington Post* from 1971 to 1979, set out to repudiate the common diagnosis of his countrymen that late twentieth-century Britain is suffering from a particularly debilitating and possibly fatal, illness:

Far from being sick, the place is healthy, democratic, productive, as stable as any of its size in Europe. It is transforming the heritage of the industrial revolution, shedding its plants, the mills and some of the values that made them work. It is slowly becoming a post-industrial society where a decreasing number of men and women are concerned with the production of goods and an increasing number with things of the mind and spirit.[5]

Ralf Dahrendorf, director of the London School of Economics from 1974 to 1983 and one of the leading liberal thinkers in Europe in the post war era, takes a similarly optimistic view of Britain's prospects. Surveying the state of the country for his BBC television series in 1982, he wrote:

> If I was asked what I regard as the main opportunities for the next twenty years, if one wants to advance the cause of liberty in the rich countries of the world, I should mention three: the transformation of work into activity; the growth of new social ligatures; the strengthening of the market society. In all three, the traditions and realities of Britain promise greater hope of success than most rich countries can hope for.[6]

Progress in these three important areas is not on the whole coming at the macro-economic level or from the actions of Governments and other large corporate bodies, but rather from a host of local initiatives and informal networks, which individually may seem small and insignificant, but which together add up to a clear national trend.

The transformation of work into activity is already well under way. As we have already seen, a growing number of people are deriving their livelihoods from the informal economy and leading lives in which conventional work occupies a relatively small amount of time. Within the conventional economy, some employers are introducing work-sharing schemes, following the lead of early pioneers like the Lothian Health Board which since 1975 has encouraged joint applications by two people for single medical posts. Several education authorities, most notably Oxfordshire, are taking up courses first developed at Dartington School in Devon which prepare children for a world where there will not be enough conventional jobs to go round and equip them with a range of social and practical skills as well as purely vocational ones. Meanwhile, a growing number of writers and thinkers are calling into question the continuing validity of the traditional work ethic and extolling the merits of a lifestyle which combines elements of self-sufficiency, barter, 'odd-jobbing', and participation in a variety of voluntary activities.[7]

There is equally positive evidence for the development of the new social ligatures which Ralf Dahrendorf rightly identifies as another key to advancing the cause of liberty. Once again it comes in the form of thousands of local community initiatives, often in some of the most depressed of our inner-city areas. In Walsall in the West Midlands, the residents of a housing estate with an unemployment rate of over eighty per cent have set up a co-operative to sell staple commodities like bread and milk and to manage their crumbling tower blocks. The profits are being used to provide common rooms, telephones and badly needed washing and drying facilities. In Brixton those who live along the riot-ravaged Railton Road have got together to build playgrounds and gardens. All over the country, in both urban and rural areas, acting sometimes on their own initiative and sometimes stimulated by community workers, people are joining together to set up playgroups, car-sharing schemes, community bus services, food co-operatives, local newsletters and a host of other enterprises.

The market society is also flourishing. Increasing voluntary and community involvement in the health and social services is bringing nearer the achievement of a welfare society. In rural North Norfolk the 200 elderly and infirm patients of Dr Anthony Allibone have been provided with a lunch club, home nursing, physiotherapy and other services as a result of local fund raising and the mobilisation of more than 250 other patients as volunteer workers. In Hoylake, Cheshire, a cottage hospital closed by the National Health Service has reopened as a pre-1948 style voluntary hospital, run by a charitable trust and by local doctors and with volunteers helping out as cleaners, cooks and gardeners. New voluntary organisations are springing up like the Hospice at Home movement. So are crusading pressure groups like the new environmental lobby which has gathered strength in the wake of the successful campaign against lead in petrol.

You have to hunt hard in newspapers and television news programmes to find much mention of these and the thousands of other experiments and practical initiatives which are taking place across the length and breadth of the country. Unlike strikes and arguments among politicians they are not judged to be news. Yet they are the signposts which point to the future state of Britain, the stepping stones to liberty.

Of course there are still many obstacles and hindrances to the liberalisation of Britain. The entrenched corporate might of trade unions, big business and public officialdom all too often kills liberal initiatives and ideas with a mixture of narrow-minded conservatism and sectional self-interest. Trade union bloody-mindedness has killed off Granada Television's Reports Action programme which pioneered the use of television as a catalyst for social action and involvement. It has also prevented the Workers Education Association from undertaking an exciting range of projects with the unemployed under the auspices of the Government's Voluntary Project Programme. The imaginative plans of the Lucas Aerospace Joint Shop Stewards Combine for socially useful products were met with almost total indifference by the company's management. A similar fate has more recently greeted an interesting study by bus drivers in Leeds of ways in which their job could be made easier and more satisfying. The Government is also inclined to display a similar narrowness of vision and lack of openness to liberal ideas. Two examples may suffice. The Home Office resolutely refuses to allow the teaching of transcendental meditation in prisons, even though there is strong evidence from the United States that it leads to a fall in aggression and recidivism. The Ministry of Agriculture has recently axed the Land Settlement Association, which provided smallholdings for the unemployed, precisely the kind of venture that ought to be encouraged as we move towards an economy based more on self-sufficiency.

But there are also encouraging examples of a much more positive approach on the part of the big battalions. Trade unions are by no means all negative in their attitudes. The trade union council at British Airways devised a way of turning the airline's Highlands and Islands division from loss to profit by getting staff to double up on jobs and abolishing rigid demarcation lines. The managements of many large companies have actively involved themselves in the Government's Youth Training Scheme for unemployed school leavers, and particularly in the

Community Action Programmes in which local business leaders work together on a variety of schemes to stimulate training and employment. Traditionally conservative corporate bodies are beginning to show a new liberal spirit, like the British Medical Association with its more sympathetic and open-minded approach towards alternative medicine. The Government is showing a similarly imaginative spirit in employing radical community activists like Ed Berman of Inter-Action to advise on the regeneration of inner cities and in backing the construction of alternative energy projects like the giant wind turbine at Burgar Hill in Orkney.

There are other signs that the tide may at last be turning against collectivism, materialism and passive consumerism. A recent study by Professor John Gennard, *The Closed Shop in Britain* (1984), suggests that compulsory trade unionism is dying, with a steady fall since the late 1970s in the number of workers who are in closed shops. The response to several recent strike calls suggests that the old 'one out, all out' mentality may be breaking down and that there is more sense of individual choice among trade unionists. Television seems to be loosening its grip on society. Viewing figures have declined steadily through the early 1980s. There have also been significant falls in the last few years in attendance at bingo games, sales of pornographic magazines and in the consumption of alcohol. It is not just that people are watching video nasties instead. The Government's latest Social Trends survey shows a dramatic increase in participation in sport, do-it-yourself activities and other active and practical hobbies. Local councils report increasing demands for allotments and playing fields, voluntary organisations a growing number of offers of help and politicians a rise in attendance at public meetings. It seems that we are becoming participators once again.

Even the metropolitan media establishment is becoming more liberal in the proper sense of the word. It is more tolerant, more concerned with moral and spiritual values and more respectful of the worth and integrity of the human personality. The publication of *Sex and Destiny* by Germaine Greer, the high priestess of the feminist movement, marked an important shift from the stridency and selfishness of the 1960s and a recognition that the permissive society had not liberated women but rather enslaved them in frantic pressures to deny their humanity in the striving for casual sex and instant excitement. Participants in television discussion programmes are even daring to assert moral and spiritual values and to suggest that not every problem in the world is amenable to purely material solutions. It is true that at first they are often a little hesitant and even embarrassed about making such statements, but more often than not it transpires that most of their fellow-pundits agree with them.

Of course there is much mean spiritedness and narrow mindedness to be found in Britain today. There is a particularly worrying streak of selfish materialism among the young. The idealism and altruism of the 1960s and early 1970s has faded in the harsher and more cynical climate of the 1980s. But there is still a good deal of generosity and openness. And despite the high unemployment and the urban squalor, the prevalence of terrorism and militancy, the bitterness of industrial unrest and class feeling and the threat that looms over all of us of annihilation in a nuclear holocaust, there is also a surprising measure of optimism, perhaps that most liberal of all states of mind and certainly a necessary condition for the spread of other liberal values. 1984 has come and gone and, although it was hardly a year of harmony and understanding, we have at least found that we are not living in the kind of totalitarian state which George Orwell feared and predicted. Nor are we anywhere near it.

A poll carried out for the *Sunday Times* on the eve of 1984 found that on the whole people feel that there is more liberty in Britain now than there was a few years ago and that there will be more still in a few years time.[8] Public opinion, it seems, recognises and welcomes the rebirth of Liberal Britain and expects it to continue – which is just as well, for it is on the attitudes and actions of all of us that its continuation depends.

PART FOUR

TOWARDS A
MORE LIBERAL FUTURE

———————

— 17 —

THE LIBERAL WAY FORWARD

Britain is not bound to become a more liberal society in the coming years. Certain contemporary trends may point in that direction but there are also powerful counter-forces at work which could push us towards greater conformity, coercion and intolerance. The increasing polarisation of the population into haves and have-nots, the growing appeal of nationalism, the increasing recourse to militancy and violence and the deadening and debilitating influences of consumerism and the mass media could, if they are not checked, produce an atmosphere more illiberal than anything we have so far experienced this century.

If liberal values are to flourish and grow again, it will be largely as a result of the attitudes, aspirations and activities of individuals and communities rather than because of anything that the Government does. To quote Ralf Dahrendorf:

> Governments cannot do very much to advance human liberty. They can guarantee the basic rules of living together, and the citizenship rights of all including a decent standard of living for the old, the infirm and the disadvantaged . . . But above and beyond these elementary needs, governments must withdraw from our lives . . . Less government means more initiative by, and autonomy for, individuals, groups, businesses, organisations, decentralised units of all kinds.[1]

This is not to say that liberalism will just arrive spontaneously if the government only gets off people's backs. It will require much effort and constant vigilance. Much of the final part of this book is devoted to an examination of some of the reforms that are needed if Britain is to become a more liberal society. Some of them involve action by the Government. But we should be ever-mindful of the limitations of purely mechanical reforms and remember that true liberalism is an affair of the hearts and the minds of the people.

A few years ago it was fashionable to argue that Britain was becoming ungovernable. Most of those who used this phrase had in mind the waning respect for law and order and the challenge which powerful vested interests like the trade unions posed to democratically elected governments by their use of force and intimidation. This threat remains. The appalling scenes of violence and hatred which appeared almost nightly on our television screens last year during the long and bitter miners' dispute were a frightening reminder of what happens when respect for the rule of law breaks down. So are the terrible atrocities perpetrated by the Irish Republican Army and other terrorist groups. As was pointed out at the beginning of this book, liberalism depends for its existence on a common respect for the rule of law and the sovereignty of the democratic process. Without this respect societies degenerate into anarchy, the rule of the strong, and totalitarianism.

But there is another sense in which Britain is becoming less governable that liberals should welcome and applaud. The emerging post-industrial society may also prove in many ways to be a post-political society. The clash of labour and capital, which has provided the great theme of politics in the twentieth century, is likely to diminish as more people work on their own account, in co-operatives and in the informal economy. The fragmented, diversified, decentralised economy which is already beginning to emerge as a result of microchip technology will be much less susceptible to centralised management and direction than the more homogeneous and compact work-based society which it is replacing. Localised initiatives will become increasingly important, and so therefore will the role of local government, while macro-economic management and the role of central government will become progressively less important.

Where does this leave the Liberal Party, traditionally the vehicle for the translation of liberal principles into practice through the medium of politics? In some respects the party is already adapting itself to the new pattern of society which is emerging. Its strength is at the grassroots rather than at the centre. The thousand or so Liberal local councillors in many ways represent a stronger force for liberalism in the country than the party's handful of MPs at Westminster. Much agonising goes on among Liberals nowadays as to how the campaigning style of local community politics can be introduced into national politics. To some extent this is unnecessary. It is within the local sphere that the principles of liberalism can most appropriately be put into practice, and it is this sphere also which is becoming more and more important in political terms.

This is not to say that the Liberals should abandon national politics altogether. But the party nationally needs to change its emphasis and approach. The Liberals have become a party of too much organisation and too few ideas. Tactics tend to predominate over policies. This is out of keeping with their historic role as the seekers of new wisdom for a new age.

Paradoxically, alliance with the Social Democratic Party has made the Liberals more concerned with organisational matters and short-term electoral calculations when it should have had the opposite effect. The two parties in the alliance should be complementary, contributing to each other the particular strengths of their traditions, as summed up by Mrs Shirley Williams: 'The Liberal Party has been a party of ideas, challenging the orthodoxy of the times. The SDP is a party conscious of the constraints of economic circumstances and the harshness of changing priorities in Government'. Yet so far it is the Social Democrats who are showing more radicalism and more interest in ideas when their natural role, as Mrs Williams suggests, is to temper the crusading idealism of the Liberals. It is time for the Liberals to resume their historic mission and to plunge themselves once again into intellectual ferment and moral passion.

The chapters that follow contain some suggestions for policies which the Liberal Party might consider taking up in the next few years. But first the party needs to rid itself of two cherished shibboleths which are at best irrelevant to the future needs of society and at worst positively illiberal. Support for a statutory incomes policy, of the kind that still seems to form the basis of much of the Liberals' current economic thinking, falls into both these categories, I regret to say, and must be at the head of the list of policies to be discarded. There is everything to be said for introducing a guaranteed national minimum income scheme of the kind outlined in the next two chapters. But there is virtually nothing to be said in favour of re-introducing the kind of controls on wage rises which were attempted in the 1960s and 1970s. This type of centralised and restrictive policy, to which the Liberal Party at national level still seems curiously wedded, has all the failings of the mechanical approach to reform. It is inflexible and unworkable at the best of times, and particularly inappropriate to a society where fewer and fewer people are likely to have the status of employees and be in receipt of wages for conventional full-time jobs. An incomes policy is also a negation of liberalism, as Jo Grimond has pointed out in his *Personal Manifesto*: 'It shows that common feelings, the bonds of a liberal society, have collapsed. It renounces the market and one important liberty, the liberty of everyone to sell his labour.'[2]

Another contemporary Liberal nostrum which needs to be abandoned is the demand that there should be more government rather than less. This cry is heard from the community politics activists as much as from the national party establishment. As Jo Grimond has commented, 'the constant complaint in the local sheets usually called *Focus* which Liberals have been producing is that government is not doing enough'.[3] This incessant demand for the creation of new public agencies and the adoption of new regulations and laws needs to be stemmed. So does Liberal enthusiasm for reforming the machinery of government and establishing new tiers and structures of administration. Such a mechanistic approach is wholly alien to the traditions of British liberalism, as Vernon Bogdanor has recently pointed out in an illuminating contribution to his book, *Liberal Party Politics*:

The Liberal approach to constitutional reform is marked by a profound rationalism which is hostile not only to the adaptive nature of the British constitution, but also to the openness and resilience of the philosophical tradition of liberalism itself. The liberal case for freedom is founded ultimately upon a view of the diversity of human nature which makes it impossible for any authority to draw up definitive rules for the regulation of human conduct. So also to impose upon society a definitive course of constitutional development ought to be regarded as artificially limiting the flow of change and in this way pre-empting possibilities of choice in the future. To urge otherwise is to betray a misunderstanding both of the nature of the British constitution, largely a product of the practical reforms of previous generations of Whigs and Liberals, and of liberalism itself.[4]

Modern Liberals would do well to study the tradition of which they are part. They might be surprised at how many radical ideas it encompasses. Speaking at a party summer school in 1931 Keynes said that he saw only two planks of the traditional Liberal programme as being still seaworthy, and those were free trade and the crusade against drink. Both those policies are, if anything, even more relevant now than they were fifty years ago and cry out for resurrection and re-assertion. So too do many other traditional concerns of British liberalism like trust in the people, the voluntary principle in social welfare, international-ism, liberal education, redistribution of wealth, co-operation in industry and land reform. To this list must be added the development of new policies to meet the specific needs of the present age: the re-distribution of work, the liberalisation of the post-industrial society, and the rescue of individuality from the grip of commercialism and the mass media.

There is much to be done. Beveridge's five giants of Want, Squalor, Disease, Ignorance and Idleness have still to be banished from the world. They can only be combated with effort, with imagination and with a spirit of buoyant and energetic optimism. It is perhaps that last quality, so central to the British liberal tradition, that more than any other needs to be rekindled and applied today.

There are at least three important benefits which would spring from the rediscovery of optimism. First it would help to overcome the extraordinarily timid and defensive conservatism which seems to reign in many areas of our national life. At present we cling to the familiar and the long-established, even when it has clearly outlived its purpose, and resist the idea of change and radical reform. Consider the outcry which greets any proposals for reforming our health and social services. Sensible suggestions for changes in this area are rejected out of hand as an assault on the Welfare State which is invested with a strange sanctity and inviolability despite its manifest weaknesses and inadequacies.

Secondly, there is an urgent need to break out of the paralysis of will which seems to grip us, collectively at least, when it comes to translating proposals for reform into action. Countless Royal Commissions and Think Tank study groups have been set up by Governments and have produced sensible and liberal recommendations on subjects as diverse as industrial democracy, financing local government and stemming the rising tide of alcohol abuse. Yet these recommendations remain almost entirely unimplemented. Governments feel no inhibitions about commissioning enormous quantities of research, yet they draw back at the prospect of taking any action on the basis of the findings which have been so expensively and exhaustively obtained. We need the boldness and the confidence to rectify this debilitating combination of too much research and not enough action. If the constraints are too great to permit uniform action at a national level, then let us start experimentally at a local level. Let one local authority raise finance through a local income tax, let another experiment with education vouchers, and a third embark on a programme for the redistribution of land and the creation of smallholdings and allotments. Let us, indeed, allow a thousand flowers to bloom, accepting that some will blossom and others will perish. That is surely better than doing nothing.

The third and perhaps the most important of the contributions which a return to the spirit of optimism would make to our lives today is by inducing both a more positive and a calmer attitude towards the future. If we contemplate the present state of the world there is much to be angry, anxious and depressed about. It would, of course, be hopelessly naive in the face of mass starvation, the threat of nuclear holocaust and the rising tide of violence and intolerance to adopt a comforting complacency or even a hope that something will turn up to save us from catastrophe. But at the same time we must not lose our faith in mankind and our sense of the worthwhileness of life and the progress of humanity. Fear is the most destructive of all emotions, inducing passivity, panic and violence. Scarcely less destructive is the habit of looking always on the negative side, a habit which we in Britain have made something of a national speciality in the last decade or so.

Without becoming smug and falsely bullish, we need to develop that positive mentality which will enable us to see the opportunities for human progress and liberation which are created by what we are now inclined to see just as problems. We need the optimism and the imagination to welcome the introduction of new technology and the decline of conventional employment and to realise, in the words of Francis Pym, that where we now read 'unemployment up a million', we could read 'leisure time doubled for two million'.[5] We need to grasp and embrace the opportunities for human altruism and voluntary effort which are presented by the inability of the Welfare State to meet ever rising expectations and demands in the field of care. We need to build on the common concern that the build-up of nuclear stockpiles has given to both East and West about the paramount necessity of avoiding all-out war and preserving civilisation. Think positive – that is the simple message of liberal optimism. It is also, perhaps, the overwhelming need of our age.

But how can this message be spread? By the media, and television in particular, concentrating rather more on the achievements and the potential of the human race and rather less on its failings and weaknesses. By a determined assault in the world of education on the doctrines of fatalism, necessitarianism and Marxist determinism so that children, and adults, feel that there is a point and purpose to their lives and that they are not just the victims of circumstances trapped in the iron grip of immutable laws. Perhaps above all by the breaking down of large institutions and the building up of small-scale communities, where the direct effects of individual and communal effort can be seen and where man is not dwarfed and reduced to near-insignificance. Then perhaps more of us will begin to see opportunities where now we only see difficulties and will start to walk forward boldly to embrace the challenge where now we prefer to flee and forget.

THE ECONOMIC FUTURE:
COMING TO TERMS WITH
INFLATION AND UNEMPLOYMENT

Economic matters, as we have seen, have never been the first priority of liberals. Yet they cannot be ignored in thinking about the future. The two great economic problems which preoccupied Keynes in the 1930s, and which he rightly saw as obstacles standing in the way of the creation of a liberal society, are with us once again. Until inflation and unemployment are cured, or until our view of them has altered and they cease to be regarded as problems, we will remain obsessed with economic matters rather than with the other more important aspects of human life.

One important point needs to be made at the outset. The state of the British economy depends to a large extent on world economic trends and on events largely outside our control. There is relatively little that any Government can do to have a major impact on our overall economic performance. This is not to say that there is no role for government – it can through monetary policy bring down the rate of inflation, it has an important part to play in the redistribution of wealth and it is in a position to help break down protectionism and monopolies of both capital and labour. What it cannot do, however, is to affect by the regulation of demand real variables in the economy like the level of output or the level of employment. There is no point in trying to return to the kind of macro-economic demand management that has been attempted by both Labour and Conservative governments since the war. What is needed rather is the pragmatism of the traditional liberal approach to economic matters coupled with the radicalism implicit in Keynes' insistence on new wisdom for a new age.

The fact is that many of the concepts which now dominate economic thinking and debate are wholly outmoded and irrelevant to the circumstances of the emerging post-industrial society. This is pre-eminently true of the much vaunted commitment to securing full employment, still clung to by politicians of all parties, which is at best a dangerous delusion and at worst a deliberate piece of dishonesty. Full employment does not lie within the gift of governments, and, as we shall see, it is unlikely that we shall return to it in the foreseeable future. Like the spurious 'right to work' which is championed by so many in the Labour Party and trade union movement, it is an outmoded concept which belongs to the old work-based economy which is now passing away. Where trade unionists now press unrealistically for policies to create full employment and for the right to work, they should be calling for policies which will enable people to pursue a whole range of activities and give everyone the right to a full and satisfying life which may, in many cases, involve very little conventional paid employment. The National Union of Miners did no real service to its members by bringing them out on strike last year to protect jobs in uneconomic pits. It should rather have supported those many miners who wished to take the generous redundancy terms offered by the National Coal Board and devote themselves to pleasanter occupations than hewing coal, whether they be choral singing, tending their allotments or starting up a small business.

Incomes policy is another essentially irrelevant and unworkable idea which is still put forward by many people, including many Liberals, as a solution to the problem of inflation. It should be clear from the experience of the 1960s and early 1970s that incomes policies, however flexible, do not curb inflation but merely dam it up for a short period. Nor do they redistribute wealth in society; rather they freeze and perpetuate arbitrary differentials and anomalies. They are also thoroughly illiberal, representing wholly unjustified interference by the Government in agreements which have been freely made by workers and their employers.

But if the idea of incomes policy is to be jettisoned, how should the problem of inflation be tackled? Control of the money supply by the Government is clearly an important element in keeping down the level of prices. But inflation is not just a monetary phenomenon, it is also a social and moral question, a matter of human expectations and behaviour. It induces a vicious cycle of greed, of grabbing what you can while you can, what one trade union leader has graphically described as the philosophy of the pig trough. In seeking to tackle inflation neither the neo-Keynesian advocates of incomes policies and demand management nor the free-market apostles of monetarism have paid enough attention to this aspect of the problem. Liberals, with their stress on human values, their anti-materialism and their preference for moral rather than mechanical reform, have a very important role to play both in identifying the importance of these human causes of inflation and in pointing the way for their removal.

Part of the reason for our persistent high levels of inflation is surely the general expectation, encouraged by advertisers, politicians and others, of a constantly rising standard of material prosperity for everyone. Equally important, perhaps, is the view that many people have of their work as a boring and alienating experience the sole justification of which is to provide money. Lacking interest or satisfaction in their job, they concentrate much of their energy on securing higher wages. Another damaging attitude which encourages inflation is the widespread obsession with relativities and differentials that shows itself in a desire to leap-frog other groups of workers and a prevailing spirit of envy and discontent.

To some extent, the structural changes which are already beginning to take place in the economy should help to alter some of these attitudes. The growth of self-employment and the spread of co-operative ownership, profit-sharing schemes and employee participation will give more and more people a direct interest in the enterprise for which they are working.

In an important paper on 'Employment, Inflation and Politics' published by the Institute of Economic Affairs in 1976 Peter Jay argued that in a future market economy where the economic units are owned, controlled and managed by workers, people 'will come to terms with the entrepreneurial realities which concern their present employers, so that they will accept a non-inflationary market-determined environment in setting the level of rewards that can be afforded'. More recently Professor James Meade, winner of the 1977 Nobel Prize in economics, has argued in similar terms.[1]

Of course, not everyone will want to work in a co-operative and no one should be forced into this particular form of organisation. But it is important that people should be given the opportunity to have a direct stake in the business for which they work. The present Government has already made some significant advances in this area, most notably in turning over the National Freight Consortium to be run by managers and employees and in giving preferential treatment to employees at the time of the flotation of shares in British Telecom. The privatisation of British Telecom was also very important in promoting the wider ownership of shares in Britain, an objective which all Liberals must surely have at heart although this was hardly evident from the response which some of them made to the sale. Future privatisation schemes should embody the principle of offering a significant allocation of shares and a significant say in management to those employed in the enterprise concerned.

There may possibly also be a case for legislation, of the kind long championed by Liberals, to establish works councils in firms over a certain size. Certainly there is no doubt that in West Germany laws establishing full-scale worker participation in industry which date, ironically enough, from the period of British occupation after the war, have led to a far stronger realisation of commercial realities by workers and trade unions and have helped to prevent free wage bargaining from being an inflationary stimulus. Ideally, the setting up of more such councils over here should be an entirely voluntary matter but it may be that a legislative push is needed to help the current trend towards greater participation and consultation in industry.

Government can also help the fight against inflation by determinedly assaulting monopolies, and promoting a vigorous competition policy which eliminates subsidies and protection. The excessive concentration of capital in the hands of certain large institutions, like pension funds, insurance companies and building societies, is injurious to the health and vitality of the British economy just as are the immunities and monopoly bargaining powers enjoyed by certain trade unions. In both areas there is room for more competition and less privilege and special treatment. There is also an overwhelming case for ending the subsidies paid to certain special groups, most notably, perhaps, farmers who are currently subsidised to the extent of around £5 a week in taxes and artificially high food prices by every family in Britain. Genuine free trade, like genuine free wage-bargaining, is still a cause for which Liberals must fight with all their strength.

But what is just as important as anything that the Government does is a fundamental change of attitude on the part of everyone, employers, employed and the growing body of self- employed and unemployed. We need to end our expectations of constantly rising material prosperity. The message that we cannot afford more than we earn is rammed home often enough by Mrs Thatcher. At the moment the answer is seen largely in terms of earning more, through increased productivity and higher levels of growth. But, as Ralf Dahrendorf has pointed out, there is another interpretation of the message and that is that we must learn to afford less:

It is unlikely, to say the least, that there will be enough growth to match human expectations at the rate at which they rose in the 1950s and 1960s. Some stabilisation of expectations is inevitable and even desirable. What Bertrand de Jouvenal called *la société de toujours plus*, the society of more and more of the same things, cannot and probably should not continue for ever . . .

. . . Expectations of gain and of growth must be scaled down to match possibilities. One of the obsessions of the modern world is that with 'relativities'; if we were to abandon it rather than give it theoretical ('relative deprivation') and institutional ('comparability commission') dignity, we might discover that quite a few economies in OECD countries already provide a satisfactory level of welfare, and quite large groups have a satisfactory income. The discovery would at least relieve frustration.[2]

We need, in fact, to rediscover the joys of John Stuart Mill's stationary-state economy. Instead of seeing the reward for what we do mainly in material terms, we need to think more of the satisfaction or the companionship that it gives us. New technology should help in this respect by removing many of the more routine and dead-end jobs and greatly increasing the possibilities for people to fill their time in a way that they find satisfying and enjoyable. As Professor Dahrendorf's remarks remind us, we should also count our blessings and remember that by the standards of most of the world's population we have a superabundance of wealth and possessions. Then perhaps the inflationary impulse will cease to grip us quite as much as it does at present.

A similar change of attitude will be needed if we are to come to terms with unemployment. It is now clear that the present high level of unemployment in Britain, and indeed in the developed world as a whole, is no mere temporary aberration that will disappear when the current recession is over. A recent report by Henley Centre for Forecasting predicts a long-term unemployment level of around five million in Britain. Technological change is creating considerably fewer jobs in the new 'sunrise' industries of the future than it is sweeping away in older, traditional industries which are being mechanised. Plessey, one of the most successful companies in the booming field of electronics, took on 1,600 new staff in 1980 – but it also shed 2,500 whose jobs had been taken over by machines. In future, economic growth will not necessarily mean more jobs. Employment, as it has traditionally been understood, as full-time paid work in a factory or office from nine in the morning to five in the evening, five days a week from the time of leaving school to retirement at 65, is on the decline and is likely to be the lot of fewer and fewer people.

The implications of this development are considerable. One of the most important, and most urgent prerequisites for coming to terms with the kind of society we are likely to be living in by the end of this century is to rid ourselves of the so-called work ethic. The particular set of values summed up in

205

this oft-quoted phrase was entirely appropriate for the circumstances of the industrial society in which we have lived for the last 200 years. But it is highly inappropriate for a post-industrial society where paid employment will not have the same central position. The work ethic teaches us that work done for pay is the central feature of our lives. It also leads to regarding those who are not in conventional employment as unproductive loafers and parasites. Both these views need to be changed.

Liberals are in a good position to help in the dethroning of the work ethic. Within the liberal tradition man has never just been seen as a worker, but rather as a thinker, a player, a participator and a person of infinite capacities and possibilities. The traditional liberal stress on the fullness and diversity of the human personality will have a major part to play in creating the activity-based society, to use Ralf Dahrendorf's words, that must replace our present work-based economy. So, one might add, will traditional religious teachings, both Western and Eastern, which stress the many different 'works' of man, contemplation, exercise, worship, refreshment and enjoyment as well as manual and mental labour.[3]

One of the most effective ways of diminishing the hold of the work ethic will be to restore domestic and community activity to the status which they had in times past. Among the most significant social trends in Britain over the last thirty years has been the removal of millions of women from the domestic economy into the world of full-time work. It is, of course, totally wrong to suggest that a woman's place is necessarily and exclusively in the home, and a man's out at work, but there is little doubt that the feminist movement has done society a disservice by devaluing the status and role of those engaged in full-time activity at home and suggesting that fulfilment and liberation is only to be found in the world of work. The satisfactions to be derived for both men and women from looking after a family and from other home and community-based activities need to be trumpeted abroad rather more loudly.[4]

Another important aspect of the work-based society also needs to be changed. At present work, in the form of paid jobs, is the main method of distributing wealth throughout society. Unless we change this then one of the main consequences of new technology will be a growing polarisation of society into haves and have-nots, with more and more wealth being concentrated in the hands of a relatively small technocratic élite. We need to establish a new means of distributing the national wealth which takes account of the fact that a maximum of wealth can now be produced with a minimum of human intervention.

The answer is to introduce a guaranteed national income which goes to every single adult and represents his or her share of the nation's wealth, regardless of whether their contribution has been through conventional work, through giving up a job to a more productive machine, or by contributing to the wellbeing of society by bringing up children, running a household or helping in the community. In a sense, of course, we are already providing this income in the form of unemployment and supplementary benefits. Yet these are seen as 'dole' handouts to unemployed and a drain on the Exchequer. If we rather saw them for what they really are, redistribution payments which represent a transfer of the national wealth, we would be well on the way to establishing a just and equitable basis for spreading the wealth of a society where not everyone needs to be in work.[5]

The implementation of a guaranteed national minimum income scheme, as part of a comprehensive reform of the taxation and social security systems of the kind described in the next chapter, would do much to end the tyranny of the work ethic and to remove the stigma of unemployment. There are also other concrete ways in which unemployment can be relieved. Perhaps the most obvious is by redistributing work itself so that it is shared out more evenly throughout the population.

This redistribution can take several forms. The working week could be shortened. There is nothing magical about a five day week. Many Victorians worked a six or even seven day week and it seems quite reasonable that we should now be ready to move to a four day week. The working life can also be shortened, either by delaying the time at which young people are released on to the labour market by extending education and by the introduction of a period of social service, or by bringing forward the retirement age. Existing jobs can be shared, so that what is now a full-time job becomes a part-time job for two people. There are already four million part-time jobs in Britain. If the number were doubled by splitting up existing full-time jobs unemployment could be reduced by two million.

Much useful study has already been undertaken on the economics of distributing work, and specifically on the concept of job sharing. The OECD produced an encouraging survey in 1982, and many positive ideas have come from the Work and Leisure Society, set up by Kathleen Smith in 1980.[6]

What is now needed is not so much Government direction and compulsion, but rather greater flexibility and imagination on the part of both employers and employees. It would be intolerable, and very illiberal, for people to be forced to share their jobs or retire early if they do not want to, but there is everything to be said for enabling them to do so if that is their wish. Some employers are already pioneering interesting schemes in this area like Rank Xerox's 'networking' plan which enables executives to work part-time from their homes. What the Government can do to help is remove the restrictive regulations in the fields of taxation and National Insurance which at present make it difficult or unattractive to opt out of conventional employment patterns. Chief among the obstacles to a wider distribution of work is the state pension scheme which effectively locks up people's savings and strongly discourages them from giving up their job before the statutory retirement age.

The more even distribution of work in society will also require a willingness to trade a loss of earnings for an increase in leisure time. In fact, this trade-off may not be as great as is sometimes supposed. If productivity growth can be maintained at the present rate of two per cent a year for a century, the average worker in a hundred years time will be seven times more productive than he is today. With the greatly increased affluence that this will bring he is unlikely to want to work for as many hours in the week, or as many years of his life, as he does now. A 30 hour working week, and a 25 year working life may well be quite enough to provide sufficient current income to live on comfortably and sufficient savings on which to retire. But quite apart from this consideration, it may prove easier to trade greater leisure time for lower earnings than might be imagined. A large-scale survey recently conducted in EEC countries found that when offered a choice between more pay and shorter hours, a majority of workers in Britain, France, West Germany, Belgium, Denmark and the Netherlands chose the latter. The British, as we have already noted, seem particularly prepared to sacrifice higher earnings for more leisure time. It is up to government, employers and trade unions to take note of this and to ensure that increases in productivity, which are often at present achieved at the expense of unemployment, are not in future translated into higher earnings for those left working but rather into greater leisure time for a larger group of workers.

An increasing amount of economic activity, and indeed a growing number of jobs, will in future be centred in the informal economy. Already much is being done to stimulate this sector. Through the enterprise allowance scheme, the voluntary projects programme and the community enterprise scheme the Government is supporting and encouraging initiatives among the unemployed in the field of voluntary and community work and in such unconventional jobs as busking and bottling spring water. There is scope for even more activity and support in this area. It is unfortunate, for example, that programmes run by voluntary organisations and public bodies as part of the Youth Training Scheme are currently being axed. They may well be preparing youngsters better for the lifestyle of the future than the more conventional employer-based schemes which the Government favours.

Those employed in the formal economy at present receive a number of subsidies and benefits which are not available to the self-employed and those in the informal sector. They include participation in pension schemes and payment of employers' National Insurance contributions. If these benefits are to continue, it is quite reasonable that those in conventional employment should be more highly taxed for the security and perquisites which they enjoy. At present the self-employed are unfairly penalised by both the taxation and social security systems. There is room for considerable reforms in both these areas to remove the privileges which employees enjoy.

Traditionally selective capital investment in public works of the kind advocated by Keynes has been seen as an important means of reducing unemployment. There is no doubt that some such investment is needed and should be part of the programme of a future Alliance Government. Capital spending, rather than current spending, has been the main victim of public spending cuts by both Labour and Conservative governments in the last ten years and has reached a dangerously low level. The renovation of our largely Victorian sewerage system is fast becoming an urgent necessity, and there are strong social and environmental grounds for substantial programmes of housing rehabilitation, rail electrification, home and office insulation, hydro-electric installations and other schemes to develop recyclable energy sources. A public works programme of this kind would have the incidental benefit of giving work to the relatively unskilled, who are less likely to have the initiative to start up their own business and thrive in the informal economy. But it is important not to be too sanguine about its overall effect on unemployment figures. It has been calculated that a £20.4 billion package of public works (at 1982 prices), involving the construction of a third London airport, a Channel tunnel, a barrage across the Severn, a new North Sea gas pipeline, railway electrification and a 33 per cent increase in spending on roads, houses and sewers would directly create only 173,000 new jobs.[7] Investment in public works should be undertaken where there is a clear benefit to be gained from it and not for the sake of creating jobs which it is not very good at doing anyway.

There is one particular area where a substantial number of satisfying and permanent job opportunities could be created. Before the Industrial Revolution most people in Britain earned their living from the land. As we move towards becoming a post-industrial society is it not logical that we should look once again to the land to provide employment for those who can no longer find jobs in factories or offices?

The United Kingdom has a lower proportion of its workforce

employed on the land than any other country in Europe. Mechanisation has systematically reduced the number of agricultural and horticultural labourers. At the same time, a process of amalgamation encouraged by Government subsidies has drastically reduced the number of individual farms and market gardens. In 1953 there were 454,000 agricultural holdings in Britain. By 1981 there were only 242,300. There has been a particularly steep decline in the number of small proprietors farming less than 100 acres, down from 250,000 in 1964 to only 120,000 today.[8]

This agricultural revolution has been disastrous not only in its contribution to unemployment but also in its damage to the environment and to the quality of our food. A relatively small number of farmers are encouraged by massive subsidies and artificially high prices to contribute to the EEC's ever-growing mountain of dairy products and to grub up hedges and drain wetlands to create arable prairies on which they grow unwanted wheat which is shipped to Russia with a subsidy of £60 a ton. Yet there is a lack of home-grown vegetables which are more labour-intensive to produce and which we are now importing in ever increasing quantities from abroad. There is also an increasing realisation of the damage that is being done to our soil by the over-use of fertilisers and a rising demand for organically-grown food which has not been liberally sprayed with pesticides. Despite an increase in the number of its farmers' groups from 300 to 1,000 in the last year, the Organic Growers Association is unable to meet the demand for its produce.

We are reaching the stage when it makes economic as well as nutritional and ecological sense to reverse the trend of the last fifty years and make agriculture and horticulture labour-intensive industries again. A study by Robert Vale of the Open University has shown that Britain could grow all its own food organically by employing one million people in vegetable growing (each with one acre), 500,000 in livestock farming (each with 20 acres) and 250,000 on arable farms (each with 62 acres). If this scheme was implemented, 7 per cent of the working population would be employed on the land, a figure which would still be below the average in the EEC as a whole.[9]

What is needed is a major initiative along the lines of previous Liberal campaigns to extend the ownership and productive use of land. Taxation of land values should be introduced to discourage hoarding and speculation and to break up large estates. Local authorities should be acquiring small-holdings to rent out, as they did under the Liberal Smallhold-ings Act of 1918, not selling them off to large farmers as they are at the moment. Most important of all, subsidies encouraging the amalgamation and concentration of farms and the over-production of cereals and milk should be ended forthwith and entry into farming should be made much easier for those without large amounts of capital. The recent Agricultural Holdings Act goes some way towards achieving this last object by removing over-protection of tenancies, but there is still much to be done to break the hold of the large institutions which now dominate landowning in Britain and to restore the land to small proprietors and tenants.

Already several of those who are out of work are deriving both satisfaction and some small profit from growing fruit, vegetables and flowers both for their own consumption and for their friends and neighbours. There is an enormous demand for local authority allotments and smallholdings. It is not just in rural areas that the land exists to provide these. A recent report published by Earth Resources Research and Growing in Hackney estimated that there are over 500,000 acres of derelict inner-city land which could be transformed into allotments, urban farms, garden centres and even trout rearing ponds. At present, this land is just standing idle. There must be ways of making it available for the benefit of the community. A system of site-value rating would help, as would more vigorous action by local authorities to rent or buy land for letting out.

There are other ways in which employment opportunities on the land could be increased. The traditional Scottish practice of crofting, whereby the cultivation of a smallholding is combined with some other activity or occupation, could usefully be extended to other parts of the country. There is also scope for the establishment of mobile labour gangs which farmers could hire on a contract basis to do labour-intensive jobs like crop-sowing or harvesting at particular times of the year.[10]

The reforms which have been urged in this chapter are all within the traditions of British liberalism. The idea of dividing up the national wealth by giving everyone a guaranteed minimum income recalls the arguments of Belloc and the distributists, the notion that 'God gave the land to the people' can be traced back through Lloyd George to Cobden, while the need to scale down expectations of constantly rising material wealth and the virtues of a steady state economy were preached by Mill nearly 150 years ago. Yet traditional though these policies and perspectives may be, they involve a more radical approach from politicians than that which has characterised any administration since the war and certainly than that which is currently displayed by the Liberal Party. But even more they involve a fundamental change of attitude on the part of all of us. The society of the future will only be fair and liberal if we can discard our expectations of an ever-increasing standard of living, our obsession with relativities and differentials, and our view that paid employment should remain both the principal means of distributing wealth and a central feature of our lives. If we can change our attitude on these and other matters, then we can look forward to a future which offers a fuller and a freer life for all and from which the ghosts of inflation and unemployment which have haunted us throughout the twentieth century will finally have been banished.

TOWARDS A WELFARE SOCIETY – REDISTRIBUTION AND VOLUNTARYISM

The outlook for the provision of social welfare in Britain presents formidable problems but it also offers considerable opportunities. The relatively high levels of economic growth which have sustained the expansion of the Welfare State over the last forty years are unlikely to return. Yet the demands on welfare services are set to increase. The proportion of elderly people in Britain will rise steadily over the next forty years, while there seems little likelihood, in the foreseeable future, of a substantial fall in the number of those unemployed. On present trends, some experts foresee the Welfare State running out of money as early as 1990. Already it is showing signs of cracking under the strain imposed by diminishing resources and ever-increasing demands. Hospital waiting lists lengthen. The number of claims for benefits threatens to engulf social security staff in a mountain of paperwork. Every week 23 million individual benefits are paid, and every year 24 million new claims are processed. Meanwhile, despite the vast panoply of benefits and allowances, more and more people are slipping into poverty. There are now over six million people at or below the level at which supplementary benefit is paid, more than four times as many as when the social security system was established in 1948.

This impending crisis in the Welfare State has already forced a radical re-appraisal of prevailing attitudes. The Government has produced a wide-ranging series of proposals for reform of the whole welfare system and there is much talk about the need for a new comprehensive Beveridge-style plan. A growing number of people accept that the time has come for the principle of universality to be replaced by one of selectivity, with help being given much more specifically to those most in need. There is also widespread acceptance of the increasingly important role that voluntary community effort must play in the future provision of welfare. There are strong grounds to hope that this rethinking may produce a revival of the principle of voluntaryism and an overall approach which embraces the liberal ideal of a partnership between professional services, voluntary community effort and the agency of the enabling state to create a welfare society which provides both the material and the moral basis for the pursuit of liberty by all its members. Before such a society can come about, however, there will have to be both a substantial shift of attitudes, and a substantial shouldering of new responsibilities, by both Government and people.

The establishment of an effective means of distributing the national wealth more equitably and justly throughout the population must be the Government's first priority. For a long time successive governments have not taken their role as redistributors as seriously as they should have done. This is partly because until recently they have been able to rely on steady economic growth raising the absolute, if not the relative living standards of the poor. Now that prospects for growth are much less certain, there needs to be a more conscious and direct effort by Government to ensure that the poor have an adequate standard of living. There is another reason why this particular responsibility will assume much greater importance in the coming decades. As was mentioned in the last chapter, paid jobs can no longer necessarily be relied on as a satisfactory mechanism for distributing the nation's wealth throughout society. Because of the technological revolution, we now face the real possibility of an increasingly polarised society where those in employment gain all the benefits of increased productivity and mechanisation while a large and growing group of unemployed get nothing. We need to find ways to ensure that the increased wealth created by the replacement of men by machines is spread more evenly across the whole population and does not just go to those lucky (or unlucky) enough still to be in a job.

At present the Government redistributes wealth in a two-stage process. It collects taxes and it pays out benefits. Liberals have argued for some time that these two operations should be merged into a single simple transfer scheme which would also incorporate the collection of National Insurance contributions. All social security benefits and allowances would be turned into tax credits along with existing personal tax allowances. Those whose total income was greater than the total of their tax credits would be net tax payers, those whose income was less than their credit entitlements would be net beneficiaries. The introduction of such a scheme would have a number of clear advantages over the present system. It would abolish the poverty trap which exists when low-paid workers find that they are worse off after a pay rise because of a loss of benefits and end the present absurdity whereby many poor families are paying tax at the same time as they are receiving supplementary benefit. It would also enormously reduce bureaucracy and paperwork by establishing one simple system run by a single government department.[1]

But could we be even bolder and work towards establishing a national minimum income or social dividend payable as of right to every adult in the country? The introduction of such a scheme has long been a liberal dream – it was vigorously canvassed by Mill nearly 150 years ago – and, as we have already seen, it would be particularly appropriate in a society where one of the most important sources of new wealth is the shedding of jobs to achieve greater productivity.

Such a scheme could be relatively simple to operate. A national minimum income, or social dividend, would be declared which would be deemed to be every adult citizen's deserved slice of the gross national product. It would be set at a level which would provide the material means for a simple but adequate existence – in present terms perhaps around £4500 a year. This would not be a hand-out but an absolute entitlement of everyone over eighteen. People could either use it as their sole means of financial support or they could supplement it in any legal way they wished, paying tax on all that they earned above the level of the national minimum.

Provision of such an income would liberate people by giving them flexibility and choice about how to use their time. Those who wished to devote themselves to looking after elderly or infirm relatives or neighbours, or engage in other forms of community service, either for a relatively limited period or as a long-term commitment, would have the economic wherewithal to do this. Those who wished to spend much of their time at home, looking after a growing family and engaged in housework and other activities which, as we have already noted, deserve to be counted as contributions to the Gross National Product just as much as jobs in the formal economy, would receive an income for this work. Those who wanted sabbaticals from their jobs, periods of further education and learning, or who simply preferred to live simple and relatively self-sufficient lives without work would be enabled to pursue these objectives.

Two objections are normally raised to the introduction of a tax credit or minimum income scheme. The first is the administrative and practical difficulties involved in setting up and running a single transfer system. With the full computerisation of Inland Revenue records, which is due to be completed in 1988, a merger of the income tax and social security systems no longer looks as daunting as it used to. Computerisation should also make it possible to produce a weekly or monthly tax assessment, which would be required if either the tax credit or minimum income schemes were to be implemented. Annual adjustments would also be necessary to cope with under or over payment of tax during the year, but overall a single transfer system should prove much easier to administer than the present mish-mash of allowances and benefits.

The more serious objection is that of cost. It has been pointed out that raising existing tax allowances to a level which would provide a decent standard of living, which is effectively what a minimum income scheme does, would be prohibitively expensive and could only be paid for by raising both the standard and

217

higher rates of income tax by at least fifty per cent. It is undoubtedly true that providing a guaranteed minimum income for everyone would place a much heavier burden on the shoulders of those who earn, and on high earners in particular. But quite apart from the strong moral argument that in a society where there is not enough paid work to go round, it is incumbent on those who are earning to support those who are not, there are a number of other points which should be borne in mind before the idea of a guaranteed national minimum income is dismissed as being too costly to contemplate.

The first is that the implementation of such a scheme would considerably reduce the need for many of the benefits which are at present paid out by Government. It would eliminate completely the need for supplementary benefit. It would also enable the principle of selectivity to be applied to other benefits which are at present universal, such as child allowances and state old age pensions, if, indeed, these were needed at all once everyone had a guaranteed and adequate income. So long as such an income is provided, there are, in fact, strong arguments for working towards the abolition of both these benefits. Child allowances encourage large families at a time when there is growing agreement that our population is too big for comfort, while state pensions, as we have already seen, do not allow individuals to retire when they want to but rather specify the same terms for everyone, regardless of personal preferences and circumstances.[2]

It is perhaps worth adding at this point that, irrespective of whether or not a minimum national income scheme is introduced, there is, in fact, an overwhelming case for heeding Beveridge's recantation of his early preference for universality and moving towards much greater selectivity in the provision of benefits. At present both child allowances and state pensions go to many people who do not really need them; indeed in the case of pensions, because they are earnings-related, the well-off actually derive more benefit than the poor. The cost of providing these universal benefits is high and will rise considerably in the coming decades – the Government Actuary estimates that the cost of earnings-related pensions will rise in real terms from the present £0.1 billion to around £10 billion by the year 2030 because of demographic trends. Liberals should be calling now for these benefits to be made selective. More radically, they should be asking whether we really want them at all.

Secondly, it needs to be said that the burden of personal taxation in Britain has shifted steadily away from the rich and towards middle and low income earners in the last forty years. Equity demands that those with high incomes should pay higher taxes. It also demands the ending of the various forms of tax relief which provide what is effectively a second welfare state for the better off members of society. The present Government has made a start by abolishing relief on life assurance premiums. There is a strong case for going further and abolishing all relief on both mortgage interest payments and company car expenses, which together accounted for some £4 billion or more lost revenue to the Treasury in the tax year 1983 to 1984.

The ending of many existing benefits, the conversion of others from universal to selective payments and the abolition of all forms of personal tax relief would make a substantial contribution towards financing a guaranteed national minimum income scheme. So also would the introduction of a tax on land values of the kind outlined in Henry George's classic *Progress and Poverty* and long championed by Liberals, most recently by Fred Harrison in his book *The Power in the Land* (1983). As we have already seen, Liberals have traditionally seen the land as a source of public wealth, much of the value of which owes nothing to the work of individual owners but rather to good luck or to the efforts of the community. As an illustration of the truth of this principle, one need only point to the enormous increase which has taken place over the last fifteen years or so in the value of land within easy reach of the M4 motorway. Taxing the unearned increment of the land would provide a substantial sum of money for spending on the welfare of the community.

There is no escaping the fact that a scheme which provided everyone with a guaranteed minimum income would be expensive and would mean higher taxation for those earning. It is also conventional political wisdom that promises of higher taxation lose votes. The Conservatives, in particular, hold that we are already an over-taxed society and that there is a need to create incentives by reducing income tax levels particularly for those in higher rate brackets. Liberals should firmly resist this line of argument and should honestly and boldly follow their traditional commitment to redistribution, accepting that it means higher taxation. They may well find that the public mind is less resistant to this principle than most politicians seem to think. Recent opinion polls show that a clear majority of people would rather pay higher taxes and see welfare services maintained than see a drop in taxation and a diminution in the public provision of welfare. A MORI poll at the end of 1983, for example, found that 61 per cent of respondents preferred to maintain spending on public services even if it meant an increase in taxation, while a Gallup Poll taken at the same time found that only 17 per cent of the public favoured a cut in taxes and a reduction in services. Interestingly, both polls found that the proportion of people favouring the tax-cutting option had declined significantly since Mrs Thatcher's election as Prime Minister in 1979.[3]

If people are, indeed, prepared to pay higher taxes to preserve the Welfare State, then they may also be willing to pay higher taxes to achieve the redistribution of wealth which is fundamental to the creation of a welfare society. Of course, the introduction of a national minimum income scheme is not something that could be done overnight. It would have to be phased in gradually. But it is surely worth thinking about as a long-term target. Yet again, what is needed to set this particular reform in motion is a change of attitude, a determination to look forward, as Mill did more than a hundred years ago, to a time

when the division of the produce of labour . . . will be made by consent on an acknowledged principle of justice; and when it will no longer be, or thought to be, impossible for human beings to exert themselves strenuously in procuring benefits which are not to be exclusively their own, but to be shared with the society they belong to. The social problem of the future . . . (is) how to unite the greatest individual liberty of action with a common ownership in the raw material of the globe, and an equal participation of all in the benefits of labour.[4]

One important side-benefit of a minimum national income

scheme is that it would open the way for introducing more flexibility and choice into the welfare services and make it much easier to charge fees for specific services and increase the element of funding from voluntary sources. In fact, irrespective of whether or not such a scheme is introduced, there is a strong case for charging for certain health and welfare services along the lines suggested in Arthur Seldon's book *Charge* (1977). It is also important that more flexibility and choice is introduced. In the field of education, for example, there is at present considerable parental dissatisfaction with the large all-in comprehensive schools which are the only option open to many children. Although there may well prove to be practical difficulties involved in implementing a voucher system of the kind advocated by the somewhat alarmingly named pressure group FEVER (Friends of the Educational Voucher in English Regions), it is surely worth experimenting with the idea in at least one local education authority area. There is also room for more experimentation and openness on the part of education authorities and of the education establishment as a whole towards unorthodox and 'alternative' approaches to schooling like the 'free school' movement and the systems devised by Maria Montessori and Rudolf Steiner. There are, in fact, some encouraging signs of a more liberal attitude emerging in this area just as in the health services there is now more interaction, and more mutual regard, between the practitioners of conventional and alternative medicine.

The growing voluntary and community involvement that is already taking place in many areas of social welfare is rightly being welcomed by many professionals and experts. It should also be welcomed by trade unions representing workers in the public sector. The trend towards community care and more use of volunteers and voluntary fund-raising in health, education and the social services is not simply a response to economic constraints. It is a reflection of a more pluralistic and voluntary-ist approach to social welfare and a more committed and responsible attitude on the part of many people towards the needs of their fellow human beings. This attitude needs to be encouraged and directed, particularly as we move into a period when we will have more time to devote to helping one another.

One way in which these naturally altruistic feelings could be encouraged might be by establishing a national community service scheme somewhat along the lines of the old National Service. At present we stand virtually alone in Europe in not requiring young people to spend a year or more in military service. Liberals rightly oppose the re-introduction of compulsory soldiering for all school leavers. But there is much to be said for introducing a national scheme, perhaps as part of an overall education and training package for 16 to 18-year-olds, which offers a choice between military service, with a strong stress on outward bound and practical skills, social and community service and conservation and environmental work of the kind undertaken by President Roosevelt's Civilian Conservation Corps in the 1930s. Such a national community service scheme was proposed by David Steel ten years ago and recent opinion polls suggest that the idea is supported by nearly eighty per cent of the population. There are, of course, already many exciting and valuable opportunities for young people to spend a period in full-time community service under the auspices of organisations like Community Service Volunteers, but the majority of school-leavers miss out on this experience. The recent study undertaken by Professor David Marsland on behalf of Youth Call shows that there are a considerable number of worthwhile jobs which could be undertaken by those taking part in community service schemes in which local authorities, voluntary bodies and public services could all be involved.[5] It may be unrealistic to think in terms of implementing a national scheme immediately, but it is surely worth initiating one or two experiments locally.

Giving much more prominence to both the principle and the practice of community service is just one aspect of a major change that needs to take place in our approach to education and training if we are to move towards the liberal goal of creating a welfare society. At present young people are prepared at school and through further education for conventional jobs of which we are running out and to be largely passive members of a Welfare State which is already creaking under the strain of the demands made on it. Indeed, one might add that they are not even being prepared very well for the former function – we still lag badly behind other developed nations in our provision of vocational training and the teaching of skills with the result that only a third of our workforce possess vocational qualifications, compared to more than sixty per cent in West Germany. We need, young and old alike, to be taught not just how to work, but how to live and how to give in a society where there is likely to be both the opportunity and the necessity for more independence, more self-reliance, and more harnessing of that spirit of altruism and co-operation which lies at the heart of the human personality. It is worth recalling again Mill's observation, quoted in Chapter Four, that 'a people among whom there is no habit of spontaneous action for a collective interest . . . have their faculties only half developed; their education is defective in one of its most important branches'.

Educationists and others are only just beginning to wake up to the magnitude of the changes that need to be made both in theory and in practice. Intellectual pressure groups like Work and Society are arguing for a much broader and more imaginative approach to education and training which embraces preparation for life and social activity as well as greater attention to practical and vocational skills. At a practical level, several local education authorities are implementing new curriculum projects which embody these wider perspectives. One of the most interesting is the three-year scheme operating in the secondary schools in Dudley which aims to make young people feel that they can deal with life competently even though they may not get a job after school. The scheme, which has brought local police officers, community workers, parents and others into the classroom and involved pupils designing their own bedsitters and working out how best to live in them, is already credited with contributing to a significant drop in the local juvenile crime rate. Those who have taken part in it have gained confidence by learning how to be active agents in their own lives, not just passive recipients.[6] It is through the extension of this kind of imaginative and liberal approach to education that we will lay the surest foundations for a true welfare society.

20

PUTTING MORE TRUST
IN THE PEOPLE –
REASSERTING THE DEMOCRATIC
PRINCIPLE

How can Britain be made a more democratic society with power and responsibility diffused more widely throughout the community? Certain constitutional changes would undoubtedly help in this direction, but ultimately what is needed is a change of attitude in which people are seen, and see themselves, less as passive consumers and more as active and responsible participators in the complex business of managing their affairs.

The most important and urgently needed constitutional reform is the introduction of the principle of proportional representation into our electoral system on the basis of a single transferable vote in multi-member constituencies. As we have already observed in Chapter Three, this method of voting accords much better than our present first-past-the-post system with traditional liberal trust in the people and concern for widening the scope of individual choice and ensuring the representation of minorities.

There are many good reasons for replacing our present system of voting. For a start it is grossly unrepresentative. It seriously distorts the expressed preferences of the electorate by over-representing majorities and under-representing minorities, even when they are quite sizeable. It exaggerates the degree of conflict in the country and minimises the extent of consensus and agreement. As is all too well known, the British first-past-the-post system has helped to produce an adversary style of politics, artificially polarising the country into two opposing blocks of opinion and reinforcing the confrontational atmosphere of other aspects of the nation's life such as relations in industry. It has also led to a see-saw pattern of government, with each new administration often reversing much of the work of its predecessor, which has promoted instability and seriously inhibited long-term planning.

There is also considerable evidence to suggest that our present voting system induces public apathy about elections and disillusionment about the whole democratic process. This is hardly surprising when so many people are effectively disfranchised by the system and made to feel that their votes count for nothing and might as well not be cast. It is surely no coincidence that in elections for the European Parliament, the turn-out in Britain, the one country in the European Economic Community to have a plural system of voting, is markedly lower than anywhere else.

The undemocratic nature of our existing system of voting can be seen particularly clearly in the sphere of local government. Here, thanks to the block vote system whereby each elector is given one vote for each vacancy to be filled in a multi-member ward, the distortions produced are often even greater than in parliamentary and European elections. It is not at all uncommon for one party to gain almost all of the seats on a local council having won only just over fifty per cent of the votes cast. Worse still, it not infrequently happens that the party which gains control of the council wins fewer votes than its main competitor. In 1978, for example, this occurred in ten of the thirty-six metropolitan districts. As at the national level, the use of the first-past-the-post system exaggerates and exacerbates conflict and division in local communities. It also produces conflict between local and central government by exaggerating the swing against the government of the day.

Without being too starry-eyed over what is, after all, only a mechanical reform, we are surely right to expect several clear benefits to result from the introduction of proportional representation into British elections. It should certainly make our electoral system more democratic and representative. It should help to diminish the role of party and enhance the role of the individual elector. It should give more force and authority to the decisions of both central and local government. Perhaps also, as Vernon Bogdanor argues in his recent book *The People and the Party System* (one of the most eloquent and persuasive statements of the case for proportional representation that I have ever read), it might even bring nearer the fulfilment of the long-held liberal dream in which democracy becomes an educative process, with the act of voting inducing a sense of responsibility and maturity in every individual who takes part in it. [1]

Certain other specific constitutional reforms would also help to make Britain a more liberal society. Despite the reservations of several eminent liberally-minded individuals like Lord Denning, there is probably on balance a case for the incorporation into British law of the European Convention on Human Rights. Although this would to some extent circumscribe the common law tradition and the flexibility of the unwritten constitution, the time may well have come when the threat to individual liberty posed by the growing power of the state and of corporate interests is such as to justify the positive assertion of certain legal rights. Lord Hailsham may have been exaggerating somewhat when in his 1976 Dimbleby Lecture he described Britain as an elective dictatorship, but the long list of cases brought against this country and declared admissible by the European Commission, which range from criminal sanctions against homosexual conduct in Northern Ireland to the dismissal of workers from British Rail because of the oppressive operation of the closed shop, suggests that we have nothing at all to be complacent about.

If there is to be a British Bill of Rights, then it should certainly include the right to privacy. This should cover not just the invasions of privacy which occur through telephone tapping and the misuse of personal information stored on computers, but also the intrusions into the private lives of individuals by the press and television. It is sadly clear that the system of voluntary controls and self-censorship operated by the Press Council does not work against some of the more hardened

226

exponents of cheque-book journalism and 'door-step' report-
ing. Perhaps we should follow our Continental neighbours and
give formal legal protection to what they call 'the right of the
personality', making it an offence for the media to harass
individuals and invade their privacy.

Another useful constitutional reform would be a Freedom of
Information Act of the kind which operates in the United States
and which is now advocated by both the SDP-Liberal Alliance
and the Labour Party. There is no doubt that governments at
present cloak themselves in an excessive veil of secrecy which
could be substantially lifted without any threat to national
security. People should be trusted with much more 'official'
information, not least information which directly concerns
themselves.

All these reforms would help the cause of liberty and
democracy. The same cannot be said, however, about some of
the other proposals for constitutional change canvassed by
contemporary Liberals. I am thinking particularly of plans for
new regional assemblies. Overall, the need is for less government, not more. The experience of the reorganisation of local
government that took place in the early 1970s should serve as a
standing warning to those who think that by re-organising the
machinery of government they can bring it closer to the people.
The net result of that particular exercise was bigger bureaucracies and more remote administrations. The present Government has been quite right to abolish the metropolitan councils
which its own Conservative predecessor created. It has been
equally wrong to impose centralised control on local authority
spending through the device of rate-capping. What is wanted is
more genuine local government, and less regulation from the
centre.

The most liberal way for local government to develop in the
coming decades would be in the direction of greater diversity
and experimentation with different councils doing things in
different ways. There is much to be said for a 'mixed economy'
which combines directly provided services with others that are
privatised or contracted out. The mixture does not need to be
the same in every area. In some places there will be considerable scope for the extension of community and neighbourhood

politics with a high level of public participation, but this will depend on the energy and enthusiasms of local activists and cannot be uniformly applied or imposed from above. Overall, the accent should be on diversity. As David Walker, *The Times* local government correspondent, has written:

> In recent years all sense of experiment and progress has gone out of local government and one reason is the depressing uniformity often imposed by 'professional' standards and precepts.
> If central government were to lift some of its obligations, then local authorities might be able to vary their activities. Would it be so shocking if school buses were provided in one area but in another they were done by a private firm, and in another by a parents' co-operative? If it means anything at all, local government means the state's functions being fulfilled differently in different geographical areas.[2]

The democratisation of industry should ideally proceed in a similarly diverse way. We have already seen that there has been an increase over the last ten years in the number of firms establishing company or works councils. There may conceivably be a case for legislation requiring managements to keep their workers continuously informed about the state of their firms, their plans and prospects, and even establishing supervisory boards elected in part by the workforce. But this coercive approach should be avoided if at all possible. Far more important, and far more effective, than legislation is a change in the attitude of both managers and workers.

There is certainly plenty of scope for a more positive approach to industrial democracy. Although a recent survey by the Confederation of British Industry found that nine out of ten managers agreed that involving their employees more in the running of their companies had improved productivity, reduced energy usage and brought a readier acceptance of new technology, it also found that less than one in five of company chairmen chaired their firm's works council, only one in four had annual profit sharing schemes and less than half trained their supervisors and managers in this area. In the words of Sir Raymond Pennock, past president of the CBI and chairman of BICC Ltd:

> The time has come for British management, and particularly top

management, to recognise that the understanding of economic reality, where the money comes from and goes to, and then the involvement of employees in contributing to decisions affecting business performance is an area in which much more time and effort must be spent. This priority rests on a philosophical conviction that in Britain, which is one of the most advanced political democracies in the world, with a passion for individual liberty, you cannot expect people to behave differently within the factory fence, the office and laboratory.[3]

That is indeed the nub of the liberal argument for industrial democracy. Surely we should trust people in their role as employees with the information and responsibility with which we trust them as voters and citizens. The attitude of the trade unions is as important here as that of managers. They have so far shown very little interest in the whole subject of industrial democracy. It suits the confrontational ethic which the unions are so keen to perpetuate for workers not to be actively participating in the management of their firms but rather to be more detached and locked in an antagonistic relationship with their employers. But this is surely not in the best interests of employees. It is time that, either collectively through their unions or individually outside them, they insisted on participating more in the affairs of their workplace and signalled their readiness to shoulder the responsibilities involved.

In industry, as in politics, it is a fundamental change in people's attitudes that is required to bring about greater democracy and participation. In his book *The Life and Times of Liberal Democracy* (1977), Professor C. B. Macpherson suggests that the establishment of a genuinely participatory democracy is the only hope for the survival for liberal democracy as we have known it in the West. He lists the essential prerequisites for the achievement of this state as the development of a stronger sense of community, a reduction in inequalities, a rise in neighbourhood and community movements and participation in workplaces and, above all, 'a change in people's consciousness from seeing themselves and acting as essentially consumers to seeing themselves and acting as exerters and enjoyers of the exertion and development of their own capacities.'[4]

We are back yet again to changing human expectations and

aspirations, to education, exhortation and example as the key elements in the continuing renaissance of Liberal Britain. Already, as we have seen, much is happening in the way of local community action and neighbourhood movements. More and more people are becoming participators and are involving themselves in the running of their place of work, the area where they live or one of the numerous voluntary groups and societies which are still among the chief glories of Liberal Britain. They must be encouraged to even more involvement and trusted with even greater responsibilities.

For in the end it is voluntary individual action which is the source of all human progress. What John Stuart Mill said of the state in one of the noblest passages in *On Liberty* is true also of the large company, the trade union, the local authority, and all the other collectivist agencies of the modern world which can so easily suffocate humanity in the name of benevolence and protection. His words remain an eternal reminder to liberals to hold fast to the principle of trust in the people:

The worth of a State, in the long run, is the worth of the individuals composing it; and a State which postpones the interest of their mental expansion and elevation, to a little more of administrative skill, or of that semblance of it which practice gives, in the details of business; a State which dwarfs its men, in order that they may be more docile instruments in its hands even for beneficial purposes – will find that with small men no great thing can really be accomplished; and that the perfection of machinery to which it has sacrificed everything, will in the end avail it nothing, for want of the vital power which, in order that the machine might work more smoothly, it has preferred to banish.[5]

A NEW INTERNATIONALISM

It is a sorry state of affairs that our main preoccupation in the field of foreign affairs has come to be haggling with our Common Market partners about the size of our contribution to the Community's budget. It is true that the EEC is in a mess, and that Britain has suffered unfairly, but the spirit with which we have approached this issue has done little to enhance our reputation and influence. Nor does it accord with our tradition and our still considerable potential as a force for internationalism. Reduced in circumstances and influence as we undoubtedly are, Britain still has an important role in the world community by virtue of our unique triple links with Europe, the Commonwealth and the United States of America and because of our historic commitment to the rule of law and justice, the promotion of free trade and the strengthening of international organisations. It is a role which is likely to become increasingly important in a world that is badly in need of more links and better understanding between its members.

One area where more links are clearly needed is that of East-West relations in the face of the continuing build-up of nuclear weapons. As a nuclear power Britain has a particular responsibility to work for a halt to the horrendous build-up of nuclear arsenals. As a prominent member of the European Community and a country with considerable diplomatic experience we also have a potentially important role to play in helping to bring the two super-powers closer together.[1] Liberals today are divided over the question of nuclear disarmament between unilateralists and multilateralists. This is not surprising – the British liberal tradition can be said to encompass both positions. The pacifist strain represented by John Bright and many other Nonconformists supports the unilateralists, but there is an equally strong element in British liberalism which stands for collective security and for not disarming in the face of aggressors. On two points all liberals must surely agree, however: one is the futility of maintaining Britain's so-called independent deterrent and of buying the costly Trident missile system to replace the existing Polaris set-up, and the other is the need to pursue nuclear disarmament much more assidu-ously and vigorously than the present Government is doing.

There is still much truth in what William Beveridge said forty years ago: 'Freedom from war cannot be obtained either by pacifism or by nationalism; it depends upon carrying into the international field essentially Liberal ideas of the rule of law, and of making the world safe for small nations by justice and the policemen'.[2] For all its shortcomings, the United Nations remains the most effective international policeman and peace-keeper that we have. Its machinery for maintaining peace and security in the world has not worked as well as it might have done largely because of the failure of member states to use it properly or to enable the UN Charter to operate in the way that its drafters intended.

The United Nations badly needs one country to take the lead in building a coalition of member states across the world which will make it their business to implement the Charter and use and improve its machinery for international peacekeeping and co-operation. Here is a role almost tailor-made for Britain with its particular links and traditions. We might also usefully play a similar role in helping to galvanise other international agencies like the World Bank and the International Monetary Fund into more active efforts to redress imbalances in the world economy.[3]

Together with a strong commitment to making the United Nations work more effectively, Britain should also be taking the lead in calling for the establishment of a new world economic order to redress the growing imbalance between rich and poor nations. The gap between the developed and the developing world is widening. Both prudence and justice demand that it be narrowed. In particular ways must be found to secure fair commodity price agreements and to relieve Third World nations of their crippling debts, which are threatening the stability of the world's financial systems. It is very sad that the plan of action for a new international economic order which was drawn up by special sessions of the United Nations General Assembly in 1975 has been frustrated by the refusal of certain rich countries, including Britain, to allow a body to be set up to monitor the policies of specialised agencies like the International Monetary Fund and the World Bank. Liberal principles of redistribution need to be applied on a global as well as a national scale. The recommendations of the Brandt Report must commend themselves to all liberals and it is high time that they were implemented. At the very least we in Britain should be committing ourselves to increasing official overseas development aid to 0.7 per cent of our Gross National Product immediately, and to one per cent by the end of the century.[4]

Britain should also be taking a lead in resisting the growing trend throughout the world towards protectionism. There is a very real danger that we are about to enter a round of tariff increases and trade restrictions comparable to that in the 1930s which is estimated to have caused the volume of world trade to contract by 60 per cent. For the present recovery in the world economy to be sustained, it is vital that markets stay open. This is particularly important for the debt-pressed nations of the Third World seeking to export their way back to recovery, but it is also vital for the developed countries transforming themselves into post-industrial societies on the basis of the export of information technology and services.

There is an urgent need for a major new multi-lateral round of tariff reductions on the lines of the GATT agreement of 1947. Of course the key nations in such negotiations will be the United States and Japan. But Britain's voice will also be important, particularly if it articulates the liberal argument which underlay the great campaign against the Corn Laws and other protectionist measures of the last century – the argument that free trade is an agent for peace as well as prosperity, bringing much closer links between nations and breaking down barriers and hostilities.

There is, of course, a great deal that we can do to promote free trade in the EEC. For an institution which calls itself a Common Market, the European Community is a remarkably protectionist body, both in terms of its internal trading arrangements and its relations with the outside world. A recent report from forty-four British businessmen, *A Europe Open to the World*, rightly warned that increasing resort to protectionism in the EEC would militate against employment opportunities, higher standards of living and innovation. Yet there is little sign of this warning being heeded by the Community.

The most urgent target for reform in the EEC is, of course, the Common Agricultural Policy which operates against the interests of consumers within the Community and of producers outside it. Mrs Thatcher has made a start at securing a reform of the policy. What is now needed is a concerted effort by all EEC Governments founded on a common conviction that the present highly protectionist system is inimical to the best interests of everyone. The CAP has given the European Community a bad name and induced a dangerous xenophobia, not least in Britain. With its reform we can, perhaps, begin to rebuild our Europeanism and shed some of our narrow nationalism.

There are other ways in which we need to become less nationalistic. We should repeal the British Nationality Act with its blatantly racist overtones. Organisations like the British Council and the External Services of the BBC should be strengthened and supported, not cut back as they have been by the present Government. We should be encouraging overseas students to come and study in this country, not putting them off by charging prohibitively high fees. We would do well to recall Cobden's adage and to promote as much intercourse as possible between the peoples of the world and perhaps rather less extravagant and often rather empty summitry between their rulers. There is room for far more cultural and professional exchanges, twinning arrangements between schools and towns

and overseas contacts under the auspices of voluntary organisations like the United Nations Association and the International Council of Women.

The kind of thing that I have in mind is being pioneered by
the Centre for International Peacebuilding which was set up a
few years ago by Brigadier Michael Harbottle, former commander of the UN peace keeping forces in Cyprus. Believing that
the key to ending the Cold War lies in breaking down mutual
fears and misunderstandings and building up confidence
between East and West, Brigadier Harbottle has devoted
himself to organising exchanges and collaborative projects.
Perhaps his centre's most notable achievement to date has been
to bring together in Vienna former generals from both NATO
and the Warsaw Pact to discuss their common commitment to
nuclear disarmament. There have also been a number of
interesting joint projects in the field of ecology and medicine.
A successful form of treatment for spina bifida sufferers
developed by the Peto Institute in Hungary, for example,
has been publicised and introduced in the West.

These ventures may seem small and insignificant but they
help to break down barriers and to change attitudes and, once
again, it is attitudes that are all important. If we respond to
those people who have a different coloured skin or speak a
different language or who live in a different kind of regime from
our own with a mixture of fear and suspicion, then we are acting
not only very illiberally but also very dangerously. For it is out
of fear and suspicion that conflict and war are bred. In
welcoming and rejoicing in the diversity of races, creeds and
customs that are found across the globe, and indeed within our
own country, we do not need to compromise our own values
and traditions. We simply need to display those qualities of
sympathy, open-mindedness and tolerance which are the
hallmarks of the liberal temper. In this spirit we can build a new
internationalism.

22

A NEW LIBERAL CRUSADE

Throughout the writing of this book I have been troubled by one persistent and nagging doubt. Have I not been hopelessly and naively optimistic about human nature, blind to the reality of Original Sin and to the apathy, the passivity and the conformity which is the natural state of mankind? This book has argued that Governments and other external authorities can do relatively little to create a more liberal society and that it is the spontaneous and voluntary actions of individuals and communities which are the source of all true progress. But is not this the great liberal delusion, attractive enough in theory but totally misconceived in reality? Do not most people lack the capacity for originality and self-direction and need to be led, if not actually coerced? Do they, indeed, really want to be free at all, in the liberal sense, with all the responsibilities involved, or are they not much happier to be slaves to custom and convention?

It is true that liberalism has always been the creed of an élite – not an élite of birth or wealth, but of the open-minded, the sensitive and the optimistic. The Victorian Age may in many ways have been more liberal than our own, but even then those who clung to the dictates of the Nonconformist Conscience, the invigorating spirit of Celtic Radicalism and the passionate pursuit of liberty and individuality were a minority of the population. So it has been in our own century an even smaller

236

minority who have kept alive the liberal tradition against the prevailing tides of secularism and materialism, that hardy band of old-fashioned Liberals to whom this book is dedicated.

But are we then to say that there is no hope of real liberty for the mass of our countrymen? Is it inevitable that most will pass their lives in a state of apathy and conformity, slaves to the mass media and the pressures of commercialism? The faces which stare out from the buses and the underground, which fill the shops and streets of cities and towns, particularly the faces of the young, are all too often without animation or hope, set in listless and bored expressions, seemingly lacking any enthusiasm or sensitivity. Is this the natural state of mankind, or is it rather a result of the de-humanising message of the media and the commercialism of modern society where excitement is sought in video nasties and escape in drink or drugs? Surely we cannot just shrug our shoulders and ignore these faces which cry out for liberation and fulfilment. Growing up around us is a generation desperate for the freedom, the absorption and the peace of mind that are the privilege and joy of the unfettered liberal spirit. It must be our task as liberals to help them set themselves free.

The means towards this liberation will be very different from that held out in the so-called 'swinging' sixties. That way, the path of permissiveness and licence, has been tried and found only to lead into a blind alley of emptiness and despair. We must go back to the original liberal ideal of liberty as a condition in which one can make the most of oneself, obeying the highest dictates of one's conscience, and responsibly exercising one's free will, that supreme gift with which we have all been endowed. To help us reach that condition, erring and frail humanity that we are, will require discipline and control, most of which must come from within ourselves but some of which will need to be imposed by external authorities.

One area where greater restriction and external control is fully justified is that of drink. Excessive consumption of alcohol is one of the major social problems of our age. The Department of Health and Social Security officially recognises problem drinking as having reached epidemic proportions, with over three-quarters of a million people directly affected not to mention the many spouses, children, friends, work-mates, road users and others who feel the indirect effects. There is abundant evidence that the growth in the levels of violent and anti-social behaviour, both at home and in the streets, which has taken place over the last thirty years is directly linked to the dramatic rise in alcohol consumption. Between 1950 and 1976 annual consumption of pure alcohol in Britain almost doubled from 5.2 litres to 9.7 litres per head. Over the same period, convictions for drunkenness and for drunken driving doubled, deaths from cirrhosis of the liver rose by 60 per cent and hospital admissions for alcoholism rose by 2,500 per cent.

It is not difficult to pinpoint the major cause of this epidemic. Alcohol has become steadily cheaper and more accessible over the last three decades. In 1950 a bottle of whisky cost 22.2 per cent of average male earnings. In 1981 it cost only 4.3 per cent. Duties on alcohol have failed to keep up with inflation. As Professor Robert Kendell, Professor of Psychiatry at the Royal Edinburgh Hospital, told a conference of doctors last year, 'The most important single act would be for the Government to increase the price of alcohol slowly year by year for a decade'.[1] It is high time for the Liberals to take up again their historic role as the party of temperance reform and to campaign for much higher duties on alcohol and for restrictions on the number and nature of outlets at which drink can be sold.

There is an equally strong liberal case for external controls and restrictions to curb drug and solvent abuse. As we have seen, the drug addict or the habitual glue sniffer, like the alcoholic, is in no real sense a free man. His so-called 'freedom' to indulge in his addiction is rather a form of slavery which deprives him of his liberty and capacity for self-development just as surely as if he had been imprisoned. To that extent depriving him of that 'freedom' may well be justified. Yet such external coercion can, of course, never really solve the problems of addiction. The only real and lasting way out of the slavery caused by drink or drugs is by the moral reformation of the individual addict, helped by the sympathy, the support and the encouragement of those around him. Ultimately it is to inner resources rather than external constraints that we must look for help in tackling what are among the most pressing human problems of modern society.

The same is true when it comes to the question of what control should be exercised over the content of television programmes and home videos. There may well be a case for legislation to ban certain kinds of video 'nasty' and for strengthening existing codes on advertising and on the portrayal of sex and violence on television. Yet just as Victorian Liberals had to accept the development of the sensational press as one of the consequences of Mr Gladstone's abolition of the tax on knowledge in the shape of newspaper stamp duty, so modern liberals must accept that the free interchange of ideas which is at the heart of their faith must perforce include the freedom to broadcast rubbish. It is not external controls or censorship which will curb the illiberal influences which are at present spread by the mass media, but rather inner controls provided by individual discrimination and taste.

This is, of course, why education is so important to Liberals. Its central role is well summed up in a declaration of liberal faith issued just after the last war by a group of Young Liberals who pointed out that a man could not be free unless he possessed, among other things, 'a mind educated to enjoy and discriminate and hands trained to some useful occupation.' In both respects it has to be said that at present education is failing in its job. Young people are fed, in many cases almost force-fed, an over-academic diet which gives them little enjoyment or stimulation and few if any practical skills. It is little wonder that several of them turn to vandalism and violence in their boredom and frustration.

Some welcome steps are at last being taken to loosen the grip of academicism on the British educational system. Pilot schemes have been introduced to develop more practical courses at school for less academically able pupils, and to establish community tutors to link schools with the local community around them. These initiatives are to be welcomed. But overall, our approach is still too narrowly vocational. The main priority in education seems to be to prepare children for jobs – in many cases, one has to say, for jobs that will simply not be there for many school-leavers – rather than to prepare them for life.

We need to return to the principles of liberal education, to the idea that school should provide a training for life in all its aspects and a developing of the whole personality. This will mean moving away from the present increasingly examination-dominated system and dropping our growing obsession with qualifications. It will mean giving much more priority in schools to such areas as community service and to the 'life and social skills' which are currently incorporated in the Youth Training Scheme. It will also mean much less sitting at desks in the classroom and much more practical activity to prepare future generations for lives where there is likely to be much more opportunity, and also a greater necessity, for cooking, gardening, odd-jobbing and self-sufficiency generally. What are now the Cinderella subjects in the curriculum must be given much more status and priority. There is, indeed, much to be said for the practice adopted in the schools of many Third World countries where classroom lessons alternate with periods out in the fields or in other practical activities.

This approach should not just apply in schools, of course. The new style of society which is emerging will offer enormous opportunities for adult learning. One of the saddest and most short-sighted actions of the present Government has been its cutdown on the funding of this area. Liberals should be demanding the expansion of all forms of adult and continuing education.

Belief in the central importance of education is a corollary of the liberal conviction that people are capable of growth and development. Depraved and corrupted man may be, but liberals also remember that he is created in the image of God and that he has been brought into this world and given free will in order that he may grow in wisdom, love and understanding, help his fellow men and develop to the full his God-given talents. Much of the last part of this book has been a call for a change in the hearts and minds of people towards a greater tolerance and concern for others, a more flexible approach towards jobs and work, and a greater readiness to take on more responsibility and participate more in the community. Such changes of attitude do occur – one can point, for example, to the significant shift which is now taking place in our approach to diet and health. It is up to liberals to exhort, educate and persuade people that the good life is to be found not just through avoiding saturated fats and eating more fibre but also through pursuing less materialistic goals and taking more part in voluntary and community activities.

It is a familiar adage, but a vitally true one, that people behave in the way that is expected of them. If they are treated like passive consumers or faceless units in some collectivist mass, then that is how they will be. That way lies the road to conformity, to apathy and to totalitarianism. But if they are excited, challenged, consulted, given responsibilities, their hearts and minds uplifted and moved, then they will begin to take the highroad of liberalism.

There can be no blueprint for the society that lies at the end of this road. It would be nice and neat if this book could end with a picture of liberal Britain as it might be in fifty years time. But by its very nature that is an impossibility. Such a society, if it comes about, will be the creation of millions of different individual aspirations, not of some central authority, nor even of some Rousseauesque General Will. Variety and unpredictability will be its hallmarks. But that does not diminish in any way our responsibility here and now to teach, to preach and to proclaim and live out the liberal faith. It matters not that we may often feel ourselves to be in a tiny minority almost engulfed by the forces of commercialism, corporatism and dull, passive conformity. We should remember John Stuart Mill's cheering words that 'one person with a belief is a social power equal to 99 who have only interests'.[2]

It is also worth recalling the words of another great Liberal that have already been quoted in these pages (on page 66 to be precise). In proposing an agenda of reforms for the coming decades I have found myself, quite unconsciously, echoing the list of remedies suggested more than eighty years ago by C. F. G. Masterman for the problems of the twentieth century: a move back to the land, more scattered industry, temperance reform, a new system of education and the elimination of the submerged portion of the population, the have-nots who consistently miss out on the opportunities and freedoms that the rest of us enjoy. But even more I find myself agreeing with

241

Masterman's conclusion that while those essentially mechanical reforms are the immediate necessities of our age, what we need above all is 'a real and living religion, some outpouring of spiritual effort'.

It may seem odd to end a book about liberalism, supposedly that most rational and matter-of-fact of creeds, with a plea for more religious faith and greater spiritual awareness. But the greatest obstacles of all to the creation of a truly liberal society are the forces of cynicism, fatalism and despair. We need to meet those forces head on in a crusading spirit and with a conviction of the utter worth of human life and endeavour. Let my final text be from William Ewart Gladstone, that noble exemplar of liberal thought and action who combined a deep Christian sense of the reality of Original Sin with an equally deep-rooted optimism about the potential and dignity of the human condition:

Be inspired with the belief that life is a great and noble calling; not a mean and grovelling thing that we are to shuffle through as we can, but an elevated and lofty destiny.[3]

NOTES

Except where otherwise stated, the place of publication of all books mentioned is London.

INTRODUCTION

1. J. Grimond, *The Future of Liberalism* (Lecture delivered to the Eighty Club in the National Liberal Club in October 1980).
2. R. Dahrendorf, *After Social Democracy* (Unservile State Group pamphlet, 1980), p. 20.
3. R. Muir, *An Autobiography and Some Essays*, ed. S. Hodgson (1943), p. 213.

CHAPTER ONE

1. E. Dodds and E. Reiss, *The Logic of Liberty* (Unservile State Paper, no date), p. 3.
2. J. Grimond, *The Future of Liberalism* (typescript of Eighty Club lecture, October 1980), f. 10.
3. Quoted in G. E. Fasnacht, *Acton's Political Philosophy* (1952), p. 19.
4. E. Dodds, *Is Liberalism Dead?* (1920), p. 48.
5. Quoted in D. Thomson, *Political Ideas* (1969), p. 76.
6. Quoted in G. Watson, *The English Ideology* (1973), p. 84. The fifth chapter of this book, entitled 'Laissez-Faire and the State' convincingly debunks the idea that Victorian Liberalism was an

ideology of *laissez-faire*.

7. J. S. Mill, *Three Essays*, ed. R. Wollheim (Oxford, 1975), p. 14;
   J. S. Mill, *The Principles of Political Economy*, ed. W. J. Ashley
   (Oxford, 1920), p. 978.

8. J. Harris, *William Beveridge* (Oxford, 1977), p. 312; J. M.
   Keynes, *Essays in Persuasion* (1952), pp. 312–3.

9. Quoted in P. Bartram, *David Steel* (1981), p. 89.

10. J. S. Mill, *Three Essays*, ed. R. Wollheim (Oxford, 1975), pp. 75–
    6.

11. *Ibid.*, p. 18.

12. *Ibid.*, pp. 133–5.

13. *The Works of T. H. Green*, ed. R. L. Nettleship (1888), III,
    p. 370.

14. *Ibid.*, pp. 371–4.

15. *Ibid.*, II, pp. 39–40.

16. L. T. Hobhouse, *Liberalism* (Oxford, 1942), pp. 146–7.

17. J. A. Hobson, *The Crisis of Liberalism* (reprint, 1974), p. 94.

18. L. T. Hobhouse, *Liberalism*, p. 137.

CHAPTER TWO

1. *Liberal Party Politics*, ed. V. Bogdanor (Oxford, 1983), p. 16.

2. *The Political Correspondence of Mr Gladstone and Lord
   Granville 1868–1886*, ed. A. Ramm (Oxford, 1962), I, p. 3,
   Significantly, this remark was made about the campaign over the
   Bulgarian atrocities.

3. *Nineteenth Century*, L (September 1901), p. 370.

4. G. M. Trevelyan, *The Life of John Bright* (1925), p. 19.

5. W. E. Gladstone, *Gleanings of Past Years* (1879), I, p. 158.

6. A splendid exemplar of Colne Valley Liberalism was the late
   Harry Senior, constituency chairman from 1978 to 1981. As
   Richard Wainwright put it in his obituary note in *Liberal News*:
   'Harry Senior was liberalism personified. A deep concern for his
   community, and for people everywhere, was underpinned by his
   cheerful Christian faith . . . His local patriotism (was) centred on
   Linthwaite Methodist Chapel'.

7. G. W. E. Russell, *Portraits of the Seventies* (1916), p. 177.

8. F. Whyte, *The Life of W. T. Stead* (1925), I, p. 201.

CHAPTER THREE

1. J. S. Mill, *Three Essays*, ed. R. Wollheim (Oxford, 1975),

pp. 247, 254.

2. V. Bogdanor, *The People and the Party System* (Cambridge, 1981), p. 134. I commend this book as a powerful and scholarly exposition of the case both for proportional representation and for more use of referenda.

3. Quoted in *ibid.*, p. vi.

4. Quoted in E. Stead, *My Father* (1913), p. 80.

5. Preface to the *Parish Councillor's Handbook*, 1894, quoted in Bryan Keith-Lucas' essay 'The Liberal Party and Local Government' in *Liberal Party Politics*, ed. V. Bogdanor (Oxford, 1983).

6. J. L. McCabe, *The Life and Letters of G. J. Holyoake* (1908), II, p. 98.

7. J. S. Mill, *Principles of Political Economy*, ed. W. J. Ashley (Oxford, 1920), p. 764.

8. Cobden's remark is quoted in A. V. Dicey, *Lectures on Law and Public Opinion* (1914), p. 199; Mill's in John Gray's article 'J. S. Mill and the Future of Liberalism', *Contemporary Review*, September 1976, p. 142.

9. T. H. Green, *Liberal Legislation and Freedom of Contract* (Oxford, 1881), p. 7.

CHAPTER FOUR

1. J. S. Mill, *The Principles of Political Economy*, ed. W. J. Ashley (Oxford, 1920), p. 949.

2. E. Baines, *Letters to Lord John Russell on State Education* (1847), p. 41. On the campaign of Baines and Miall and the general development of the doctrine of voluntaryism among Victorian Liberals see chapter eight of my book, *The Optimists: Themes and Personalities in Victorian Liberalism* (1980).

3. Quoted in B. H. Abbott, *Gladstone and Disraeli* (1972), p. 59.

4. J. Chamberlain, 'Favourable Aspects of State Socialism', *North American Review*, XV (1891), pp. 536–7.

5. *The Works of T. H. Green*, ed. R. L. Nettleship (1888), III, pp. 374–5.

6. Gladstone propounded this idea in an article in the *Nineteenth Century* in 1890 in which he commended the doctrine of the Scottish-born industrialist and philanthropist, Andrew Carnegie.

7. W. S. Churchill, *Liberalism and the Social Problem* (1909), p. 82.

8. Quoted in Philip Waller's article 'Charles Booth, the Calm Investigator' in *New Society*, 11 August 1983, p. 207.

9. L. T. Hobhouse, 'The Contending Forces', *English Review*, IV

THE STRANGE REBIRTH OF LIBERAL BRITAIN

(1909–10), p. 368.
10. J. A. Hobson, *The Crisis of Liberalism* (1909), p. xii.

CHAPTER FIVE

1. J. S. Mill, *Dissertations and Discussions, Political, Philosophical and Historical* (1859), II, p. 381.
2. *The Political Writings of Richard Cobden* (1867), I, pp. 282–3.
3. J. Morley, *The Life of Richard Cobden* (1881), II, p. 10.
4. G. M. Trevelyan, *The Life of John Bright* (1925), p. 256.
5. W. E. Gladstone, *Midlothian Speeches*, ed. M. R. D. Foot (Leicester, 1971), pp. 115–7.
6. F. Whyte, *The Life of W. T. Stead* (1925), I, p. 155.
7. Quoted in J. L. Hammond, *Gladstone and the Irish Nation* (1938), p. 64.
8. Quoted in P. Knaplund, *Gladstone's Foreign Policy* (new edn., 1970), p. 56.
9. Quoted in G. E. Fasnacht, *Acton's Political Philosophy* (1952), p. 130.
10. *Hansard*, 3rd series, CCXXXI (1876), 184.
11. W. E. Gladstone, *Gleanings of Past Years* (1879), IV, p. 249.
12. J. L. Sturgis, *John Bright and the Empire* (1969), p. 108; F. Whyte, *Life of Stead*, I, p. 156.
13. F. W. Knickerbocker, *Free Minds: John Morley and His Friends* (Cambridge, Mass., 1943), p. 258.
14. L. T. Hobhouse, *Liberalism* (1911), p. 105.
15. W. E. Gladstone, *Midlothian Speeches*, p. 129.

CHAPTER SIX

1. G. Murray, *A Conversation with Bryce* (Oxford, 1944), p. 10.
2. C. F. G. Masterman, *The Heart of the Empire* (1902), pp. 50–1. The extent to which the New Liberals thought in spiritual terms is well brought out in Michael Freeden's excellent book, *The New Liberalism* (Oxford, 1978).
3. There is an illuminating account of Mill's advocacy of a stationary-state economy in John Gray's article 'John Stuart Mill: Traditional and Revisionist Interpretations' in *Literature of Liberty*, April–June 1979, p. 27.
4. J. Morley, *On Compromise* (1913 edn.), p. 127.
5. M. Arnold, *Culture and Anarchy*, ed. J. Dover Wilson (Cam-

bridge, 1971), p. 41.

6. *Ibid.*, p. 64.

7. M. Moorman, *George Macaulay Trevelyan: A Memoir* (1980), p. 232.

8. Quoted in Lord Trevelyan's article 'The History Man' in *The Times*, 14 February 1976.

9. G. M. Trevelyan, *Garibaldi and the Thousand* (1936), p. 6.

10. M. Howard, *War and the Liberal Conscience* (1978), p. 11.

CHAPTER SEVEN

1. For an expression of this view see J. L. Garvin, *The Life of Joseph Chamberlain*, Vol. II (1933) and N. Mansergh, *The Irish Question* (1965).

2. For an expansion of this thesis see P. Stansky, *Ambitions and Strategies* (Oxford, 1964), D. Hamer, *Liberal Politics in the Age of Gladstone and Rosebery* (Oxford, 1972) and H. C. G. Matthew, *The Liberal Imperialists* (Oxford, 1973).

3. H. Pelling, *Popular Politics and Society in Late Victorian Britain* (2nd edn., 1979), p. 120. K. O. Morgan, *Wales in British Politics* (Cardiff, 1963) also has some useful thoughts on this point.

4. P. Clarke, *Lancashire and the New Liberalism* (Cambridge, 1971).

5. G. Dangerfield, *The Strange Death of Liberal England* (1935 and many subsequent editions); T. Wilson, *The Downfall of the Liberal Party 1914–1935* (1966).

6. Quoted in R. Douglas, *The History of the Liberal Party 1895–1970* (1971), p. 91. There is a moving account of the part played by the Great War in destroying the atmosphere of hope and tolerance in Edwardian Britain in J. B. Priestley's *The Edwardians* (1970), p. 289.

7. H. C. G. Matthew, R. I. McKibbin and J. A. Kay, 'The Franchise Factor in the Rise of the Labour Party', *English Historical Review*, xci (1976), p. 723.

8. M. Bentley, *The Liberal Mind 1914–1929* (Cambridge, 1977).

9. J. Morley, *On Compromise* (2nd edn., 1886), pp. 21, 37.

10. *Ibid.*, p. 20.

11. Quoted in D. A. Hamer, *op. cit.*, p. 223.

12. L. T. Hobhouse, *Liberalism* (1911), p. 214.

13. J. H. Morgan, *John, Viscount Morley* (1924), p. 99.

14. R. Muir, *The Faith of a Liberal* (1933), p. 1.

15. Quoted in A. Brown, *Essays in Anti-Labour History* (1974), p. 39.

16. J. M. Keynes in the *New Statesman*, January 1939, quoted by David Marquand in his article 'Four Liberal Heroes' in *The Listener*, 23 November 1978.

17. Quoted in M. Bentley, *op. cit.*, p. 127.

CHAPTER EIGHT

1. Quoted in H. C. G. Matthew, *The Liberal Imperialists* (Oxford, 1973), p. 126–7.

2. H. Pelling, *Popular Politics and Society in Late Victorian Britain* (1968), p. 165.

3. This point is made with considerable force in C. B. Macpherson's *The Life and Times of Liberal Democracy* (1977), especially pp. 78–9.

4. Quoted in *The Times Literary Supplement*, 4 November 1983, p. 1209. Martin Skidelsky's new biography of Keynes shows the extent to which he was influenced by moral and ethical philosophy.

5. From Keynes' *Economic Possibilities for Our Grandchildren*, quoted in *British Book News*, November 1983, p. 659.

6. J. M. Keynes, *The End of Laissez-Faire*, quoted in A. Bullock and M. Shock, *The Liberal Tradition from Fox to Keynes* (1956), p. 255. On Keynes' monetarism and the distortion of his views by Neo-Keynesians, see Tim Congdon's article 'Are We Really All Keynesians Now?' in *Encounter*, April 1975, pp. 23–32.

7. Quoted in A. Peacock, *The Welfare Society* (Unservile State Paper, 1961), p. 3.

8. *Manchester Guardian*, 7 July 1889.

9. L. T. Hobhouse, *Democracy and Reaction* (1905), p. 230.

10. Quoted in W. H. Greenleaf, *The English Political Tradition*, II (1983), p. 472.

11. J. M. Keynes, 'Liberalism and Labour' reprinted in *Essays in Persuasion* (1931), p. 341.

12. A. Briggs, *Seebohm Rowntree* (1961), p. 335.

CHAPTER NINE

1. Quoted in G. Lishman, 'Economic Resources and the Welfare Society', *New Outlook*, September 1981, p. 31.

2. H. Belloc, *The Servile State* (1912), p. 183.

3. Quoted in R. Barker, *Political Ideas in Modern Britain* (1978), p. 99.

4. W. Beveridge, *Why I Am A Liberal* (1945), p. 9.
5. Quoted in J. Harris, *William Beveridge* (Oxford, 1977), p. 420.
6. W. Beveridge, *Full Employment in a Free Society* (1944), p. 36.
7. W. Beveridge, *Report on Social Insurance and Allied Services* (1942).
8. W. Beveridge, *Voluntary Action* (1948), p. 304.
9. *Ibid.*, p. 320.
10. J. Grimond, *The Future of Liberalism* (Eighty Club lecture, 28 October 1980), f.6.
11. W. Beveridge, *Why I Am A Liberal*, p. 10.

CHAPTER TEN

1. G. and M. Clutton-Brock, *Cold Comfort Confronted* (1972), p. 9.
2. Quoted in J. Morley, *Miscellanies*, Fourth Series (1908), p. 278.
3. C. Trevelyan, *From Liberalism to Labour* (1921), p. 43.
4. Quoted in M. Howard, *War and the Liberal Conscience* (1978), p. 85.
5. Quoted in Philip Noel-Baker's essay 'The League of Nations' in *The Baldwin Age*, ed. J. Raymond (1960), p. 109.
6. G. Murray, *A Conversation with Bryce* (Oxford, 1943), p. 30.
7. Sir Nicholas Henderson's dispatch, which provides a penetrating analysis of post-war British foreign policy, was published in *The Economist*, 2 June 1979, pp. 29–38.
8. There is a good account of the Liberals' commitment to European union in the post-war period in Alan Butt Philip's essay, 'The Liberals and Europe' in *Liberal Party Politics*, ed. V. Bogdanor (Oxford, 1983).

CHAPTER ELEVEN

1. J. Morley, *On Compromise* (2nd edn., 1886), p. 34.
2. G. Dangerfield, *The Strange Death of Liberal England* (new edn., 1966), p. 123.
3. *Essays in Liberalism by Six Oxford Men* (1897), p. 272.
4. M. Bentley, *The Liberal Mind 1914–1929* (Cambridge, 1977), p. 156.
5. W. Beveridge, *Voluntary Action* (1948), p. 323.
6. *Ibid.*, p. 322.
7. J. Seabrook, 'The valley without the chapels', *New Society*, 24–31 December 1981, pp. 527–30.
8. R. Hoggart, *The Uses of Literacy* (Penguin edn., 1977), p. 246.

9. Quoted in A. J. Lee, *The Origins of the Popular Press 1855–1914* (1976), p. 15. Lee's book is an excellent study of the Liberal origins of the popular press in Britain and its decline into vulgar commercialism in the early twentieth century.

10. *Ibid.*, p. 104.

11. Quoted in Krishan Kumar's fascinating study 'The Nationalisation of British Culture' in *Culture and Society in Contemporary Europe*, ed. S. Hoffman & P. Kitromilides (Harvard, 1981).

12. A. J. Lee, *op. cit.*, p. 160.

13. R. Hoggart, *op. cit.*, p. 241.

14. *Nonconformist*, 17 December 1879.

15. B. Webb, *Our Partnership* (1948), pp. 162–3. Stephen Yeo's book *Religion and Voluntary Organisations in Crisis* (1976) explores the retreat of the middle classes from participation in civic and voluntary activities during this period.

16. J. Morley, *op. cit.*, p. 30.

17. J. Morley, *The Life of W. E. Gladstone* (2nd edn., 1905), II, p. 715.

18. A. Briggs, *Seebohm Rowntree* (1961), p. 312.

19. E. M. Forster, 'What I Believe' in *Two Cheers for Democracy* (Penguin edn., 1965), p. 81.

20. G. Murray, *A Conversation with Bryce* (Oxford, 1943), pp. 44–5.

CHAPTER TWELVE

1. One index of this is the proportion of the working population employed in central and local government which increased from 14.5% in 1951 to 23% in 1976.

2. Quoted in R. Barker, *Political Ideas in Modern Britain* (1978), p. 181.

3. *Listener*, 25 March 1976, pp. 357–9.

CHAPTER THIRTEEN

1. F. Gladstone, *Voluntary Action in a Changing World* (1977), p. 123.

2. There is a useful summary of these and other similar proposals in *A Brief Review of Workers Plans* published by the Centre for Alternative Industrial and Technological Systems in 1981.

3. Quoted by Graeme Shankland in *Our Secret Economy* (1980), p. 59.

4. The idea of television as a medium for stimulating voluntary action

and community involvement came originally from Holland. On the pioneering Dutch programme 'Werkwinkel', and the application of the principle to British broadcasting see Francis Coleman's study *Social Action in Television*, published by the Independent Broadcasting Authority in 1975.

CHAPTER FOURTEEN

1. E. P. Thompson, *Out of Apathy* (1960), p. 194.
2. R. Williams, *The Long Revolution* (1961), p. 328.
3. F. von Hayek, *The Constitution of Liberty* (1960), p. 11.
4. S. Brittan, *Capitalism and the Permissive Society* (1973), p. 36.
5. *Guardian*, 13 September 1982.
6. *Observer*, 26 September 1982.
7. Iain Macleod Memorial Lecture delivered to Greater London Young Conservatives, 4 July 1977. Typescript issued by Conservative Central Office, p. 4.
8. *Ibid.*, p. 7.
9. *Ibid.*, p. 14.
10. *Ibid.*, p. 14.
11. P. Riddell, *The Thatcher Government* (Oxford, 1983), p. 231.
12. *Illustrated London News*, September 1980.

CHAPTER FIFTEEN

1. J. Grimond, *The Common Welfare* (1978), p. 12.
2. Ed. G. Watson, *The Unservile State* (1957), p. 7.
3. A. Peacock, *The Welfare Society* (1961), p. 7.
4. J. Chamberlain, 'A New Political Organisation', *Fortnightly Review*, XXII (1877), p. 126.
5. P. Hain, *Radical Regeneration* (1975), pp. 155–6. For a further exposition of the philosophical basis of community politics see the same author's *Community Politics* (1976).
6. *Foundations for the Future* (1981), pp. 3, 4.
7. R. Samuel, 'The SDP's Escape from the Christian Heritage of Socialism', *Guardian*, 29 March 1982.
8. M. Meadowcroft, *Social Democracy – Barrier or Bridge* (1981), p. 1.
9. *Liberal Clarion*, February 1982.
10. Tom McNally, quoted in BBC Radio 4 programme 'File on Four', 20 January 1982.

11. Chris Muir, quoted on the same programme.
12. E. Luard, *Socialism at the Grassroots* (Fabian Tract 468), p. 1.
13. E. Luard, *Socialism Without the State* (1979), p. 282.
14. D. Owen, *Face the Future* (paperback edn., Oxford, 1981), p. 260.
15. *Spectator*, 27 June 1981.
16. *The Times*, 4 September 1982.
17. *The Times*, 6 September 1983.

CHAPTER SIXTEEN

1. The liberal potential of the microchip is the theme of an interesting discussion paper published by the Vanier Institute of the Family in Canada which was the subject of an article by Charles Stainsby in *Liberal News*, 23 August 1983. See also Auriol Blandy's article in *Employment Gazette*, vol. 92, no. 10.
2. There are two particularly useful and illuminating short studies of the informal economy: *The Informal Economy* by Charles Handy, published by the Association of Researchers in Voluntary Action and Community Involvement in 1982 and *Our Secret Economy* by Graeme Shankland (Anglo-German Foundation, 1980).
3. On Consett's enterprising attempts to come to terms with high conventional unemployment, see Chris Tighe's article 'Farewell, Satanic Mills' in *The Sunday Times*, 10 June 1984.
4. See particularly the polls reported in the article 'Do the British Sincerely Want to be Rich?' in *New Society*, 28 April 1977, and those in *The Times*, 23 and 26 June 1980.
5. B. Nossiter, *Britain, a Future That Works* (1978), p. 196.
6. R. Dahrendorf, *On Britain* (1982), p. 185.
7. Among those who have challenged the conventional work ethic are Charles Handy and Graeme Shankland in the works mentioned above, Kathleen Smith, founder of the Work and Leisure Society, and the Rev. Alan Webster, Dean of St Paul's, in an important letter to *The Times* on 3 February 1984.
8. The poll carried out by MORI for the *Sunday Times* in December 1983 found that 39% of those questioned thought there was more freedom in Britain than there had been a few years ago, 27% less, and 30% the same amount. In answer to another question, 38% of respondents said that Britain would have even more freedom in a few years' time, 23% less, and 23% about the same.

CHAPTER SEVENTEEN

1. R. Dahrendorf, *On Britain* (1982), p. 186.

2. J. Grimond, *A Personal Manifesto* (Oxford, 1983), p. 75.
3. Quoted in *New Outlook*, Vol. 22, No. 4 (Spring 1984), p. 2.
4. V. Bogdanor, *Liberal Party Politics* (Oxford, 1983), pp. 189–90.
5. F. Pym, 'The Revolution Laissez-Faire and Socialism Cannot Handle', *Guardian*, 10 October 1983.

CHAPTER EIGHTEEN

1. P. Jay, 'Employment, Inflation and Politics' (IEA Occasional Paper No. 46, 1976), p. 13.
   See James Meade's article, 'How to achieve full employment without stoking up inflation', in *The Times*, 20 January 1982. It is interesting to see the stress that Meade puts on a change of attitudes in the battle against inflation.
2. R. Dahrendorf, *After Social Democracy* (Unservile State Paper, 1980), pp. 15–16.
3. There are some interesting reflections on this theme, and particularly on the relevance to our present needs of the ideal of work put forward in the Benedictine monastic rule, in James Robertson's *The Sane Alternative* (1978), p. 95.
4. This theme was the subject of an interesting letter from Mrs Lea Briggs published in *The Times* on 27 January 1983.
5. The argument for such a system of redistribution payments is made with particular force in letters published in *The Times* on 28 July, 1983 by Mr Harry Hodgkinson and Mr Francis Bennion.
6. On the benefits to be derived from a major programme of job-sharing, see Christopher Johnson's article 'Work Sharing: Half a Job is Better than None', in *The Times*, 29 July 1983, and 'The Economics of Worksharing' by Paul Blyton and Stephen Hill in *National Westminster Bank Quarterly Review*, November 1981.
7. Computation made by Simon and Coates for BBC 2 *Newsweek* programme, 16 April 1983.
8. These figures are taken from Richard Body's splendid book *Agriculture: The Triumph and the Shame* (1982).
9. Robert Vale's study is published as the Open University Technology Policy Group's Paper No. 1. It is discussed in another excellent document, 'Four Million Low-Growth Jobs', published by the St Ives Ecology Group.
10. The idea of mobile labour gangs has been canvassed by Mr Ivan Holmes, who farms in the Yorkshire Dales. He wrote about it in

the *Sunday Times*, 21 December 1980, and his ideas formed the basis of an article I wrote in *The Times* on 23 February 1981.

CHAPTER NINETEEN

1. Liberal Party proposals for a tax credit scheme are set out in '*To Each According . . .*' *The Liberal Plan for Tax and Social Security* (1983).
2. For a powerful, and liberal, blast against the whole concept of state pensions, see Tim Congdon's article 'Why State Pensions Should be on the Road to Oblivion' in *The Times*, 15 August 1984.
3. The MORI poll was carried out for the *Daily Express* in November 1983, the Gallup Poll, and the whole subject of public attitudes to taxation, was discussed in an article in the *Guardian* in December 1983 by Brian Gosschalk and Stewart Lansley ('Tax Cuts Welcome, but not at any price').
4. J. S. Mill, *An Autobiography* (1879), pp. 231–2.
5. David Marsland, *Work to be Done* (published by Youth Call, 1984). See also the series of articles on community service by Colin Hughes which appeared in *The Times* between 1 and 3 October 1984 and my own article 'A New National Service: the Way to Find a Million Jobs' in *The Times*, 1 April 1982.
6. There is an interesting, though brief, report on the Dudley scheme on pages 349–50 of *New Society*, 29 November 1984.

CHAPTER TWENTY

1. V. Bogdanor, *The People and the Party System* (Oxford, 1981). Bogdanor also argues persuasively for more use of referenda in Britain. This is perhaps something that Liberals should think about although it tends to be a rather crude device.
2. D. Walker, 'Let's Make Councils Really Local', *The Times*, 1 October 1983.
3. R. Pennock, 'How to Give Workers the Profit Motive', *The Times*, 22 March 1982.
4. C. B. Macpherson, *The Life and Times of Liberal Democracy* (Oxford, 1977), p. 99.
5. J. S. Mill, *Three Essays*, ed. R. S. Wollheim (Oxford, 1975), p. 141.

CHAPTER TWENTY-ONE

1. For a concrete suggestion of how Britain might lead the way

towards East-West arms reductions, see David Steel's article 'A Nuclear Summit for Europe' in *The Times*, 27 April 1984.

2. Quoted in A. Beith, *The Case for the Liberal Party and the Alliance* (1983), p. 139.

3. This point was well put in a letter to the *Guardian* by Frank Hooley of the United Nations Association published on 19 November 1983.

4. On the development of a crusading Liberal policy on the Third World, see John Madeley's article 'The Liberal Politics of Trade and Aid' in *New Outlook*, Vol. 22, No. 4 (Spring 1984).

CHAPTER TWENTY-TWO

1. *The Times*, 29 November 1984.

2. J. S. Mill, *Three Essays*, ed. R. S. Wollheim (Oxford, 1975), p. 155.

3. J. Morley, *The Life of W. E. Gladstone* (1903), Vol. I, p. 184.

INDEX

This is largely an index of names – to index topics would be well-nigh impossible and the chapter headings should help in this regard.